[ENG]LISH FOR BETTER JOBS WORKBOOK 2

By Paul J. Hamel

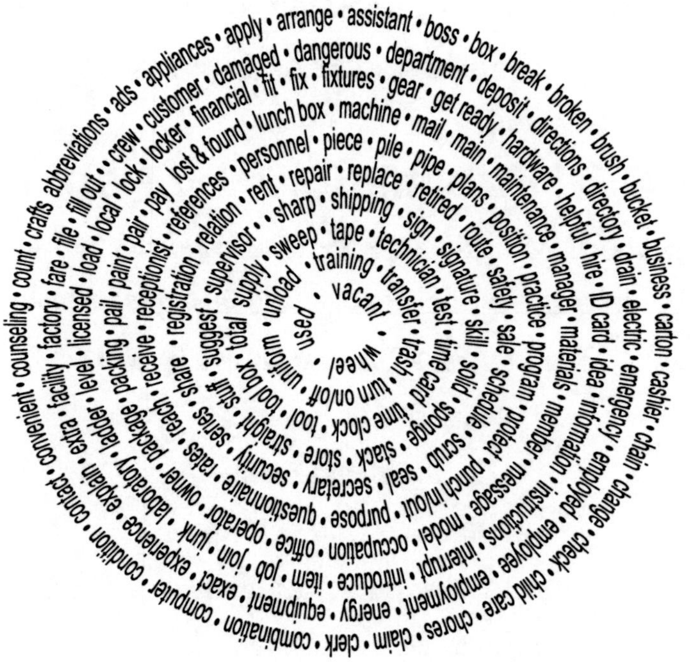

This series is dedicated to all of my former ESL Student.

Special thanks to **Mike Breyer** for his technical help and patience and to **Michael Dayton** for proof-reading.

Our Website: ESL Worksheets and Lesson Plans

eslworksheetsandlessonplans.com

Other ESL Publications by Paul Hamel

Group Activities for Advanced ESL Students (e-book)

Group Discussions for Advanced Students (e-book)

Doing the Right Thing on the Job (e-book)

ESL Bag of Tricks I & II

Listen and Write

Cleaning Up the Classroom

Better English Every Day 1, 2, 3, & Teachers Manual.

Picture That Build Stories I & 2

GAIN Manual for Educational Services, Sec. VII, California. State Dept. of Social Services

Adult ESL Handbook, Chapters 1 & 3, California State Dept. of Education

Problem Solving on the Job, Refugee Employment Training Project, LAUSD

For more information concerning this publications contact Paul J. Hamel at 310-991-2374 or at *paulhamel@twc.com.*

CONTENTS

IN THE BEGINNING ...

INTRODUCTION TO THE TEACHER

English for Better Jobs is a three-book workbook series designed for adult English learners who plan to enter the workforce. It presents the grammar, vocabulary, and language skills necessary for entry-level employment as well as getting along in an English-speaking environment. While students are learning basic English language skills in a mostly work-related context, they practice all four language skills: listening, speaking, reading, and writing. Although this series does not focus on academic goals and interests, the content of *English for Better Jobs* complies the *ESL Model Standards for Adult Education.**

For a quick look at the content of all three workbooks, go to ***At a Glance*** at the end of the ***General Teaching Notes*** below.

Workbook 2 has been designed for beginning ESL students who have mastered basic literacy skills in reading and writing. The workbooks are divided into chapters and units with common themes: a classroom, a work shop, a store, a party, and the like. Within each chapter, each unit carefully integrates grammatical structures with practical vocabulary and every-day expressions in useful situations.

The series aims at simplicity. The simple, clear page design is in black and white with large type and simple cartoon illustrations that allow students to concentrate on the lesson rather than be overwhelmed with crowded and complicated page layouts that may distract. The illustrations are timeless and help minimize the use of outdated photos, fashions, and current events. Each page measures 8 1/2 by 11 inches and is ideal for making photo copies or when using an overhead projector. Detailed teaching notes provide step-by-step explanations on how to present the lessons. The workbook is designed to be used in tutoring situations or in small group instruction. However, it can be used with larger groups, too. Although most exercises are self-explanatory, teaching notes at the back of the workbook give suggestions for class presentations and additional activities.

After opening with a class discussion and conversation that presents the topic and useful vocabulary, a reading passage or dialog is read aloud by the instructor so students can practice listening skills. Then, the students read the text and answer questions in the "Understand" section. Next, students practice student-centered oral activities such as pair or group practice. This is followed by a grammar component is presented with additional oral practice. "Challenge" activities are sprinkled throughout the series to provide students with the opportunity to go beyond the material presented. Finally, varied written exercises, dictations, and short quizzes are presented in as natural a context as possible. The lessons recycle grammatical structures again and again, with review and new vocabulary in changing contexts. Survival and work-related vocational skills are carefully balanced. Most of the vocabulary presented in work-related situations is also applicable in other real life contexts.

* *ESL Model Standards for Adult Education, California Department of Education, 1992*

GENERAL TEACHING NOTES

Detailed Teaching Notes and Answer Keys can be found starting on page 236.

INTRODUCING THE LESSON

Before starting a new chapter, introduce the topic of the chapter through a conversation. Ask general questions about the topics listed in the objectives at the beginning of each chapter.

DIALOG

Before presenting the dialog, introduce key vocabulary. You can do this by eliciting the words by means of a sentence in which the last word is not specific. For example, if you want to elicit the word "water," you can say, "when I'm thirsty, I drink something, What?" When a student guesses the word, have him/her repeat the original sentence replacing the final word with the specific noun. If nobody can guess the word, give the word and have everybody repeat the word in the original sentence. This is a valuable technique used in presenting new vocabulary because even if the students do not know the word that you are trying to elicit, they are being made aware of the context in which the word is found.

Naturally, this cannot be done with very low level classes. In this case, explain the words through pictures, flash cards, or by other means, and simply have the students repeat the words after you.

Slowly read the dialog aloud twice to your students before having them open their books. As a variation, have students cover the dialog and look at the picture accompanying the text. Then ask general comprehension questions to test their understanding of the dialog.

Direct the students to open their workbooks and follow the dialog as you read it again at normal speed. At the same time, have them underline any unfamiliar words that they come across. Then discuss the unfamiliar words.

Direct the students to the **Understand** exercise below the dialog. Have them read the questions as a silent reading exercise. Discuss and correct the answers. Expand the exercise by asking inference questions *(i.e., questions whose answers cannot be found directly in the dialog).* These kinds of questions force students to think and study the content of the dialog more closely. For example, read the dialog below then read the inference questions. The answers are not evident in the dialog.

Sue: What kind of car do you have?
John: A ten-year-old Buick. What about you?
Sue: I have a 2009 Ford.

Inference Questions
Whose car is newer?
In what year was the Buick built?

As a variation have your students ask you questions about the dialog.

For oral practice, have the whole class repeat each line of the dialog after you have modeled the sentence. Break up long sentences into segments, or use a backward-buildup technique in which you start at the end of the sentence and work toward the beginning. Here is a sample sentence:

Instructor	***Student***
in the evening	in the evening
to school in the evening	to school in the evening
go to school in the evening	go to school in the evening
We go to school in the evening.	We go to school in the evening.

Teach the second line (usually a rejoinder) in the same manner. Repeat the first line and have a student respond with the rejoinder. Then reverse roles. Select two students to repeat the two lines. Teach the next two lines in the same manner. Then return to the beginning of the dialog and review it to the point where you left off. Continue to the end of the dialog. If the dialog is too long, teach only a part of it. Do not attempt to teach dialogs that are more than eight to ten lines long.

Vary the dialog by substituting different words. Prompt new vocabulary for the dialog by oral cue, by pictures, by flash cards, by objects, or by written cues on the board.

Have students practice the dialogs in pairs. Then assign roles to individual students. Have them read and dramatize the dialog.

Finally, encourage students to paraphrase or

reconstruct the dialog in their own words.

Other Suggestions:

- Write the first part of the rejoinder on the board and have the students come up to write the second part.
- Give part of the dialog as a dictation on a subsequent day.
- As a written quiz, prepare a handout of the dialog with some of the key vocabulary missing. Have students fill them in from memory.
- Have students write their own dialogs modeled on the text presented.
- Have students rewrite the dialog as a narrative (story).

ROLE-PLAYING

Adapt the dialog to be used as the basis of a role-playing exercise. Role-playing differs from acting out a dialog because it requires students to improvise. They are forced to use vocabulary, structures, concepts, and cultural information previously presented and practiced.

Allow students to prepare themselves in pairs or small groups before having them perform before the whole class. Give the students the freedom to vary the situation and be creative. Don't over-correct. Note major mistakes; discuss and correct them later. To practice active listening, have the class note the errors, too.

Discuss the role-playing exercises afterward for students' reactions and interpretations.

READING & LISTENING

Teaching a reading text is similar in many ways to teaching a dialog. Before starting the reading passage, introduce the vocabulary and grammatical structures that students do not know. For effective visual reinforcement, use the board, flash cards, objects, and pictures. Give many contextual examples of new words.

Tell students to close their books and read the text twice as a listening comprehension exercise. Then ask general comprehension questions to test general understanding. Direct the students to open their books and read the text again. Have students underline any unfamiliar words. Discuss the vocabulary and expressions the students have identified. Have students read the **Understand** exercise below the reading text as a silent reading exercise. Call on students individually to read the answers. Expand the exercise by asking more detailed inference questions. *(See the preceding Dialog section for an explanation on how to ask inference questions.)*

Do a read-and-look-up exercise: have students read a sentence silently, then look away from the text and try to repeat as much of the sentence as they can without looking at the text.

Finally, have the students retell the story in their own words.

Other Suggestions:

- As a variation, instead of reading the passage to the students, let them read the passage as a silent reading exercise. After asking comprehension questions, have students ask their own detailed questions of each other.
- On a subsequent day, give a short dictation based on part of the text.
- Prepare a handout of the text with some of the vocabulary items missing *(cloze exercise)*. Have students supply the missing words.
- Have students write a similar story based on the reading passage.

GRAMMAR

Read through the grammar explanation with the students. Illustrate the grammar point with the use of the board, visuals, flash cards, felt board, and overhead projector to give students several different ways of understanding the structure.

You may want to have students turn to the preceding dialog and underline or circle all examples of the grammatical structure being taught.

Direct students to the **Read** exercise which are often found below the **Grammar** section in the workbook. Have them make as many correct sentences as possible with the words in the boxes. Continue and expand the exercise by having students compose original sentences.
In such a nonacademic setting, minimize the use of grammatical terms. For instance, students

are more interested in learning how to use the structures than in knowing the differences between transitive and intransitive verbs.

Constantly review previously taught grammar. Reintroduce it in another context and situations, contrast it with another grammatical structure, or build it into another lesson. Such review is important to achieve complete mastery of vocabulary and structure.

You may want to use the new vocabulary and structures for dictations during a subsequent class meeting. Such dictations will have the benefit of further reinforcing the vocabulary, grammatical patterns, and spelling.

ORAL DRILLS

Be sure that the students are familiar with the vocabulary and structures presented in the **Dialog**, **Grammar** section, and **Practice** exercises before doing oral drills.

You may want to use the Practice exercises as oral drills for general class practice to allow the students to practice on their own. Most Practice exercises consist of simple substitution and transformation drills.

When doing an oral drill, tell the students to close their books and listen.

Model the first part of the rejoinder. *(Rejoinders usually consist of a question and answer.)* Then cue the second part of the rejoinder with one of the words, pictures, or phrases provided in the drill. Model the correct response. Do two or three more examples until the students understand how the words are to be arranged.

Continue the drill by saying the first part of the rejoinder followed by the cue word or phrase. Call on individual students to supply the correct rejoinder. When all the cue words have been used, extend the drill by supplying original cue words. For maximum effectiveness, try to use flash cards, pictures, objects, or even actions as cues whenever possible.

PRACTICE

Pairing and grouping exercises give the students time, especially in large groups, to practice important speaking skills. Organizing the students to work together can be somewhat frustrating at the start, but once they clearly understand what is expected of them, subsequent pairing or grouping activities usually proceed smoothly.

Explain that this is an exercise that allows students to practice their speaking skills, not their writing skills.

Tell the students to put away all writing materials. Have each student choose a partner. (The first few times, you will probably have to go around the classroom and pair up students.) Encourage the students to pair up with different partners each time.

Direct the students to open their books, and indicate the **Practice** exercise that was used as the oral drill. Have them do the exercise in pairs. Point out that a written example for each **Practice** exercise appears to the right in a speech balloon. Also point out to your students that the series of dots (.....) at the end of the **Practice** exercises means that they are supposed to continue the exercise by supplying original words or phrases.

While students are doing the exercise, walk around the room, listen to individuals, and correct mistakes.

WRITING EXERCISES

The written exercises reinforce knowledge previously gained through the oral practice. Activities include fill-in-the-word, unscramble-the-words, choose-the-missing-word,put-in-the-correct-order, complete-the-sentence, and fill-in-the-balloon exercises.

Other less controlled types of writing exercises consist of filling out forms; finding and applying information from charts, maps, and forms; and interviewing other students. All the exercises are designed to reinforce the structures presented in the chapter.

Be sure to explain how to write in the correct answers by reading over the directions on the page and by doing a few examples with the students. For each written activity, an example is provided to insure full comprehension of the directions.

If the exercise is assigned for homework, allow the students a few minutes at the end of the day's lesson to begin the exercise. Walk around and make sure that everyone understands how to do the exercise.

Correct the sentences by having individuals read them. If an overhead projector is available, you may want to make a copy of the page on an overhead transparency to correct the exercise faster and to insure that students see the correct answers. Otherwise, write the answers on the board.

When exposing students to unstructured or free writing, be sure that the activity is short and closely related to the vocabulary, structures, and topics that you have already taught. They should be varied, practical, and related to the students' daily lives. Don't overwhelm students; begin this program with simple exercises such as addressing envelopes and writing postcards, notes, simple text/e-mail messages, and shopping lists.

Once the students have learned the basics, gradually build up to longer and more complex exercises. When correcting the students' papers, correct only serious mistakes in structure and spelling. Praise the correct use of recently taught vocabulary and structure. If you find mistakes that several students are making, note them and teach a special lesson based on these errors. To include the entire group in the correction process, copy onto the board or handout incorrect sentences taken from their papers. Have a class discussion on how best to correct the mistakes. Also keep a list of spelling errors to be used as a future dictation.

DICTATION

The dictation exercises reinforce the material that previously has been practiced orally. The correct words are usually written on the following page so that students can obtain feedback immediately. This is a very efficient type of exercise that saves precious class time normally used for correction, and makes it unnecessary for instructors to check the students' writing. It is also a useful copying exercise for any semi-literate students that you may have in your group.

When giving a dictation you may want to follow these suggestions: First read the whole dictation and tell the students to listen to it for general comprehension without writing anything. Then instruct the students to write the dictation as you slowly read the sentences in short segments or "sense groups" several times. (Three or sometimes even four repetitions should not be considered too many.) At the end of a sentence, repeat all of it at normal speed. From time to time you may want to supply the punctuation terminology. Be sure to allow the students adequate time to write the sentences. After all the sentences have been read, repeat the whole dictation once again to allow students a final chance to add any words that they might have missed.

Dictate parts of the dialogs or reading passages as a review, quiz, or test. It is especially useful as a warm-up exercise at the beginning of the class period to review previously covered material. Frequent short dictations, focusing on common words and expressions used in simple sentences and repeatedly stressing function words (such as articles, prepositions, pronouns, and auxiliary verbs), will do much to improve the students' general writing and spelling skills. Once students become accustomed to simple dictations, you may wish to vary the dictation format to keep interest high. As an example, try the following:

Dictate six questions based on the previous day's lesson. After the students have written all six questions in their notebooks, have six volunteers write the questions on the board. Then have six other students read and correct the questions. Ask for six more volunteers to go up to the chalkboard and write the answers to the questions. Have all students read and correct the answers. Finally, discuss additional possible answers to the questions.

Other Suggestions:

• Dictate the answers, then have students write the questions.

• Dictate single words that students must use in complete sentences.

• Dictate jumbled sentences that students must put in correct word order. Dictate sentences that students must change from affirmative to negative, interrogative to affirmative, etc.

CHALLENGE

The Challenge exercises consist of communicative activities that challenge students to gather necessary information, perform important life and work-related skills tasks, and practice English in a natural setting outside of the classroom.

Students should be encouraged to do the Challenge activities in small groups. This way they learn to listen to people with different accents, become aware of their own mistakes, correct one another, share opinions, experiment with the language, and become less self-conscious about asking questions that they would not normally ask in the classroom setting.

PRONUNCIATION

In teaching the lessons on pronunciation and phonics, use the following sequencing. First, clearly model the words containing the sound you want to present. Be sure not to distort intonation or rhythm. Then have students repeat the words several times. Next you may want to explain what is involved in the production of the sounds that are being taught. Use diagrams of the mouth, phonetic symbols, or demonstrations. Be sure that students can recognize the sounds before they are asked to produce them. You may want to contrast the sounds in minimal pairs to teach consonant and vowel contrasts. (A minimal pair consists of two words in which only one phoneme is different, such as *bit* and *beat*.) After sufficient oral practice, do the listening and fill-in exercises in the workbook with the students. Finally, encourage the students to think of some original sentences using as many words as they can with the sound being practiced. Have the students write the sentences on the chalkboard and practice pronouncing them. Give the sentences as a dictation on a subsequent day.

REVIEW CHAPTERS AND TESTS

This workbook contains two review chapters at midpoint and at the end. The first chapters of workbooks 2 and 3 serve as a general review of the material found in Books 1 and 2 respectively. Use these chapters as a pretest to determine the level of your students. The review chapters at the midpoint and at the end of all three books recycle the most important vocabulary and grammar found in the previous chapters. Use them for review before the midterm and final tests. The tests at the end of the review chapters were designed for simplicity and quick correction. It also exposes students to a popular method of testing used in this country.

GENERAL TEACHING SUGGESTIONS

• Create an atmosphere where students are not afraid to make mistakes. Simple communication is more important than speaking perfectly.

• Encourage students to use what they have learned in class in their speech. Encourage them to speak to one another in English during their breaks and free time. You might even reserve a special "English-speaking table" or area in your classroom where students can practice while having a snack or something to drink.

• Be eclectic. Use any method, technique, or combination of methods that work for you and your students.

• Don't be afraid to experiment, but be well-prepared.

• Use as much variety in your lessons as possible. Use other supportive materials to supplement the lessons.

• Space out your best activities throughout the course to keep interest high. Don't empty your entire "bag of tricks" early on.

• Make and collect as many teaching aids (visuals, objects, handouts, posters) as possible. Store them for future use.

• Encourage your students to use dictionaries often. Most students now have smart phones with access to sophisticated on-line programs.

• When teaching your own material, try these basic lesson planning steps.

1. First, assess the students' knowledge. Have the students demonstrate any previous knowledge of the topic. Do this through a conversation, demonstrations, pictures, songs, guest speakers, dialogs, or examples of potential situations the students may be expected to encounter at work or in daily life.

2. Present new material in short segments or units. Each chapter is divided into three to four units. Covering each unit takes about two hours. Have the students participate in the presentation of the materials as much as possible. For example, when presenting a reading passage or a dialog, teach students active listening skills by asking them to circle unfamiliar words or underline specific words and expressions as they read and listen along. Elicit new vocabulary words whenever possible. Try saying a sentence in which the students must guess the last word. For example, you might say, "When I'm thirsty, I drink ..." This is a valuable technique because even if the students cannot guess the new word, they are learning the context in which the word is used. Use realia whenever possible: food, clothing, photos, and other physical objects that can help explain new words, phrases, or concepts. Stimulate the senses of sight, hearing, smell, taste, and touch to help students learn.

3. Constantly check for understanding. Have the students demonstrate understanding of the presentation. This can be done nonverbal gestures to indicate yes or no, by physically responding to directions and commands (Stand up, sit down), and games such as pantomime (Simon Says). Also, play "stump the teacher" by having students ask questions about the material.

4. Have students reproduce the new material. For example, to improve pronunciation, have students echo words and statements. Lead chain drills. Have the students recite short dialogs or have them read orally. Have students copy information and label items. Other techniques include unscrambling words, rewriting words in the correct order, alphabetizing words, categorize phrases, place events in chronological order, and write simple dictations. Practice fluidity and intonation by ordering words and phrases into meaningful statements. All of these techniques are present in the exercises in the workbooks.

5. Have students manipulate the new material by changing words and structures. Practice vocabulary in oral substitution and patterns in transformational drills (i.e., changing nouns to pronouns). Have students continue practicing on their own in pair-practice exercises preferably using contextual cues. For review, try having students write dictated questions on the white board and others write the answers using previously learned vocabulary and structures. Other techniques include scanning for specific information, changing statements to questions and negative statements, doing fill-in-the-missing-word exercises like the ones presented in this workbook.

6. Have the students consolidate the material. At this point the students should be able to continue oral drills by substituting original words or by completing open-ended drills using their own words and phrases. Students should also be able to give original answers orally and provide written responses to their instructor or partner's questions. For example, one student fills out a food order form for another student using information on a menu. Also, have the students supply answers using other skills such as simple math. (i.e.,calculating savings using store coupons).

7. Help the students exploit the learned material. Provide opportunities to use original statements and responses based on the already-learned models. Guide the activities in which students use the new vocabulary and structures to create new dialogs, fill out forms, and write narratives based on familiar materials. At this state students should be able to participate in class discussions on familiar topics.

8. Help the students apply the learned material. Provide ways in which students can apply the new material to other situations. Try cooperative learning techniques in which students generate original language, paraphrase and participate in open discussions.

9. Evaluate the students' progress. Have the students demonstrate their ability before teaching any new material or going on to a new topic. Don't ask the students if they "understand" what you taught them. They will probably say "yes." Have them show you! Measure your students ability by applied performance in real or simulated situations, oral responses to aural (listening) cues, written responses to aural cues, written responses to written cues, and integration of language skills in which students write stories, reports, dialogs, etc.

WOOKBOOK 1 CONTENTS AT A GLANCE

WORKBOOK 1	SKILLS / COMPETENCIES	GRAMMAR / STRUCTURES	VOCABULARY / EXPRESSIONS	WORD BUILDING / PHONICS
CHAPTER 1 *Welcome to the ESL Class.*	• Meeting and introducing people	• *to be (am, is, are)* • *this / that; these / those* • Indefinite Article • Singular and Plural Nouns	• Classroom Items • Workshop items / tools • Cardinal Numbers	• Consonants
CHAPTER 2 *Isn't This the Workshop?*	• Meeting and Introducing People • Telling Time	• *to be* (neg. and question) • *to be* + adjectives • *where / when* • *in / on*	• Common Occupations • Numbers (telephone numbers, years, age) • Emergency Phone Numbers	• Short Vowels
CHAPTER 3 *Get Ready for a Dictation.*	• Common Classroom Directions • Filling Out a Registration Card • Read / Write Addresses	• Imperative (*Don't, Let's*) • Definite Article	• Common Verbs • Classroom Words	• */sh/* and */ch/* Sounds
CHAPTER 4 *Where Can I Get Some Shoes?*	• Giving Simple Street Directions • Reading a Directory & Schedule of Classes • Asking About a Job	• *can / can't* • Prepositions: *across from, next to, behind, between, near, in front of, to the right, to the left)*	• Store Names/ Shopping Terms • Common Job Positions • Expressions of Time • Ordinal Numbers	• Names of the Letters of the Alphabet • Alphabetization
CHAPTER 5 *Let's Have a Party.*	• Making a Work Schedule • Describing Household Chores	• The Present Tense (*do / don't*) • Using Expressions of Time	• Common Action Verbs • Common Household Items	• Noun Plurals • Names, Places, Days, Months • Beginning of Sentences, and the Pronoun ***"I"***
CHAPTER 6 *A Typical Day*	• Talking About Daily Activities • Writing a Simple Letter • Addressing an Envelope	• The Present Tense (*-s, does, doesn't*) • Object Pronouns • Verb + Infinitive	• Verbs Used in Daily Activities	• The Long */ā/* Sound (as in *mail*)
CHAPTER 7 *How Much Does This Cost?*	• Count Money / Read Prices • Reading a Simple Menu • Reading Advertisements • Getting Child Care Information	• *how much / how many* • *what kind of* • *a little / a few / a lot of*	• Names of Currency / Coins • Common Food Items • Child Care Terms	• The Long */ē/* Sound (as in *tea*)
CHAPTER 8 *A New Student*	• Filling out a Registration Form • Reading a Directory / Schedule • Filling Out a Simple Application • Answering a Questionnaire	• Present Tense • Can • Wh-question words	• Verbs Used in Daily Personal / Work Activities • Name of Office Positions • Application terms	• Spelling activity: Unscramble the words
CHAPTER 9 *Let's Have a Garage Sale.*	• Describing and Telling Location of Objects • Writing a Simple Letter • Addressing an Envelope	• *there is / there are* • *some / any* • Adjective Word Order	• Common Household Items • Descriptive Adjectives • Community Areas/Buildings • *both*	• The Long */ū/* Sound (as in *room*)
CHAPTER 10 *Do You Have an Apartment for Rent?*	• Renting an Apartment • Filling out an Application Form • Reading Apartment Ads	• *have / has*	• Rooms of the House • House Appliances/Amenities • Abbreviations Used in Apartment Ads	• The */k/* Sound
CHAPTER 11 *We Have a Tight Schedule ...*	• Telling Time • Taking Public Transportation • Reading Bus, Work, and TV Schedules	• *to* and *at* with Expressions of Time and Place • Word Order with Expressions of Time and Place	• Transportation Words	• Long Vowels with Final Silent *e*
CHAPTER 12 *Are You Using This Ladder?*	• Describing Basic Home and Work Activities	• The Present Continuous • The Future with *going to*	• Verbs for Common Work and Home Activities	• Doubling Consonants • Deleting Silent Letters
CHAPTER 13 *We Can't Find Our Luggage.*	• Showing Possession • Filling out a Claim Form • Trying on Clothes	• The Possessive of Nouns • Possessive Adjectives and Pronouns • *too* + Adjective	• Clothing • Common Descriptive Adjectives	• The */j/* Sound (as in *job*)
CHAPTER 14 *Who Are These People?*	• Understanding Family Relationships • Buying Furniture • Reading Newspaper Ads	• The Possessive with *of*	• Names of Relatives • Common Descriptive Adjectives	• The */s/* Sound
CHAPTER 15 *I Want to Hire a Cleaning Crew.*	• Telling Someone What to Do	• Verb + Infinitive • Verb + Object + Infinitive • *why / because* • The Simple Past	• Common Cleaning Items • Common Work Activities • *know how to*	• The Short */ŏ/* Sound (as in *wash*)
CHAPTER 16 *Moving Day*	• Moving to a New Apartment • Renting a Truck • Filling Out an Application	• Review of present tense, *to be (am, is, are), can* • *Review of object pronouns* • *Review of pronouns of place*	• Household items • Room names • Common tools	• Review of consonants • Consonant and Vowel Combinations • Silent *e* at the End of Words

WOOKBOOK 2 CONTENTS AT A GLANCE

WORKBOOK 2	SKILLS / COMPETENCIES	GRAMMAR / STRUCTURES	VOCABULARY / EXPRESSIONS	WORD BUILDING / PHONICS
CHAPTER 1 *Welcome Back (Review of Workbook 1)*	• Introducing People • Asking and Giving Directions • Reading a Directory & Schedule • Filling Out Job Application	• Simple Present & Continuous Tenses, *can, may* • Subject & Object Pronouns • Possessive Adjectives	• Basic School, Bus, Shopping, and Job Search Vocabulary	• Word Puzzle (long and short vowels)
CHAPTER 2 *It's Too Wet to Walk Home.*	• Understand / Read a Weather Forecast • Using a Fahrenheit and Centigrade Thermometers	• Adverbs if Frequency • *to be* + Adjectives + Infinitive • *too / enough*	• Frequency Words • Weather / Temperature • Common Adjectives • Basic Job Vocabulary	• Changing Nouns to Adjectives with the Suffix ***-y*** • Negative Prefixes
CHAPTER 3 *Get Ready for a Dictation.*	• Identifying Career Goals and School Subjects • Reading an Appointment Book	• *have to / has to* • *if* clause • in order to • so • without	• Common Professions • School Subjects	• Suffixes used in Occupations *(-er, -ist, -or, -ess, -man, -woman)*
CHAPTER 4 *What Do I Have to Do to Go to College?*	• Describing Future Events or Activities (Plan a picnic) • Taking a Trip • Reading an Itinerary	• Future with the Present Continuous • Future with *"will"* & *"going to"* • Prepositions: *in, across, by*	• Party Supplies • Picnic Food • Expressions of Time *(Future)* • *US States & Big City Names*	• Double Consonant Combinations *(-ss, -ll)*
CHAPTER 5 *Where Were You About 11 O'clock?*	• Reporting a Crime • Describing Emotions • Describing Levels of Difficulty	• Past Tense of the Verb *"to be" (was, were)*	• Office Equipment • Time Expressions (Past) • Emotions • Descriptive Adjectives	• The */w/* and */v/* Sounds
CHAPTER 6 *Thank You, But No Thank You.*	• Describing Past Actions • Reading a Time Card • Reading a Personal Schedule	• Regular Verbs in the Past Tense	• Common Work Related Vocabulary • Expressions of Time: *ago, last*	• The ***-ed*** Ending • Rules for Adding the ***-ed*** Ending
CHAPTER 7 *It's Nice to Be Back Home.*	• Describing Past Actions • Identifying Major States & Cities	• Common Irregular Verbs • Preposition: *through*	• U.S. Cities, States, and Areas	• The Prefix ***re-***
CHAPTER 8 *The Past, Present, and Future*	• Writing a Story about Oneself • Asking and Answering Interview questions	• Review of present simple, present continuous, future, and the simple past tenses	• Review of Prepositions of Time and Place *(in, on, to, at)*	• Crossword puzzle using words from the chapter
CHAPTER 9 *Please Follow Directions Carefully.*	• Understanding Written Directions	• Using More Regular Verbs in the Past Tense	• Commonly Used Technical Words	• The Suffix ***-al***
CHAPTER 10 *Isn't that Women's Work?*	• Identifying Daily Activities • Making a Household Work Schedule	• Expressions with *do, make*, and *get*	• Household Chores • Daily Activities	• The Suffix ***-ing*** Used as a Noun (Gerund) • Rules for adding ***-ing*** to a Verb
CHAPTER 11 *Everything Went Wrong.*	• Describing a Series of Daily Events	• Intransitive Verbs with Prepositions of Direction • Two-word Verbs	• Common Separable and Non-Separable Two-Word Verbs	• The */ər/* Sound (as in ***her***)
CHAPTER 12 *At the Supermarket.*	• Read a Directory • Use U.S. Measurements • Read a Recipe • Read Ads & Compare Prices	• The Prepositions ***"of"***	• Common Shopping Items • Food Containers and U.S. Measurements	• The Suffix ***-ish***
CHAPTER 13 *Where Does It Hurt?*	• Making a Medical Appointment • Describing Medical Problems • Filling Out Medical Forms	• ***would like*** • ***that*** with clause • More Irregular Verbs • ***say*** and ***tell***	• General Medical Terms • Parts of the Body • Symptoms and Illnesses	• The Silent ***gh***
CHAPTER 14 *What Kind of Car Are You Looking For?*	• Reading Road Signs • Requesting Information About Price/Condition of a Car • Reading Car Ads	• How long does ***it take***?	• Common Road Signs • Parts of a Car	• The Suffix ***-ward***
CHAPTER 15 *Do You Work or Do You Hardly Work?*	• Describing How People Work	• Adjectives and Adverbs • Regular and Irregular Forms of Adverbs	• Common Adjectives and Adverbs • Important Safety Signs • ***hardly***	• The Suffixes ***-tion*** & ***-sion*** • Rules for adding ***-ly*** to Words
CHAPTER 16 *English for a Better Job*	• Looking for a Job • Filling Out an Application	• Review of the simple past, expressions with ***do*** and ***get*** • Review of possessives	• Car Terms • Household Chores	• Final Exam

WOOKBOOK 3 CONTENTS AT A GLANCE

CHAPTER 1

Welcome Back;
Review of Workbook 1

SKILLS	• Introducing People
	• Asking and Giving Directions
	• Reading a Shopping Directory, Schedule of Classes, and Bus Schedule
	• Filling Out a School Registration Form
	• Filling Out a Job Application
GRAMMAR	• The Simple Present Tense
	• The Present Continuous (Progressive) Tense
	• *can, may*
	• Subject and Object Pronouns
	• Possessive Adjectives
VOCABULARY	• Basic School, Bus, Shopping, and Job Search Vocabulary

Here are some of the people in the book.

Paul Wilson

Betty Wilson

Steve Wilson

Mike Breyer

Mary Breyer

Helen Pavlos

Jen Yang

Manuel Perez

Amir Abbas

Yuri Tanaka

Vince Cartelli

Martin Ngon

Rita Lachance

Alberto Duran

Alfonso Duran

Joanne Vordale

David Morris

Tan Van

Lan Van

Carmen Martinez

Read & Listen

Yuri Tanaka and Amir Abbas meet after the semester break.

Yuri: Hi, Amir.
Amir: Hi, Miko.
Yuri: Well, here we are again.
Amir: What class are you in this semester?
Yuri: In Level 2. What about you?
Amir: I'm in Level 2, too.
Yuri: What classroom are you in?
Amir: Room 204.
Yuri: So am I. Who's our teacher?
Amir: Mr. Wilson, I think.
Yuri: Doesn't he teach Level 1?
Amir: This semester he's teaching Level 2.
Yuri: Great! He's a really good teacher.

Understand *Circle **True, False,** or **We don't know.***

1. It's a new semester.			
2. Amir and Yuri are both in the same class.	True	False	We don't know.
3. It's January.	True	False	We don't know.
4. Yuri likes Mr. Wilson.	True	False	We don't know.
5, ***"So am I"*** means ***"Me, too."***	True	False	We don't know.
6. ***"ESL"*** means ***"English as a Second Language."***	True	False	We don't know.

Read

Here's the new schedule of classes.
May I see it?
Sure, here you are.

SCHEDULE OF CLASSES

Class	Level	Room	Time	Days	Instructor
Accounting 1	1	112*	8:30-11 a.m.	M & W**	J. Younger
Keyboarding	1	109	6:30-9 p.m.	M & W	M. Brown
Keyboarding	2	110	6:30-9 p.m.	T & Th	M. Brown
Solar Energy	1	111	6:30-9 p.m.	T & Th	J. Fuller
Nursing Assistant	1	206	6:30-9 p.m.	M & W	G. Graves
ESL	1	123	8:30-11 a.m.	M - Th	M. White
ESL	2	204	8:30-11 a.m.	M - Th	P. Wilson
ESL	3	312	6:30-9 p.m.	M - TH	A. Green
ESL Conversation	2	210	2-4 p.m.	F	M. Dayton
Graphic Design	1	221	1-6 p.m.	S	N. Long

Practice *Talk with another student about the schedule above. See the example.*

Student 1: What room is (class)........ in?
or
What floor is it on?
or
What time does it begin?
or
What days does it meet?
or
Who's the instructor?

What room is the ESL 2 class in?
It's in Room 204.
What floor is it on?
It's on the second floor.
What days does it meet?
It meets Monday through Thursday.
Who's the teacher?
Mr. Wilson.

Student 2: ....

** The first number of the room number tells the floor. Example: Room 203 is on the second floor.*

** ***& = and**, (**M & W** means two days a week, **M**onday **and W**ednesday.)*

*** *"-" = through, (**M-Th** means four times a week, Monday, Tuesday, Wednesday, and Thursday.)*

Read & Listen

Mary and her friend, Carmen Martinez, join Amir and Yuri.

Mary: Hi, Amir. Hi, Yuri.
I want you to meet a friend.
This is Carmen Martinez. She's from Colombia.
Carmen, these are my friends, Amir and Yuri.

Carmen: Pleased to meet you.

Yuri and Amir: Pleased to meet you, too.

Mary: Here comes Vince Cartelli.

Vince: Hi, everybody.

Mary: Do you know Carmen?

Vince: No, I don't.

Carmen: Hello. My name's Carmen Martinez.

Vince: I'm Vince Cartelli.

Carmen: Glad to meet you.

Vince: Glad to meet you, too.

Practice *Walk around the room and practice the mini-dialog below with other students.*

Student 1: Hello, I'm ....

Student 2: Hi, I'm ....

Student 1: Pleased to meet you.

Student 2: Pleased to meet you, too.

Practice *Walk around the room and introduce one student to another.*

Student 1: This is ....
He's / She's from ....

Student 2: Glad to meet you.

Student 3: Glad to meet you, too

Read

Carmen registers for a class.

Amir: This is a new student. She wants to register for an ESL class.
Counselor: What level?
Carmen: Level Three.
Counselor: Please fill out this registration card.

Write *Help Carmen fill out her registration card.*

I'm Carmen Martinez. My middle name is Maria. I'm from Colombia. I want to study English. I want to be in a level three ESL class. I passed a placement test for level three. I live at 34 Ocean Street, Santa Monica, California. My zip code is nine-two-oh-six-nine. My phone number is three-four-two-six-zero-seven-nine. I'm nineteen years old. My birthday is November sixth.

REGISTRATION FORM

NAME ______________________________
last first middle

ADDRESS ______________________________
number street apartment

CITY __________ **STATE** ______ **ZIP CODE** ______

DATE OF BIRTH ________ / ________ / ________
month date year

CLASS ______________ **LEVEL** ________

TELEPHONE ______________ ______________
home mobile

E-mail ______________________________

Signature ______________________________

Abbreviations

St. = Street
Ave. = Avenue
Blvd. = Boulevard
Dr. = Drive
Rd. = Road
Apt. = Apartment
# = number
N. = North
S. = South
E. = East
W. = West

Understand *Circle **True, False,** or **We don't know**.*

1. Amir's a new student. True False We don't know.
2. Carmen lives in an apartment. True False We don't know.
3. Carmen's year of birth is 1999. True False We don't know.
4. Carmen's telephone number is 342-6079. True False We don't know.

Read

Amir, Mary, and Carmen go to the snack bar across the street.

We have a few minutes before our classes. Let's go to the snack bar across the street and meet Mike.
OK.
All right.

Amir, Mary, and Carmen are standing at the door of the snack bar.

Look! There are Alberto and Alfonso Duran. They're twins. Alberto lives in Los Angeles. Alfonso lives in Santa Monica. Alberto rents a house. Alfonso rents an apartment. Alberto works for a trucking company. Alfonso works in an office.
What! Can you repeat that?

Write

Help Mary describe Alberto and Alfonso Duran. Fill in the spaces with the present tense verbs. Use the **-s** *ending, and the negative with* **doesn't**. *(Remember that she is talking about regular or habitual actions.)*

1. Alberto ___*lives*___ in Los Angeles; he ___*doesn't*___ ___*live*___ in Santa Monica.
2. Alberto __________ a house; he __________ __________ in an apartment.
3. Alberto __________ for a trucking company; he __________ __________ in an office.

Write

Fill in the spaces with **does** *or* **doesn't**.

1. ___*Does*___ Alberto rent a house?
2. __________ Alfonso live in Los Angeles?
3. __________ Alberto work for a trucking company?
4. __________ Alfonso drive a truck?
5. __________ Alberto live in an apartment?

Of, course he ___*does*___.
No, he __________.
Sure he __________.
No, he __________.
He sure __________!

Read

Amir sees some friends.

... and there are Anna and Manuel Perez and Lee and Jen Yang. Anna and Manuel are from Mexico. Lee and Yen come from China. Anna and Manuel have two kids. Lee and Jen have one child. Anna and Manuel live near here. Lee and Jen live far away. Anna and Manuel walk to school. Lee and Jen drive here.
What! Please repeat that?
SNACK BAR

Write

Fill in the spaces with the present tense verbs. Use ***don't*** *in the negative.*

1. Lee and Jen _come_ from China; they _don't_ _come_ from Mexico.
2. Lee and Jen ________ only one child; they ________ ________ two kids.
3. Lee and Jen ________ far from school; they ________ ________ near school.
4. Lee and Jen ________ a car to school; they ________ ________ to school.

Write

Fill in the spaces below with the words in the box.

come	have	live	drive	do	does	don't	doesn't

1. _Does_ Anna _come_ from Mexico?
2. ________ Lee and Jen ________ from Mexico?
3. ________ Anna ________ two kids?
4. ________ Lee and Jen ________ near school?
5. ________ Anna and Manuel _____ near school?
6. ________ Lee ________ a car to school?

Of, course she _does_.
No, they ____________.
Yes, she ____________.
No, they ____________.
Yes, they ____________.
Yes, he ____________.

Write *Fill in the spaces with the correct present continuous form of the verb. (Remember that they are talking about continuous action in the present time.)*

Amir, Mary, and Carmen go to Mike's table at the snack bar. Mike is sitting with a friend, Peter Pavlos.

Amir: Hi, Mario. Hi, Peter.

Mary: How are you?

Peter: Fine. How (1) ___are___ you ___doing___? *(do)*

Amir: I (2) ____ ________ *(do)* fine. What (3) ____ you ________ *(do)*?

Mike: We (4) ____ ________ *(rest)* before class. I (5) ____ ________ *(have)* a cup of coffee, and Peter (6) ____ ________ *(eat)* dinner.

Mary: There are a lot of students here.

Peter: And the waitress is really busy. She (7) ____ ________ *(run)* from table to table. Look! The manager (8) ____ ________ *(help)* her, too. They (9) ____ ________ *(try)* to serve all of us before the classes begin.

Mary: Peter, where's your wife?

Peter: She (10) ____ ________ *(stand)* over there near the window. She (11) ____ ________ *(talk)* to Tan and Lan Van. She (12) ____ ________ *(tell)* them about our new apartment.

Waitress: May I help you?

Carmen: No, thank you. We (13) ____ ________ *(leave)* now. We don't want to be late for class.

Peter: I'll leave the tip.

Group Discussion *Talk about restaurant etiquette and tipping.*

Read

Mary, Mike, Carmen, and Amir are walking in the hall.

Write *Fill in the spaces below with the words in the box.*

Subject Pronouns:	I	you	he	she	it	we	they
Possessive Adjectives:	my	your	his	her	its	our	their
Object Pronouns:	me	you	him	her	it	us	them

That's Mr. Thompson. (1) ___He___'s your teacher. (2) ___His___ first name is Percy. The students like (3) ___him___ very much.

There's Ms. Sumner. (4) ______'s a teacher and an actress. (5) ______ classroom is next door. Mr. Thompson is speaking to (6) ______ now.

There's Mr. Wilson. (7) ________ is my instructor. (8) ________'s an excellent teacher. (9) _______ lessons are very interesting. I learn a lot from (10) ____.

Mr. Wilson, Mike and I sometimes take a break together. (11) ______ usually go to the catering truck downstairs. (12) _______ friends sometimes join (13) _________, too.

Write *Fill in the spaces below with the words in the box.*

Where's Lisa?

She (1) _'s working_ now.
work

Oh? Where (2) _does_ she _work_?
work

She (3) ______ at the hospital.
work

(4) ______ she ______ her job?
like

Yes, she (5) ______.
do

What (6) ______ you __________?
read

I (7) ________ a book about history.
read

(8) _____ you _______ history books?
like

Yes, I (9) ________. What about you?
do

I (10) ________ love stories.
like

What (11) _____ he _________?
do

He (12) ______ _________ a pen.
look for

Why (13) _____ he ______ a pen?
need

He (14) _____ to write a note to his friend.
want

Why (15) _____ you ______ here?
wait

We (16) ____ ______ for our teacher.
wait

(17) ____ you _____ to school early?
come

Yes, we (18) ________.
do

Why?

Because we (19) ______ good seats.
want

Read & Listen

Carmen is speaking to Anna.

Anna: Where do you work?

Carmen: I don't have a job. I'm looking for one now.

Anna: What kind of work do you do?

Carmen: I'm an electronics assembler.

Anna: Try the Byte Computer Company on Fifth Street.

Carmen: How can I get there? I don't have a car.

Anna: Take the #93 bus. You can catch it on First Street in front of the school.

Carmen: What time does it stop there?

Anna: Here's a bus schedule. You can keep it.

Carmen: Thanks a lot for your help.

Practice *Talk with another student about the bus schedule below.*

Student 1: When does the bus stop at .... and ....?
Student 2: It stops there at ....

When does the bus stop at the corner of First and Main?
It stops there at nineteen past three, twenty to four, ...

BUS SCHEDULE LINE 93

INBOUND TO DOWNTOWN

FIFTH ST. & MAIN ST. P.M.	FOURTH ST. & MAIN ST. P.M.	THIRD ST. & MAIN ST. P.M.	SECOND ST. & MAIN ST. P.M.	FIRST ST. & MAIN ST. P.M.
2:44	2:29	3:04	3:11	3:27
3:05	3:20	3:25	3:32	3:40
3:29	3:44	3:49	3:56	4:04
4:29	4:44	4:49	4:56	5:04
5:00	5:15	5:20	5:27	5:35
5:22	5:37	5:42	5:49	5:56
5:50	6:05	6:10	6:17	6:27
6:21	6:36	6:40	6:47	6:54

Read & Listen

An hour later, during the break, Carmen is talking to Mary.

Carmen: Mary, can you go with me tomorrow?
I want to apply for a job at a computer company on Fifth Street.

Mary: I'm sorry, but I can't. I work, you know.

Carmen: Oh, right. Before I go, I need to get a new dress, some shoes, and a haircut. Where can I get all that?

Mary: At the Lincoln Shopping Center. There's a computer store in the shopping center, and the computer company is next door to it.

Understand *Circle **True, False,** or **We don't know.***

I. Mary and Carmen are at a shopping center.	True	False	We don't know.
2. Mary can go with Carmen.	True	False	We don't know.

LINCOLN SHOPPING CENTER DIRECTORY

	FLOOR		FLOOR		FLOOR
Information Desk	1	Shoe Store	2	Women's Clothing	4
Drug Store	1	Hairdresser	3	Video & Game Store	4
Department Store	1	Barber Shop	3	Restaurants	5
Lost and Found	1	Men's Clothing	3	Toy Store	5
Security Office	1	Children's Clothing	3	TV & Appliances Store	5
Restrooms	1	Business Offices	3	Byte Computer Store	5
Coffee Shop	2	Book Store	4	Pet Shop	6
Hardware Store	2	Movie Theaters	4	Bank ATM	1

Practice *Talk with another student about the items below.*

Student 1: Where can I get .... ?
Student 2: You can get .... at the ....

Where can I get a new dress?
INFORMATION
You can get a new dress at the Women's Clothing store.

1.a new dress

2. a book

3.shoes

4. a cup of coffee

5. toys

6. a radio

7. a notebook

8.tools

Practice *Use the directory above.*

Student 1: What floor is the .... on?
Student 2: It's on the .... floor.

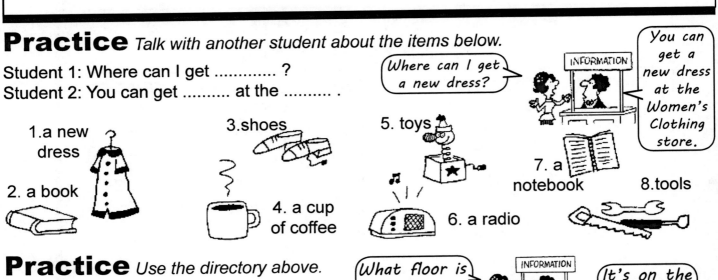

What floor is the computer store on?
INFORMATION
It's on the fifth floor.

Challenge *Alphabetize the direction above in your notebook.*

Read & Listen

Carmen is applying for a job at the Byte Computer Company.

Carmen: Is this the Personnel Office?

Receptionist: Yes, it is. May I help you?

Carmen: I want to apply for a job.

Receptionist: Please fill out this application and wait here.

APPLICATION FORM FOR EMPLOYMENT

NAME: Martinez Carmen Maria TODAY'S DATE 11/3/2016

Last First Middle *Month / Date / Year*

ADDRESS: 39 Ocean Street

Number Street Apartment

CITY: Santa Monica STATE: CA ZIP: 90269

PHONE: (310) 430-1923 (213) 342-6079

Home Other

OCCUPATION: Electronics assembler ____________

Write

Now you fill out an application for a job, too.

APPLICATION FORM FOR EMPLOYMENT

NAME: ______________________ TODAY'S DATE ____________

Last First Middle *Month / Date / Year*

ADDRESS: ______________________________________

Number Street Apartment

CITY: ____________ STATE: ____________ ZIP: ____________

PHONE: ______________________________________

Home Other

OCCUPATION: ______________ IMMIGRATION STATUS ________

When can you begin to work? ______________________

Can you work on weekends? ______________________

Can you work at night? ______________________

Your last job: ______________ Where? ______________

Do you have a job now? ______________________

SIGNATURE: ______________________

Write *Fill in the spaces below with the words in the box below.*

m	is	's	are	do	don't	can

Manager: I (1) *'m*______ the personnel manager. Please come in.

Carmen: Thank you. Here (2) _______ my application.

Manager: Let me ask you a few questions.

Carmen: OK. Please do.

Manager: (3) _______ you know how to work with electronic equipment?

Carmen: Yes, I (4) _______. I (5) _______ an electronics assembler.

Manager: How much experience (6) _______ you have?

Carmen: Two years.

Manager: (7) _______ you working now?

Carmen: No, I (8) _______not. I (9) _______ have a job. I (10) _______ new in America. I need a steady job. I like to work. I work very hard, and I work very well.

Manager: When (11) _______ you begin?

Carmen: Immediately.

Manager: (12) _______ you work on weekends?

Carmen: Yes, I (13) _______.

Manager: How (14) _______ your English?

Carmen: I go to school and my English (15) _______ better every day!

Manager: Good. Come in tomorrow at eight o'clock. I have a job for you.

Practice *Fold this page along the dotted lines. Practice with a partner.*

Student 1

Ask your partner the questions below.

1. What room is the Auto Shop in ?
2. What floor is the ESL 1 class on?
3. Who is the ESL 1 instructor?
4. What time is the ESL 3 class?
5. What room is Electronics class in?
6. What time is the English 1 class?
7. Who teachers ESL 3?
8. Who is the teacher for ESL 2?
9. Who is Mrs. Brian?

Fill out the Identification card for your partner. Listen to the information.

IDENTIFICATION CARD

Name ______________________________

Address ____________________________

______________**State**___**ZIP** _______

PHONE _____________________________

Date of Birth ________________________

Class _______________ **Level** _______

E-mail ____________________________

Signature __________________________

FOLD HERE

FOLD HERE

Student 2

Listen to the questions. Find the answers in the schedule of classes.

SCHEDULE OF CLASSES

Class	Room	Time	Instructor
ESL 1	123	2:30 pm	Ms. Wood
ESL 2	210	6:30 pm	Mr. Wilson
ESL 3	303	8:30 am	Mrs. Khan
English 1	130	8:30 am	Mr. West
Auto Shop	130	6:30 pm	Ms. Monte
Electronics	207	2:30 pm	Mr. Sax
Keyboarding	137	8:00 am	Mrs. Brian

Your partner fills out an identification card for you. Tell your partner your:

1. First name
2. Last name
3. Middle Name
4. Street address
5. City and State
6. Zip Code
7. Telephone number
8. Date of Birth
9. Your class and level
10. E-mail address
10. Check the card and sign it.

Group Activity

Walk around the room and ask questions. Find the students with the following characteristic(s). Then, write their names on the lines below.

1. ______________________ has a job.
2. ______________________ doesn't work.
3. ______________________ lives near here.
4. ______________________ lives far away.
5. ______________________ is wearing a white shirt.
6. ______________________ is wearing a necklace.
7. ______________________ is smart
8. ______________________ has a quarter in his / her pocket.
9. ______________________ has a brother and a sister.
10. ______________________ can drive a car.
11. ______________________ takes the bus to school.
12. ______________________ can't speak my language.

Write

Find as many words as you can. Write the words below.

m	a	n	y	e	s	p	r	a	c	t	i	c	e	s
n	i	n	e	a	r	e	a	n	o	t	s	i	u	i
w	m	a	n	t	b	i	g	s	a	y	u	r	e	t
c	a	t	o	o	l	m	d	a	t	e	n	u	s	e
e	p	i	c	t	u	r	e	d	h	s	d	c	p	a
n	o	t	t	h	e	e	s	e	a	t	a	k	e	s
t	s	i	z	r	m	s	k	n	t	r	y	m	a	y
h	s	t	r	e	e	t	i	m	e	n	m	a	k	e
i	o	f	r	e	e	x	r	i	g	h	t	a	p	e
s	a	b	o	u	t	z	t	w	e	i	v	e	i	l

1. *man*	11. ______	21. ______	31. ______	41. ______
2. *nine*	12. ______	22. ______	32. ______	42. ______
3. *wait*	13. ______	23. ______	33. ______	43. ______
4. *cat*	14. ______	24. ______	34. ______	44. ______
5. *eat*	15. ______	25. ______	35. ______	45. ______
6. ______	16. ______	26. ______	36. ______	46. ______
7. ______	17. ______	27. ______	37. ______	47. ______
8. ______	18. ______	28. ______	38. ______	48. ______
9. ______	19. ______	29. ______	39. ______	49. ______
10. ______	20. ______	30. ______	40. ______	50. ______

CHAPTER 2

It's Too Wet to Walk Home.

SKILLS
- Understanding a Weather Forecast
- Reading a Weather Fore0cast
- Using a Fahrenheit and Centigrade Thermometers

GRAMMAR
- Adverbs if Frequency
- *to be* + Adjectives + Infinitive
- *too / enough*

VOCABULARY
- Frequency Words
- Weather / Temperature
- Common Adjectives
- Basic Job Vocabulary

WORD BUILDING
- Changing Nouns to Adjectives with the Suffix ***-y***
- Negative Prefixes

Read & Listen

The personnel manager introduces Carmen to Vic Pontrelli, her new supervisor at work.

Welcome to our company. Let me introduce you to our supervisor. Vic, this is Carmen Martinez. She's a new employee. Please give her an orientation to the company.
PERSONNEL MANAGER

Vic: Here's your badge.

Carmen: You must always wear it at work. We usually work eight hours a day, and we sometimes work only half a day before holidays. We never work on legal holidays. We punch in at 8:00 a.m. and we punch out at 5:00 p.m. Sometimes we work overtime, but only two or three times a month.

Manager: We take fifteen minute breaks twice a day, mid-morning and mid-afternoon. We seldom take our breaks before 10:00 a.m. or after 4:00 p.m.

Carmen: How many times a month do we get a paycheck?

Vic: Twice a month, and we generally get a raise once a year.

Understand *Circle **True, False,** or **We don't know.***

1. ***"Not often"*** means ***"seldom."***	True	False	We don't know.
2. The employees work eight hours a day.	True	False	We don't know.
3. The employer pays the workers for holidays.	True	False	We don't know.
4. Lunch is one hour.	True	False	We don't know.
5. A ***"raise"*** means ***"more money."***	True	False	We don't know.
6. ***"Overtime"*** means ***"extra time."***	True	False	We don't know.

Grammar Adverbs of Frequency

• Adverbs of frequency tell how often an action happens. The percentages below show approximately what frequency of occurrence each word represents.

always - 100%	***sometimes*** - 50%
generally - usually 90%	***seldom*** - 20%
often - 75%	***never*** - 0%

• Adverbs of frequency come before the main verb of a sentence.

Examples:	We	***usually***	work eight hours.
	We	***sometimes***	work half a day
	We	***never***	work on holidays.
	We	***seldom***	take breaks before 10 a.m.
	We	***generally***	get a raise every year.

• But they follow the verb ***be*** and modal verbs.

Examples:	It isn't	***often.***	
	You must	***always***	wear the badge at work.

• Adverbs of frequency can appear at the beginning of a sentence.

Example: ***Sometimes*** we work overtime.

• We often use the adverb ***ever*** in questions. We never use ***ever*** in positive statements.

Example: Do you ***ever*** work overtime?

I Employees We They	always generally usually often sometimes seldom never	take a break work work overtime get a raise go home come to work arrive at school	on time. early. late. eight hours. every day. every month. every year.

Practice

Talk with another student. Use adverbs of frequency with the phrases below. See the example.

Student 1: How often do / are you ....?
Student 2: I ....

How often do you work overtime?
I seldom work overtime.

1. work overtime
2. be sick
3. come to school late
4. come to school early
5. be on time
6. get a paycheck
7. sleep late
8. get e-mails
9. ask questions
10. speak English
11. read a newspaper
12. work on the weekend

Grammar Adverbial Expressions of Time

• Long adverbial expressions of time generally come at the end of the sentence.

Examples:	We	work	***eight hours a day.***
	We	work overtime	***two or three times a month.***
	We	take a break	***twice a day.***
	We	get a raise	***once a year.***

Read *Make logical complete sentences with the words in the box.*

I Employees We They	take a bus get a paycheck work overtime work get a raise come to work early come to work late	once twice three times four times five times eight hours a few hours	a day. * a week. a month. a year.

Practice *Talk with another student. Use adverbial expressions of time with the phrases below. Answer the questions in your own words. See the example.*

Student 1: How often do you ....?
Student 2: I ....

1. work overtime
2. see your parents
3. see your relatives
4. come home late from work (or school)
5. come home early from work (or school)
6. miss the bus
7. miss school or work
8. get a haircut
9. take a vacation
10. write a dictation
11. take a test
12. go shopping for food

Practice *Use adverbial expressions of time with the phrases below. Answer the questions in your own words. See the example.*

Student 1: How many times a .... do you ....?
Student 2: .... a ....

1. get a paycheck
2. take a shower
3. eat
4. go to a restaurant
5. go to a movie
6. call a friend
7. read a book
8. work
9. clean the house
10. take out the garbage
11. pay your bills
12. *(Use your own words.)*

---

* Do not use the preposition ***"in"*** before these expressions. For example, it is not correct to say "*once in a day.*"

Read

Here's a page from Carmen's calendar.

FEBRUARY						
Sunday	Monday	Tuesday	Wednesday	Thursday	Friday	Saturday
1 call parents	2 work, school	3 work, school	4 work, school	5 work, school	6 work, market	7 clean house, date
8 movie date	9 work, school	10 work, school	11 work, school	12 work, school	13 work, paycheck, market	14 clean house
15 call parents	16 work, school	17 work, school	18 work, school	19 work, school	20 work, laundry, market	21 clean yard, restaurant
22 text parents	23 work, school	24 work, school	25 work, school	26 work, school	27 work, paycheck, market	28 clean house, market

Practice

Work with a partner. Use the calendar above. See the example below.

Student 1: How often does Carmen ....?
Student 2: ....

How often does Carmen have a date?
About three times a month.

Practice

Work with a partner. Use ***always, usually, often, sometimes,*** *and* ***seldom*** *in your answers. Use the calendar above. See the example below.*

Student 1: Does Carmen ever ....?
Student 2: Yes, she does. She ....
or
No, she doesn't. She never ....

Does Carmen ever go to the movies?
Yes, she does. She usually goes about once a month.

Practice

Work with a partner. Talk about your own monthly schedules. Answer the questions in your own words with ***always, usually, often, sometimes,*** *and* ***seldom.*** *See the example below.*

Student 1: How often do you ....?
Student 2: I ....

How often do you go to a restaurant?
I go about once a month.

Read & Listen

Carmen is taking a break. Vic Pontrelli is coming into the lunch room.

Carmen: Vic, you're all wet. How is it outside?

Vic: It's terrible. It's raining and windy.

Carmen: Does it rain very often here?

Vic: Not very often, but when we have a winter storm, it rains hard.

Carmen: Isn't it always warm and sunny in California?

Vic: No, not always. It's usually nice, but the weather's sometimes bad here, too.

Carmen: How are the seasons here?

Vic: It rains in the winter, and it snows in the mountains. It's cloudy, foggy, and cool in the spring. In the summer, it's hot, dry, and sometimes smoggy. My favorite season is the fall or autumn. It's cool at night and warm and clear in the daytime.

Carmen: How hot is it in the summer?

Vic: Here in Los Angeles, it's about 65 degrees Fahrenheit at night and about 80 degrees in the daytime.

Carmen: How many degrees Centigrade is that?

Vic: I don't know. I don't understand Centigrade. I use my smart phone.

Understand *Circle **True, False,** or **We don't know**.*

1. It's always sunny and warm in California.	True	False	We don't know.
2. It sometimes snows in California.	True	False	We don't know,
3. ***"Fall"*** means ***"autumn."***	True	False	We don't know.
4. Vic understands degrees in Fahrenheit.	True	False	We don't know.

Challenge *What the average body temperature in Centigrade and in Fahrenheit?*

** To change Fahrenheit to Centigrade (Celsius), subtract 32 and multiply by 5/9.*
To change Centigrade to Fahrenheit, multiply by 9/5 and add 32.
Examples: (65°F - 32 x 5/9 = 18.3°C), (27°C x 9/5 + 32 = 80.6°F)

Read

QUESTIONNAIRE

Use Fahrenheit Degrees

1. What's the temperature of this room?__________
2. What's a good room temperature?__________
3. What's the temperature outside? __________
4. How's the weather today? __________
5. What season is it? __________
6. What's normal body temperature? __________
7. Are you sick if you have a 102ºF temperature? ________
8. Is 100 degrees hot or warm? __________
9. Is 70 degrees warm or cool? __________
10. Is 60 degrees cool or cold? __________
11. Is 40 degrees cool or cold? __________
12. Is 32 degrees cold or freezing? __________
13. How much is 16 degrees Centigrade? ________

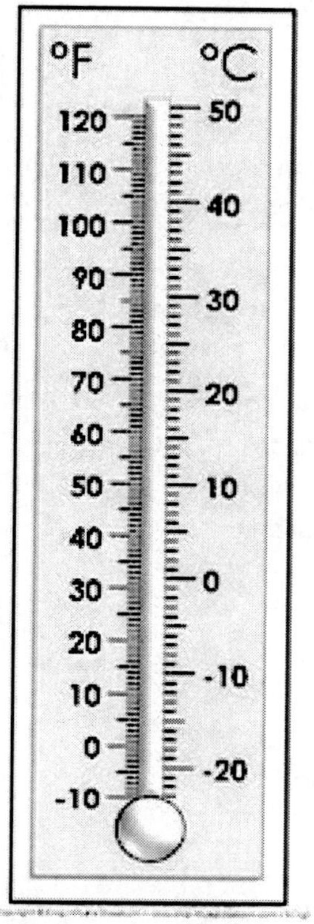

Group Discussion *Talk about your answers in a small groups.*

Practice *Work with a partner. Use the thermometer above. See the example below.*

Student 1: How much is .... degrees Centigrade?
Student 2: It's about .... degrees Fahrenheit.

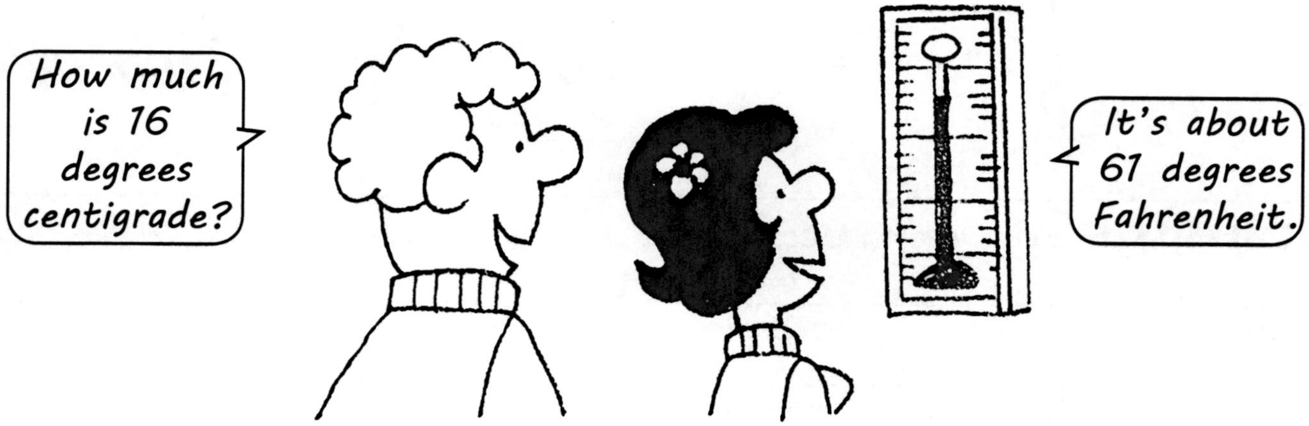

How much is 16 degrees centigrade?
It's about 61 degrees Fahrenheit.

Read

Weather Forecast

Today - rain in the early evening
Temperatures: High: 73; Low: 55

Tomorrow - clear with morning low clouds
Temperatures: High: 78; Low: 54

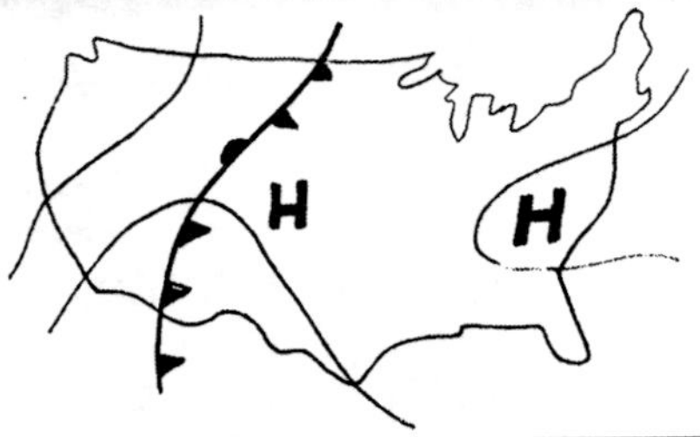

Today's Weather Around the Country

City	*High*	*Low*	*Weather*
Chicago	31	15	snowy
Dallas	56	37	cloudy
Denver	38	15	icy
Fairbanks	10	-5	freezing
Los Angeles	70	55	rainy
Miami	75	60	sunny
New Orleans	65	49	stormy
New York	40	28	hazy
San Francisco	60	45	fair
Seattle	40	30	windy
Washington, D.C.	44	32	foggy

Practice *Work with a partner. Use the weather forecast and the map above. See the example below.*

Student 1: What's the high / low temperature in .....(city)....?
Student 2: It's .... degrees.

Practice *Work with a partner. Use the weather forecast and the map above. See the example below.*

Student 1: How's the weather in ....(city)....?
Student 2: It's ....

How's the weather in Chicago?
It's snowy.

Challenge *Find a weather forecast for your city in the newspaper. Share it to your classmates.*

1. ______________________________
City *Weather* *Temperature*

2. ______________________________
City *Weather* *Temperature*

3. ______________________________
City *Weather* *Temperature*

4. ______________________________
City *Weather* *Temperature*

Read & Listen

Carmen begins her training with Betty Kogan.

Betty: I'm glad to meet you, Carmen. Let me show you the shop and your job. It's nice to work here. It isn't dangerous, and the job isn't hard to do. We try to fix circuit boards. When a circuit board doesn't pass inspection, it comes to us. It's expensive to throw away parts, and it's possible to fix some of them. It's interesting to work with electronics, and it's challenging to find the problems, too. Some parts are easy to fix and some are hard to fix. We're able to fix about 80 percent of the boards. After we fix a board, it's necessary to test it. Then it's important to test it a second and a third time before we send it to the shipping department.

Understand *Circle T**rue, False,** or **We don't know.***

1. Betty likes her job.	True	False	We don't know.
2. Betty is training Carmen.	True	False	We don't know.
3. It's easy to work with electronic parts.	True	False	We don't know.
4. It's dangerous to work with circuit boards.	True	False	We don't know.
5. They are able to fix all the boards.	True	False	We don't know.

Grammar *to be* + Adjective + Infinitive

• We use the infinitive to complete the meaning of the adjective. It expressess feelings and reactions, and it gives a reason for the adjective.

Examples:

	to be	*Adjective*	*Infinitive*	
I	*'m*	*glad*	*to meet*	you.
The job	*isn't*	*hard*	*to do.*	
Some parts	*are*	*easy*	*to fix.*	

• Many sentences with infinitives begin with ***"it."***

Examples:

It	*'s*	*nice*	*to work*	here.
It	*'s*	*expensive*	*to throw away*	the parts.
It	*'s*	*difficult*	*to find*	the problems.
It	*'s*	*important*	*to test*	it a second time.

Read *Make logical complete sentences with the words in the box.*

It	is	possible	to begin	the broken parts.
	isn't	interesting	to fix	a new job.
		hard	to work	with you.
		easy	to test	English.
		important	to learn	early.

Word Building Negative Prefixes

• We can change the meaning of a word from affirmative to negative with prefixes such as ***un-***, ***im-***, and ***in-***.

Examples:

Affirmative		*Negative*		
1. important	➞	***un***important	=	not important
2. happy	➞	***un***happy	=	not happy
3. exployed	➞	***un***employed	=	not employed
4. expensive	➞	***in***expensive	=	not expensive
5. possible	➞	***im***possible	=	not possible

Read *Make logical complete sentences with the words in the box.*

I	'm	an	unimportant	book.
He	's		uninteresting	problem.
She	're		impossible	person.
It			unemployed	car.
You			inexpensive	worker.

Read

Betty, I'm new here. Can you tell me about this country? What do you think? Is it hard to find a good job?
Carmen, you're very lucky. It's very hard to find a good job.

Practice

Work with a partner. Use the adjectives under the question with the phrases below. See the example.

Student 1: Is it .... to ....?

easy / hard
good / bad
possible / impossible
dangerous / safe
necessary / unnecessary
interesting / uninteresting
important / unimportant
expensive / inexpensive

Student 2: Yes / No, it's .... to ....

Is it easy to find a good job.
No, it's hard to find a good job.

1. find a good job
2. work overtime
3. work part time
4. work on the weekend
5. come to work on time
6. punch out early
7. get a raise often
8. get a check every week
9. buy lunch at work
10 *(Use your words.)*

Group Discussion

What do you think? Discuss the topics below in small groups. Use the adjectives above. See the example below.

Student 1: Is it .... to ....?
Student 2: Yes, it is. / No, it isn't.
Student 1: Why?
Student 2: Because ....*(Give a reason.)*......

It is necessary to work well?
Yes, it is.
Why?
Because ...

1. work well
2. understand people on T.V.
3. begin a new life in a new country
4. find an inexpensive apartment
5. learn to drive a car
6. buy a car
7. pay your bills on time
8. be a millionaire
9. walk outside at night
10. meet some neighbors
11. know English well
12. ....*(Use your words.)*....

Read & Listen

Grammar too / enough

• ***Too*** means more than necessary, excessive or unacceptable. Use it <u>before</u> adjectives.

• An infinitive often follows an adjective with ***too*** or ***enough*** to show purpose.

		Too +	***Adjective*** +	***Infinitive***		
Examples:	The box is	***too***	***heavy***	***to lift.***		*(I can't lift it.)*
	I'm	***too***	***old.***	***to pick***	up the box.	*(I can't pick it up.)*

• ***Enough*** means sufficient, satisfying or equal to what is needed. Use it <u>after</u> adjectives.

		Adjective +	***enough*** +	***Infinitive***		
Examples:	Tom's	***strong***	***enough***	***to lift***	the box.	*(He can do the work.)*
	Jim's not	***tall***	***enough***	***to reach***	the shelf.	*(He can't do it.)*

• Do not use ***too*** or ***enough*** instead of ***very***. ***Too*** and ***enough*** imply the idea of a following infinitive even if there isn't one.

Examples:	He's	***very strong***.	*(He can lift the box.)*
	He isn't	***strong enough.***	*(He can't lift the box.)*
	He's	***too weak.***	*(He can't lift the box.)*

READ *Make logical complete sentences with the words in the box.*

He She	's isn't	too young young enough too old old enough too weak strong enough	to do the work. to work here. to pick up the box. to help us.

Practice *Work with a partner. Use the words below.*

Student 1: Why can't ..*(name)*.. work here?
Student 2: Because he / she is too ....;
he / she isn't .... enough to work here.

Axel

1. weak / strong

Moses

2. old / young

Betsy

3. young / old

Roger

4. sick / healthy

Scott

5. fat / thin

Brenda

6. dirty / clean

Carl

7. lazy / hard-working

Pat

8. messy / neat

Buster

9. dangerous / safe

Larry

10. dumb / smart

Bobby

11. small / big

Slim

12. tall / short

Write *Fill in the spaces with the words in the box.*

too expensive	***twice a month***	***hours a day***	***usually***
always	***once a year***	***twice a day***	***never***

Carmen is talking to Mary.

How's your new job? Tell me about it.

It's great to work there. I like the job very much. I (1) *always* punch in on time; I'm (2) ____________ late. We work eight (3) ____________ and we take breaks. I (4) ____________ bring my lunch with me because it's (6) ____________ to buy lunch at a restaurant or snack bar. We get a paycheck (7) ____________ and a raise (8) ____________.

Write *Put the sentences of the dialog in the correct order. Write the numbers 1 to 9 in front of the sentences. (1 is the first in order, and 9 is last.)*

________ What level are you in?

________ How many times a week does his class meet?

________ I don't, but my husband does.

________ Level Three.

________ Oh, really? What does he study?

________ I study English.

________ He's studying electronics.

___1___ Do you go to school?

________ Twice a week. What do you study, Carmen?

Dictation *Listen to the instructor (or your partner) read the dictation at the bottom of the next page. Write the sentences below. Then, check your writing.*

Mike,

1. ____
2. ____
3. ____
4. ____
5. ____

Love, Mary

Practice

Fold this page along the dotted lines. Practice with a partner.

Student 1

Ask your partner the questions below.

1. What's the high temperature in Chicago in July?
2. What's the low temperature in Miami?
3. Is it hot or warm in Dallas?
4. Where is it nice weather in July?
5. What's the temperature in New Orleans?
6. Where is it between 65 and 80 degrees?
7. Where is it cold?

Listen to the questions from your partner. Use the thermometer to find the answers.

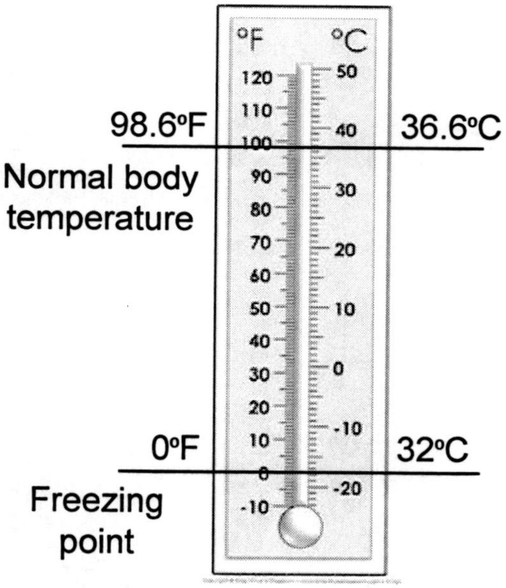

FOLD HERE

Student 2

Listen to the questions. Find the answers below.

Average Daily Temperature in July around the Country

City	*High*	*Low*
Chicago	87°F	65°F
Dallas	105	79
Denver	90	63
Los Angeles	80	65
Miami	90	76
New Orleans	95	77
New York	88	71
San Francisco	72	54
Seattle	73	54
Washington, D.C.	91	74

Ask your partner these questions about the thermometer to the left.

1. How much is 14 degrees Centigrade in Fahrenheit?
2. How much is 100 degrees Fahrenheit in Centigrades?
3. Is 72 degrees Fahrenheit a good room temperature?
4. Is 100 degrees Fahrenheit a comfortable outside temperature?
5. What's the temperature outside now?
6. How much is ...... degrees Fahrenheit in Centigrade?
7. How much is ...... degrees Centigrade in Fahrenheit?

FOLD HERE

Dictation

(from the previous page) Read this dictation to your partner.

Mike,

1. Please pick me up at work today.
2. I don't want to walk home.
3. The weather isn't very nice today.
4. The weather forcast is for rain and wind this afternoon.
5. See you at 5 pm in front of the factory.

Love, Mary

Word Building **Making Adjectives with the ending *-y*.**

• We can sometimes make an adjective from a noun by adding a ***-y*** at the end of the word.

Examples:	sun	➡	--	sunny*	weather
	rain	➡	a	rainy	day
	ice	➡	an	icy**	street

* When a word ends in a consonant-vowel-consonant pattern and the final vowel is stressed, the last consonant is doubled before adding ***"-y."***

** When a word ends in a silent ***"e,"*** before adding ***"-y."***

Write *Change these nouns to adjectives.*

1. snow snowy
2. ice ____________
3. haze ____________
4. fog ____________
5. smog ____________
6. wind ____________
7. storm ____________
8. cloud ____________
9. rain ____________
10. dirt ____________

Write *What kind of day do the pictures show?*

1. It's a rainy day.

2. ____________

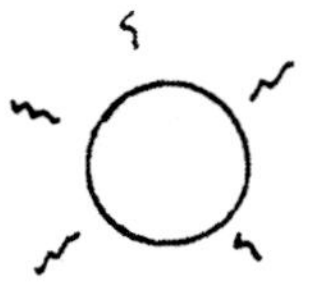

3. ____________

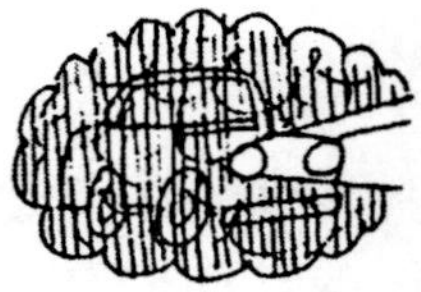

4. ____________

5. ____________

6. ____________

7. ____________

8. ____________

CHAPTER 3

What Do I Have to Do to Go to College?

SKILLS
- Identifying Career Goals and School Subjects
- Reading an Appointment Book

GRAMMAR
- *have to / has to*
- *if* clause
- *in order to*
- *so*
- *without*

VOCABULARY
- Common Professions
- School Subjects

WORD BUILDING
- Suffixes Used in Occupations

Read & Listen

Tan Tran and his son, Phuong, are talking at home.

Tan: Phuong, before you leave the house, you have to take out the garbage.

Phuong: Do I have to?

Tan: Yes, you do.

Phuong: Dad, I have to have ten dollars.

Tan: For what?

Phuong: To go out with Ann Wong.

Tan: Go out!? Why do you have to go out? Why aren't you studying?

Phuong: Why do I always have to study?

Tan: Do you want money?

Phuong: Yes, of course.

Tan: Good. If you want money, you have to get a part-time job. If you want a job, you have to look for a job. If you look for a job, you have to go on an interview. If you go on an interview, you have to have skills and know English well. If you want to have skills and know English well, you have to go to school. If you go to school, you have to study. Right?

Phuong: I guess so.

Tan: Don't you want to go to college?

Phuong: Yes, of course.

Understand *Circle **True, False,** or **We don't know.***

1. Phuong has a job.	True	False	We don't know.
2. Phuong's studying now.	True	False	We don't know.
3. Phuong likes to study.	True	False	We don't know.
4. Phuong has work skills.	True	False	We don't know.
5. ***"I guess so."*** means ***"I think you're right."***	True	False	We don't know.

Write *Underline the words "**have to**" and "**has to**" each place they appear in the dialog.*

Grammar Adverbs of Frequency

- We use ***have to*** to show necessity or strong obligation.
- The third person affirmative singular is irregular: ***has to***.
- ***Have to / has to*** are followed by the simple form of the verb.

Examples:

	have to / has to	**Verb**	
You	***have to***	take out	the garbage.
I	***have to***	have	ten dollars.
Why do I	***have to***	study	all the time?
He	***has to***	get	a job.
You	***have to***	look	for a job.
Phuong	***has to***	go	on an interview.
You	***have to***	have	some skills.
Phuong	***has to***	know	English well.
You	***have to***	go	to school.
We	***don't have to***	get up	early on Saturday.
You	***have to***	study.	

Read *Make logical complete sentences with the words in the box.*

I You We They	have to	study find a job go on an interview have work skills look for a job know English	if	I you we they	want	a job. money. to be happy. to get a job. to work here. to live here.
He She	has to			he she	wants	

Read *Make three questions with the words in the box. Then answer them.*

Why	do	I we you they	have to	study? work? have work skills? know English? get a job? go on an interview?
	does	he she		

Questions ***Answers***

1. ______________________ ______________________

______________________ ______________________

2. ______________________ ______________________

______________________ ______________________

3. ______________________ ______________________

______________________ ______________________

Practice *Work with a partner. Use the phrases below.*

Student 1: Before you leave, you have to ......
Student 2: Do I have to?
Student 1: Yes, you have to!

1. take out the garbage
2. clean your room
3. clear the dinner table
4. wash the dishes
5. close the windows
6. help me
7. put on a sweater
8. turn off the radio
9. tell me where you're going
10. *(Use your words.)*.....

Practice *Work with a partner. Answer in your own words. See the example below.*

Student 1: Why do I have to ....?
Student 2: Because ....

1. take out the garbage
2. study
3. go to college
4. have skills
5. know English well
6. get a part-time job
7. go to school
8. always stay home
9. do housework
10. *(Use your own words.)*

Practice *Work with a partner. Answer in your own words. See the example below.*

Student 1: Don't you want to ....?
Student 2: Yes, of course.
Student 1: Then, you have to ....?

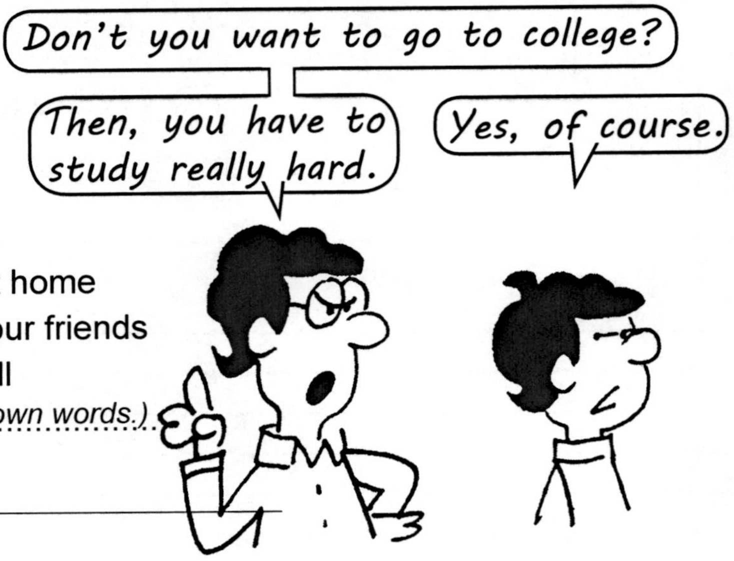

1. go to college
2. have money
3. be an important person
4. find a good job
5. learn
6. by happy
7. help us at home
8. go visit your friends
9. speak well
10. *(Use your own words.)*

Read

Phuong and his mother, Lan, are talking.

Lan: What do you want to be?
Phuong: I don't know.
Lan: You have to decide soon, before you go to college. Don't you want to be a doctor?
Phuong: What do you have to study to be a doctor?
Lan: You have to study medicine.
Phuong: I think I want to be an engineer.
Lan: Do you have plans for college?
Phuong: No, I don't.
Lan: Why don't you speak to your counselor at school?

Understand *Circle **True, False,** or **We don't know.***

1. Phuong wants to be a doctor.	True	False	We don't know.
2. You have to study math to be an accountant.	True	False	We don't know.
3. Phuong is in his last year of high school.	True	False	We don't know.

POSSIBLE OCCUPATIONS & PROFESSIONS

Career	***Subjects***
accountant, bookkeeper	accounting, mathematics
administrator	management
artist	art
chef	culinary arts
computer programmer, software developer	computer science
doctor, nurse	medicine
driver	driver training
engineer	engineering
landscaper	horticulture
lawyer, law clerk	law
salesperson, receptionist	hospitality
scientist	science
social worker	psychology, social work
teacher, teaching assistant	education

Practice *Work with a partner. Ask and answer questions about the list above. See the example below.*

Student 1: What do I have to study to be a ....?
Student 2: You have to study ....

What do I have to study to be an accountant?
You have to study math.

Read & Listen

Phuong is talking to his school counselor.

Excuse me, Ma'am. Can I make an appointment to see you tomorrow?
HIGH SCHOOL COUNSELOR
We can talk now. I have a few minutes.
I can't stay now. I have to go to my history class.
Let me check my appointment book, OK? Come in tomorrow after school.

Practice *Work with a partner. Use the phrases below. See the example below.*

Student 1: Why can't you stay?
Student 2: I have to ....

Why can't you stay?
I have to go to my history class.

1. go to my history class
2. catch the bus
3. meet a friend
4. go home
5. be home early
6. be home for dinner
7. help my father
8. take a test
9. go to work
10. *(Use your own words.)*

Read

APPOINTMENT BOOK

8 a.m.	*Register new students*
9 a.m.	*Return phone calls & e-mails*
10 a.m.	*Speak to accounting class*
11 a.m.	*Meet with the school principal*
12 noon	*Have lunch with vice principal*
1 p.m.	*Meet Mr. Rios*
2 p.m.	*Correct placement tests*
3 p.m.	*Meet with Phuong Van*
4 p.m.	*Write a report*
5 p.m.	*Pick up kids at the pre-school*

Practice *Work with a partner. Use the appointment book below. See the example.*

Student 1: What does the counselor have to do at .... o'clock?
Student 2: She has to ....

What does the counselor have to do at 3 o'clock?
She has to meet Phuong Van.

Read & Listen

Phuong is meeting with his counselor.

Counselor: Now, how can I help you?
Phuong: I want to go to college. Can you help me?
Counselor: Why do you want to go to college?
Phuong: In order to be an engineer.
Counselor: What college do you want to attend?
Phuong: UCLA.*
Counselor: You can't go to UCLA without good grades. How are your grades?
Phuong: I have a B average.
Counselor: Well, you have to do a lot of things.
Phuong: What do I have to do first?
Counselor: You have to take a special test and send an application.
Phuong: Is that all?
Counselor: No, it isn't. To go to UCLA, you have to pass the test with a high score.
Phuong: Oh!

Understand *Circle* ***True, False,*** *or* ***We don't know****.*

1. Phuong has good grades.	True	False	We don't know.
2. Phuong wants to study engineering.	True	False	We don't know.
3. Phuong is in college.	True	False	We don't know.
4. Phuong has to take a test to go to UCLA.	True	False	We don't know.
5. Phuong can't go to UCLA with low grades.	True	False	We don't know.

* The University of California, Los Angeles
** Grades: A = excellent, B = above average, C = average, D = below average, F = failure

Grammar *in order to*

- Use ***"in order to"*** to show purpose or reason. It answers the question ***"Why?"***
- ***"To"*** is the shortened form of "***in order to.***"

Examples:	I want to go to college	***in order to***	be an engineer.
	You have to take a test	***to***	go to UCLA.

Read *Make logical complete sentences with the words in the box.*

Phuong He I We Students	have to has to	take a test send an application go to college pass a test study hard	in order to to	go to UCLA. be an engineer. attend college. pass the class. finish college.

Practice *Work with a partner. Use the phrases below. Answer in your own words.*

Student 1: Why do you .... ?
Student 2: To ....

Why do you want to go to college?
To be an engineer.

1. want to go to college
2. have to take tests
3. have to pass the tests
4. come to school
5. want to be an engineer
6. talk to the counselor
7. have to have good grades
8. study hard
9. work
10. *(Use your own words.)*

Practice *Make sentences with* ***ever, never,*** *and* ***without.*** *Use your own words if necessary.*

Student 1: Can I ever .... without ....?
Student 2: No, you can never .... without ....

Can I ever go to college without good grades?
No, you can never go to college without good grades.

1. go to college / good grades
2. go to work / I.D. badge.
3. go to school / notebook
4. drive a car / license
5. go shopping / money
6. leave the house / ....
7. eat brealfast / ....
8. go on an interview / ....
9. mail a letter / ....
10. .... / .... *(Use your own words.)*

Read & Listen

Phuong is playing with his brother.

Why do people use keys?
To open locked doors.

Practice

Work with a partner. Use the words in the box to answer the questions about the things in the picture below. See the example.

Student 1: Why do people ....?
Student 2: To ....

To know the temperature.

find	clean	drink	look up	listen	light
mop	know	see	fix	go	call

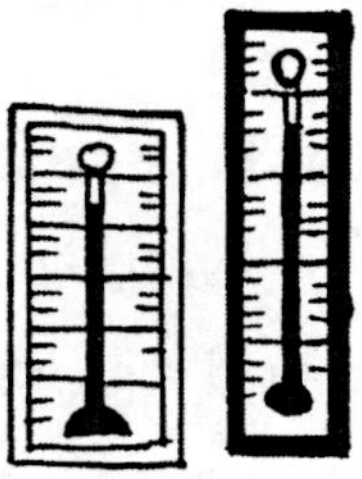
1. thermometers

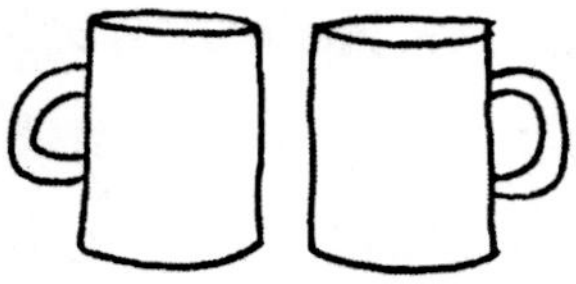
2. cups

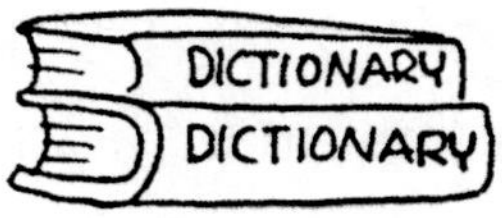

3. dictionaries

4. a computer

5. cars

6. tools

7. matches

8. lights

9. watches

10. mops

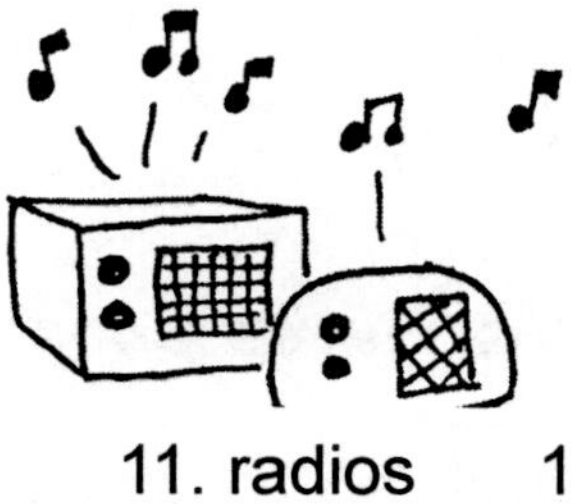
11. radios

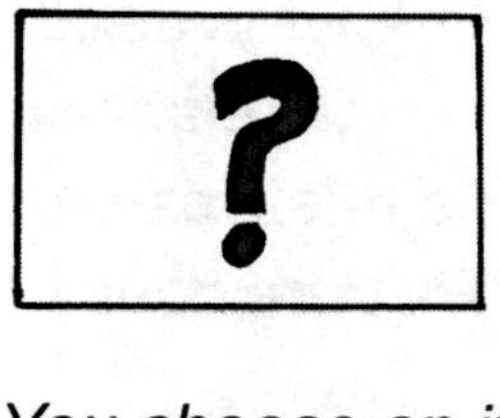
12. *You choose an item.*

Read & Listen

The counselor has an appointment with Mr. Rios.

I'm Mr. Rios. I have an appointment with you.
I want to enroll my children in this school.
Oh, yes. Please come in, sir. What can I do for you?

The secretary and the counselor are talking after the appointment.

Secretary: How are you?

Counselor: A little tired.

Secretary: Who was that man?

Counselor: That was Mr. Rios. He's new in the city. He has a lot of problems. He has two kids, so he has to enroll them in school. He doesn't have a place to live, so he has to find an apartment fast. He is a widower, so he has to find a person to stay with his kids after school. He doesn't have much money, so he has to find a job. But he has some relatives here, so maybe they can help him.

Secretary: Wow! He sure has a lot of problems.

Counselor: He sure does.

Understand *Circle* ***True, False,*** *or* ***We don't know.***

1. Mr. Rios is married.	True	False	We don't know.
2. His wife is dead.	True	False	We don't know.
3. He has relatives in this city.	True	False	We don't know.
4. His relatives can help him.	True	False	We don't know.
5. ***"He sure does."*** means ***"He really does."***	True	False	We don't know.

Write *Underline the word* ***"so"*** *each place it appears in the dialog above.*

Grammar *so*

- We use ***"so"*** to show consequence.
- ***"Therefore"*** has a similar meaning, but it is more formal.

Examples: He has two kids, **so** he has to enroll them.
He doesn't have a place to live, **so** he has to find an apartment.
He doesn't have much money, **so** he has to find a job.
He has relatives, **so** maybe they can help him.

Read *Make logical complete sentences with the words in the box.*

Mr. Rios The counselor Phuong	doesn't have money, wants to go to college, is tired, needs help, wants to pass the test,	so	he she	has to	rest. take a test. get a job. study. talk to a counselor.

Practice *Work with a partner. Use the phrases below and answer in your own words. See the example.*

Student 1: ....
Student 2: So?
Student 1: So ....

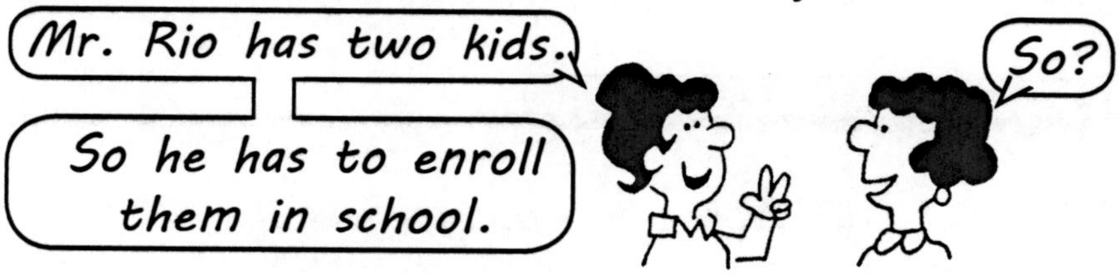
Mr. Rio has two kids.
So he has to enroll them in school.
So?

1. Mr. Rios has two kids.

2. Mr. Rios has a problem.

3. The kids don't speak English.

4. Phuong's brother want to be a firefighter.

PLEASE, DAD...

5. Phuong needs ten dollars.

NO!

6. His dad doesn't want to give him the money.

7. Mr. Rios is thirsty.

8. The counselor is tired.

9. Think of a situation.

Write *Fill out the appointment book for today and Sunday. Use the expressions **"have to"** and **"don't have to."***

THINGS I HAVE TO DO.

TODAY	SUNDAY
I have to work today.	I don't have to work on Sunday.

Practice *Work with a partner. Use the information above. Talk about what you **have to** and **don't have to do**. See the example.*

Student 1: What do you have to do today ....?
Student 2: I have to ....
Student 1: What about Sunday?
Student 2: I don't have to ....

Practice *Work with a partner. Ask and answer about the list above. Use short answers.*

Student 1: Do you have to .... today?
Student 2: Yes, I do. / No, I don't.

Do you have to work today?
Yes, I do.

Write *Put the sentences of the dialog in the correct order. Write the numbers 1 to 10 in front of the sentences (1 is the first in order and 10 the last).*

_______ They're very good students.
_______ How are you doing, Mr. Rios?
_______ I have a job and a new apartment.
___1___ Hello, this is Mr. Rios.
_______ What about them?
_______ That's wonderful news.
_______ How are they doing?
_______ I'm glad to hear that. I have some good news for you, too.
_______ Fine, thanks, I'm calling to ask about my children.
_______ What good news?

Dictation *Listen to the instructor (or your partner) read the dictation at the bottom of the next page. Write the sentences below. Then, check your writing.*

OFFICE MEMO

TO: Natalie

FROM: Claudine

DATE: Friday, March 2

REF: Appointments

1. ____
   ____
2. ____
3. ____
4. ____
5. ____
6. ____

Practice

Fold this page along the dotted lines. Practice with a partner.

Student 1

Ask your partner the questions below.

1. What's Phuong's grade in English?
2. What's his grade in science?
3. Does he study engineering?
4. Does he have a good grade in history?
5. Does he have a good grade in physical education?
6. What's his grade average?
7. What subjects does he study?

Fill in the "To Do" list for your partner. Listen carefully to the information your partner tells you.

My "TO DO" List for Today

6 a.m. ______________________

8 a.m. ______________________

10 a.m. ______________________

12 noon ______________________

2 p.m. ______________________

4 p.m. ______________________

6 p.m. ______________________

8 p.m. ______________________

10 p.m. ______________________

FOLD HERE

Student 2

Listen to the questions. Find the answers below.

SCHOOL REPORT CARD

NAME: Phuong Van

SUBJECT	GRADE
English	B
History	C
Mathematics	A
Physical Education	B
Science	A
Computer Science	A

A = excellent, B = above average, C = average, D = below average, F = failure

Your partner will fill out your "To Do" list for today. Tell your partner what you plan to do at the following times.

Question: What do you have to do at ...

6 o'clock in the morning

8 o'clock in the morning

10 o'clock in the morning

12 noon

2 o'clock in the afternoon

4 o'clock in the afternoon

6 o'clock in the evening

8 o'clock in the evening

10 o'clock in the evening

FOLD HERE

Dictation

(from the previous page) Read this dictation to your partner.

1. I'm very busy, so please don't make any appointments for me today.
2. I have a lot of things to do.
3. I don't have enough time.
4. I need the time to write a report.
5. Please get me Phuong Tran's grades.
6. I have to have them for his college application.

Word Building Suffixes Used in Occupations

• We can form many names of occupations by adding the suffix ***"-er"*** to a verb.

Examples:

Verb		Occupation
work	→	worker
teach	→	teacher
paint	→	painter

Write *Fill in the spaces with names of occupations. Use the suffix **-er.***

1. A ____painter____ paints buildings.

2. A ______________ writes books.

3. A ______________ programs computers.

4. A ______________ builds buildings

5. A truck ______________ drives trucks.

6. A driving ______________ teaches driving.

7. A ______________ waits on tables.

8. A ______________ reports the news.

9. A ______________ manages people.

Word Building Other Suffixes Used in Occupations

• Other suffixes used in occupations:

-ist	***-or***	***-ess***	***-man*, *-woman,***
typist	doctor	stewardess	policeman - policewoman
artist	director	waitress	salesman - saleswoman
dentist	instructor	actress	fisherman
chemist	actor	hostess	mailman (mail carrier)

Challenge *How many other occupations or professions can you name?*

______________ ______________ ______________

______________ ______________ ______________

______________ ______________ ______________

______________ ______________ ______________

______________ ______________ ______________

Group Discussion *Discuss the chart below. How is the U.S. system different from other countries? Write a list below.*

United States Education System

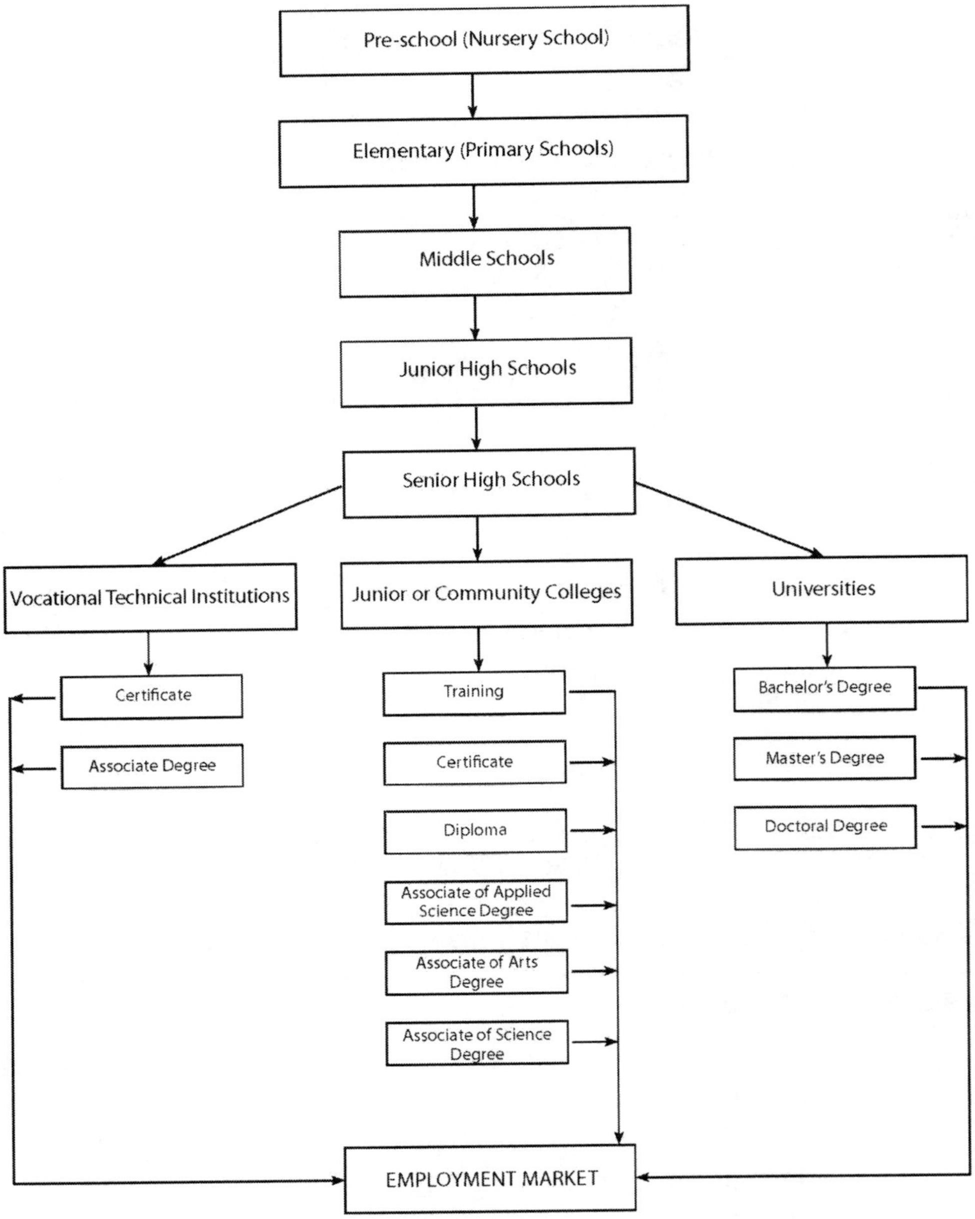

1. ______________________________
2. ______________________________
3. ______________________________
4. ______________________________
5. ______________________________
6. ______________________________

CHAPTER 4

What Are You Going To Do Tomorrow?

SKILLS	• Describing Future Events or Activities
GRAMMAR	• Future with the Present Continuous
	• Future with *"will"*
	• Future with *"going to"*
	• Prepositions: *in, across, by*
VOCABULARY	• Toys
	• Picnic Food
	• Expressions of Time (Future)
SPELLING	• Double Consonant Combinations

Read & Listen

David and Alice Morris are at home. They're talking about tomorrow's plans.

David: What are you doing tomorrow?

Alice: I'm going shopping to buy a present for Steve Wilson. It's his birthday on Sunday. What about you?

David: I'm playing golf with Paul Wilson tomorrow morning. We're planning a school picnic. What are you buying Steve?

Alice: I'm getting him a toy.

David: Are they having a birthday party?

Alice: Yes. They're giving him a small party on Sunday afternoon.

David: Are you going?

Alice: Yes, we're going.

David: Am I going, too?

Alice: Yes, you're going, too. And we're having dinner at my mother's house afterwards.

Understand *Circle **True, False,** or **We don't know.***

1. Steve is having a party tomorrow.	True	False	We don't know.
2. Steve is seven years old.	True	False	We don't know.
3. David and Alice are having dinner with the Wilson family tomorrow.	True	False	We don't know.
4. 4, David and Alice are bringing a present.	True	False	We don't know.
5. 5. David is going shopping with his wife.	True	False	We don't know.

Write *Underline all verbs in the present continuous in the sentences above.*

Grammar Future with the Present Continuous

• We often use the present continuous to show the near future.

Examples:

What	***are***	you	***doing***	tomorrow?
I	***'m***		***going***	shopping tomorrow.
I	***'m***		***playing***	golf tomorrow morning.
We	***'re***		***planning***	a class picnic.
What	***are***	you	***buying***	Steve?
	Are	they	***having***	a party?
They	***'re***		***giving***	him a small party.
	Are	you	***going***?	
We	***'re***		***going***.	
We	***'re***		***having***	dinner at my mother's.

Read *Make logical complete sentences with the words in the box.*

I You He She They You	'm 's 're	bringing buying having giving planning going playing	a party shopping to dinner a picnic golf a present at home	tomorrow. on Sunday afternoon. tomorrow morning. tomorrow afternoon. Sunday evening. afterwards. later.

Practice *Work with a partner. Use the phrases below. Answer in your own words in the present continuous tense. See the example below.*

Student 1: What are you doing ....?

Student 2: I'm ....

1. tomorrow
2. tonight
3. tomorrow morning
4. tomorrow afternoon
5. tomorrow evening
6. the day after tomorrow
7. this weekend
8. next Saturday
9. next Sunday
10. next week
11. next month
12. next ....

Read & Listen

Alice Morris is talking to Betty Wilson on the telephone.

Alice: How's everything?

Betty: We're busy. I have to do a million things before Bobby's party tomorrow. After the housework, my daughter and I will go to the market. We'll buy the food for the party, and then we'll come home and get ready for the party.

Alice: Will you make a birthday cake?

Betty: No, I won't, but Theresa will. And Paul will do all the work tomorrow, too. I won't have to clean up after the party, I won't wash the dishes, and I won't make dinner.

Alice: Why not?

Betty: Because my birthday will be tomorrow, too!

Understand *Circle True, False, or We don't know.*

1. Betty and her son, Steve, will have birthdays tomorrow.	True	False	We don't know.
2. Betty and her daughter, Theresa, will go shopping before they do the housework.	True	False	We don't know.
3. Steve will go shopping with Betty.	True	False	We don't know.
4. Paul will make dinner tomorrow.	True	False	We don't know.
5. Betty will make a birthday cake.	True	False	We don't know.
6. Betty won't work tomorrow.	True	False	We don't know.

Grammar Future with "*will*"

• We use ***"will"*** and "***won't"*** to show future time, especially of plans and promises.

Examples: ***Affirmative Statements***

My daughter and I	***will***	***go***	to the supermarket.
We	***'ll***	***buy***	food for the party.
We	***'ll***	***go***	home.
We	***'ll***	***get ready***	for the party.
Paul	***will***	***do***	all the work tomorrow.
My birthday	***will***	***be***	tomorrow, too.

Questions

Will	you	***make***	a birthday cake?
Will	they	***buy***	a present?
Will	Paul	***be***	there?

Negative Statements

I	***won't clean up***	after the party.
I	***won't wash***	the dishes.
I	***won't make***	dinner.

Short Answers

No, I ***won't,*** but Theresa ***will.***

Read *Make logical complete sentences with the words in the box.*

Steve Paul I Theresa Alice Betty It	will 'll won't	be go buy work do have make	my birthday to a party a party all the work a cake shopping a present	on Sunday. on the weekend. tomorrow. tomorrow afternoon. this afternoon. after the housework. too.

Will	they you Paul Theresa Alice Betty Steve	do buy make have work go give	a party shopping a present a cake dinner all the work a birthday	today? on Sunday? tonight? tomorrow?

Yes, No,	I he she they we	will. won't.

Read & Listen

David and Alice are talking about Betty's present.

What will you buy Betty for her birthday?
Maybe I'll buy her a blouse.

Practice

Work with a partner. Talk about the items below. See the example below.

Student 1: What will you buy Betty?
Student 2: Maybe I'll buy her ....

What will you buy Betty?
Maybe I'll buy her a blouse.

1. a blouse

2. a plant

3. an appointment book

4. a sweater

5. some glasses

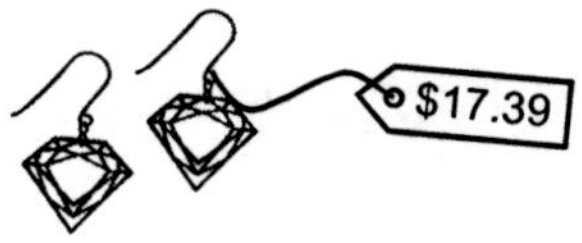

6. some earrings

7. a gift card

8. a wallet

Read

How much is this blouse?
It's fifteen dollars.
Good. I'll take it.
That'll be fifteen dollars plus tax.

Practice

Work with a partner. Use the items in the pictures above. See the example.

Student 1: How much is this ....?
Student 2: It's $..................
Student 1: Good. I'll take it.
Student 2: That'll be $........ plus tax.

How much is this plant?
It's nine dollars and ninety-nine cents.
Good. I'll take it.
That'll be nine ninety-nine plus tax.

Read & Listen

Alice is at a toy store.

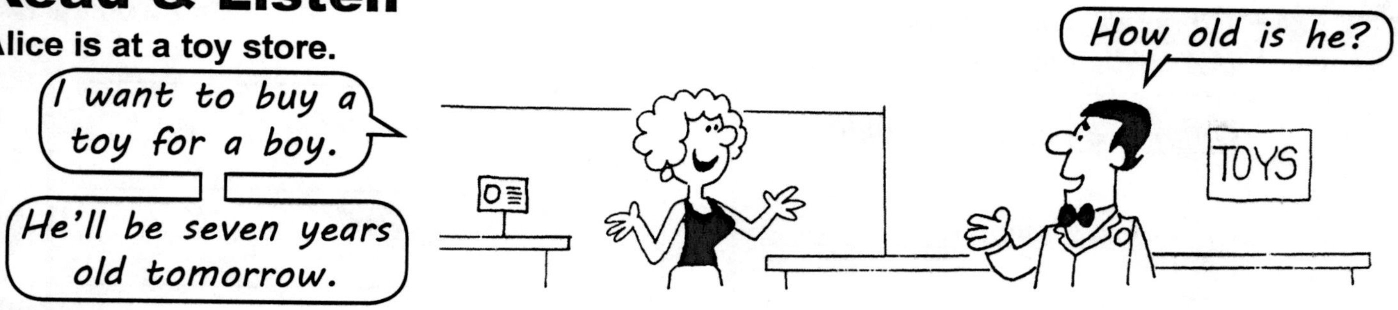

Practice

Work with a partner. Use the phrases below. See the example.

Student 1: How old is / are ....?
Student 2: He'll / she'll / they'll be ....

1. Steve Wilson / 7/ tomorrow
2. Betty Wilson / 35 / tomorrow
3. Theresa Wilson / 14 / next week
4. Mike Breyer / 40 / next month
5. Phuong Van / 17 / next June
6. Alberto and Alfonse Duran / 25 / next July
7. Amir Abbas / 49 / next September
8. Vince Cartelli / 23 / next November

Read

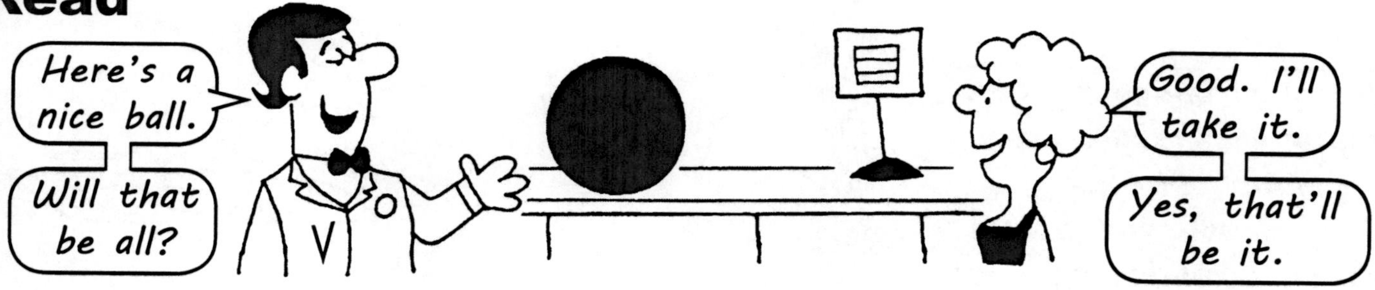

Practice

Work with a partner. Use the phrases below. See the example below.

Student 1: Here's a nice ....
Student 2: I'll take it.
Student 1: Will that be all?
Student 2: That'll be it.

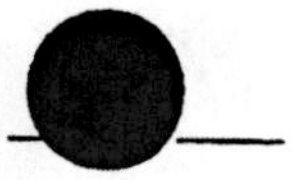
1. a ball

2. a game

3. a coloring book

4. a toy car

5. a doll

6. a doll house

7. a train

8. a bat

Group Discussion

1. Is there a local sales tax where you live? If so, how much is it?
2. It is OK to ask the age of children, young adults, or people over 40 years old? Why or why not?

Write

When will your birthday be? What will you do on your birthday? What won't you do? Write the answers below.

On my birthday, I will ...

I'll have a party.

On my birthday, I won't ...

I won't work.

Read & Listen

At the party.

Happy birthday to you.
Happy birthday to you.
Happy birthday,
Dear Betty and Steve.
Happy birthday to you!

Alice is telling Betty about the special present she is getting.

Betty: Thank you very much for the present. It's beautiful.
Alice: You're very welcome.
Betty: Guess what!
Alice: What?
Betty: I'm going on a trip!
Alice: Where are you going?
Betty: Across the country.
It's a birthday present from Paul.
I'm leaving next month.

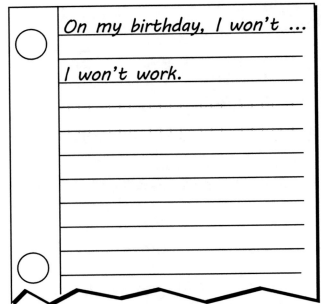

Understand *Circle **True, False,** or **We don't know**.*

1. Betty will go on a trip with Paul.	True	False	We don't know.
2. Betty will leave next week.	True	False	We don't know.
3. Betty likes Alice's present.	True	False	We don't know.

Read

Here's Betty's itinerary.

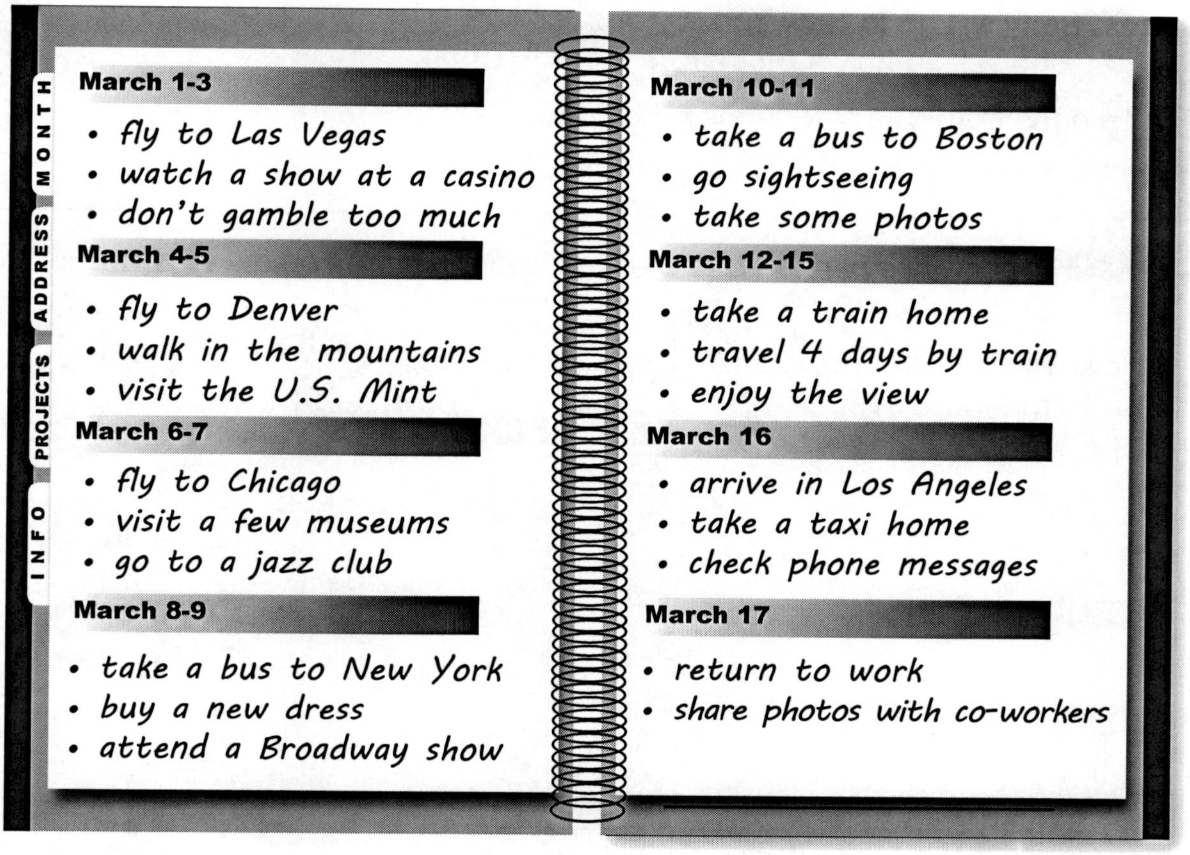

Practice

Work with a partner. Ask and answer questions about Betty's itinerary.

Where will she go on March 1?
How will she get to Las Vegas?
What will she do in Las Vegas?
Where will she go on ....?
How will she get ....?
What will she do in ....?

She'll go to Las Vegas
She'll fly.
She'll see a show at a casino.
She'll go to ....
She'll ....
She'll ....

Grammar Prepositions *"by"* and *"across"*

- We use ***"by"*** to show means of transportation.

  Examples: Betty will go to New York ***by*** bus.
  She will go home ***by*** train.

- ***"Across"*** means from one side to the other side.

  Example: Boston is ***across*** the country from Los Angeles.

Practice *Work with a partner. Use the words and pictures below. Answer with the preposition **"by."***

Student 1: How will Betty get *(to)* ....?
Student 2: She'll get there by ....

1. the airport / car

2. Las Vegas / airplane

3. New York / bus

4. Boston / bus

5. Los Angeles / train

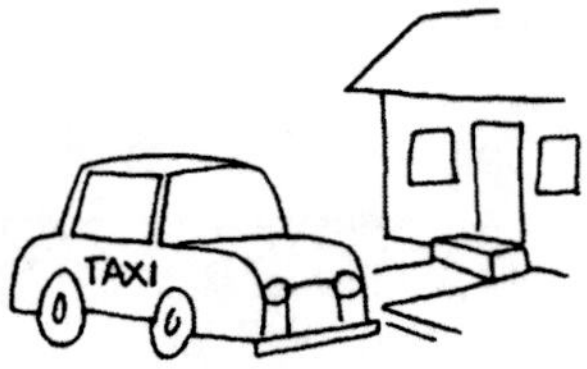

6. home from the airport / taxi

Practice *Work with a partner. Use the words and pictures. Use "across" in the answers.*

Student 1: Where's ....?
Student 2: It's across ....

1. Boston / country

2. Chicago / lake

3. restaurant / street

4. New York / river

5. the restrooms / hall

6. Japan / ocean

7. Canada / border

8. San Francisco / bridge

Read & Listen

Paul Wilson and David Morris are playing golf.

Paul: What are we going to do for our class picnic?

David: When is it going to be?

Paul: It's going to be in two weeks.

David: Where are we going to have it?

Paul: The students want to go to the lake.

David: OK. What are we going to need?

Paul: My students are going to bring hamburgers, hot dogs, and drinks. And what about your students?

David: They're going to bring salads and desserts.

Paul: Who's going to bring the paper goods?

David: I'm going to bring the plates, cups, and tablecloths.

Paul: And I'm going to bring plastic utensils and napkins, OK?

David: Good. I think we're going to have a good time.

Understand *Circle **True, False,** or **We don't know**.*

1. The picnic is going to be next week.	True	False	We don't know.
2. The picnic is going to be at the lake.	True	False	We don't know.
3. The students are going to bring the food.	True	False	We don't know.
4. David is going to bring the drinks.	True	False	We don't know.
5. The married students are going to bring their kids.	True	False	We don't know.
6. Paul is going to bring spoons, forks, knives, and napkins.	True	False	We don't know.

Grammar Future with *"going to"*

- We use ***"going to"*** to show a future action.
- We use the verb ***"to be"*** *(am, is, are)* before ***"going to"*** and a simple verb after it.
- ***"Going to"*** is sometimes pronounced ***"gonna"*** in informal speech.

Examples:	***to be***		***going to***	***Verb***	
What	***are***	we	***going to***	***do***	about the picnic?
When	***is***	it	***going to***	***be***?	
It	***'s***		***going to***	***be***	in two weeks.
What	***are***	we	***going to***	***need***?	
My students	***are***		***going to***	***bring***	hamburgers and hot dogs.
They	***'re***		***going to***	***bring***	salads and desserts.
I	***'m***		***going to***	***bring***	plastic utensils.
We	***'re***		***going to***	***have***	fun.

- We often use the preposition ***"in"*** to show a future time.

Example: The party is going to be ***in*** two weeks.

Read *Make logical complete sentences with the words in the box.*

I The students They The picnic We It	'm 's 're are	going to	be bring go have buy eat	there. at the lake. to the lake. food. fun. in two weeks.

Practice *Work with a partner. Ask and answer about the list below. Use short answers.*

Student 1: When's the .... going to be?
Student 2: It's going to be in ....

When's the picnic going to be?
It's going to be in two weeks.

1. the picnic / two weeks
2. the party / three weeks
3. the trip / one month
4. the test / a few days
5. the dictation / a few minutes
6. dinner / a few hours
7. the birthday / a few days
8. the T.V. program / one hour
9. lunch / fifteen minutes
10. the movie / half an hour
11. the vacation / one year
12. ....*(Use your own words.)*........

Read & Listen

Here's a list of people who are going to the picnic and what they are bringing.

BULLETIN BOARD

Mr. Wilson's class

Paul and Nancy Wilson (+ 2 kids)	utensils & napkins
Manuel and Anna Perez	hamburgers
Amir Abbas	juice
Mike and Mary Breyer (+ 2 kids)	hot dogs
Jen and Lee Yang	chicken
Tan and Lan Van	hamburger and hot dog buns
Yuri Tanaka	iced tea
Rita Lachance	sodas & water

Mr. Morris's class

Vince Cartelli	green salad
Joanne Vordale (+ friend)	potato salad
Martin Ngon	cup cakes
Alberto Duran (+ wife)	cookies
Alfonso Duran	potato chips

Practice

Work with a partner. Ask and answer about the list above. See example below.

Student 1: What is / are .....*(name)*....... going to bring?

Student 2: He / She / They .... going to bring ..*(item)*..

What is Amir going to bring?
He's going to bring juice.

Practice

Work with a partner. ***Ask and answer*** *about the list above. Use short answers. See example below.*

Student 1: Is / Are ..*(name)*.. going to bring ....*(item)*.....?

Student 2: Yes, ... *or* No, ...

Write *Write sentences with **"going to"** on the lines below. Use your own words.*

Roy and James are talking.

Paul: Mary and Mike are sitting at the picnic table. They're really hungry
David: What are they going to do?
Paul: (1) They're going to eat.

David: Yuri's plate is empty.
Paul: What's she going to do?
David: (2) ____________________.

Paul: Theresa's at the lake. She's wearing a bathing suit.
David: Whats she going to do?
Paul: (3) ____________________.

David: Amir's thirsty.
Paul: What's he going to do?
David: (4) ____________________.

Paul: Martin Ngon's full.
David: What's he going to do?
Paul: (5) ____________________.

David: We're finished.
Paul: What are we going to do?
David: (6) ____________________.

Paul: I'm tired. What about you?
David: So am I. What are we going to do?
Paul: (7) ____________________.

Write Fill in the spaces with ***will, won't,*** or ***want.***

Tan: Do you (1) __want__ to take a walk?

Lan: Not right now. I (2) __'ll__ take a walk later. I (3) ________ to rest now.

Anna: Do you (4) ________ some potato salad?

Manuel: Sure, and I (5) ________ a hot dog, too. I'm really hungry, so I (6) ________ come back for more food later.

Mary: What do you (7) ________ to do?

Theresa: I (8) _______ to go swimming.

Mary: Don't swim too far!

Theresa: OK, I (9) ________ .

David: (10) ________ we go to your mother's for dinner again next Sunday?

Anne: Why? Don't you (11) ________ to go?

David: No I dont. I (12) ________ to take you out to dinner.

Amir: (13) ________ you be in class tomorrow?

Yuri: Yes, I (14) ________. Why?

Amir: I have to work overtime, so I (15) ________ come to school.

Yuri: Do you (16) ________ me to call you and tell you the homework?

Amir: Thanks. I (17) ________ be home at 10 p.m. Call me then.

Write
What are you going to do next week? Write your plans below.

What are your plans for next week? What are you going to do?

MY WEEKLY SCHEDULE

DATES: From ________________ To ________________
month / date / year — *month / date / year*

Mon.	Morning	______
	Afternoon	______
	Evening	______
Tues.	Morning	______
	Afternoon	______
	Evening	______
Wed.	Morning	______
	Afternoon	______
	Evening	______
Thurs.	Morning	______
	Afternoon	______
	Evening	______
Fri.	Morning	______
	Afternoon	______
	Evening	______
Sat.	Morning	______
	Afternoon	______
	Evening	______
Sun.	Morning	______
	Afternoon	______
	Evening	______

Practice
Work with a partner. Ask and answer questions about your plans above. Answer the second question in your own words. See the example below.

Student 1: What are you going to do on ....(date).....?
Student 2: I'm going to ....
Student 1: Why are you going to do that?
Student 2: Because ....

What are you going to do on Monday?
I'm going to go to school.
Why are you going to do that?
Because I need to learn English.

Write

Put the sentences in the dialog in the correct order. Write the numbers 1 to 7 in front of the sentences (1 is the first in order and 7 the last).

The Wilson family is in the car. They're going home.

_______ Who do you want to invite?

_______ When is it going to be?

___1___ Are we going to have a picnic again?

_______ A friend from school.

_______ Yes, we're going to have a picnic again very soon,

_______ Sure, I like the beach. Will you let me invite a friend?

_______ In June at the beach. Is that OK?

Nancy is writing a postcard to a friend in New York.

Dictation

Listen to the instructor (or your partner) read the dictation at the bottom of page 68. Write the sentences below. Then, check your writing.

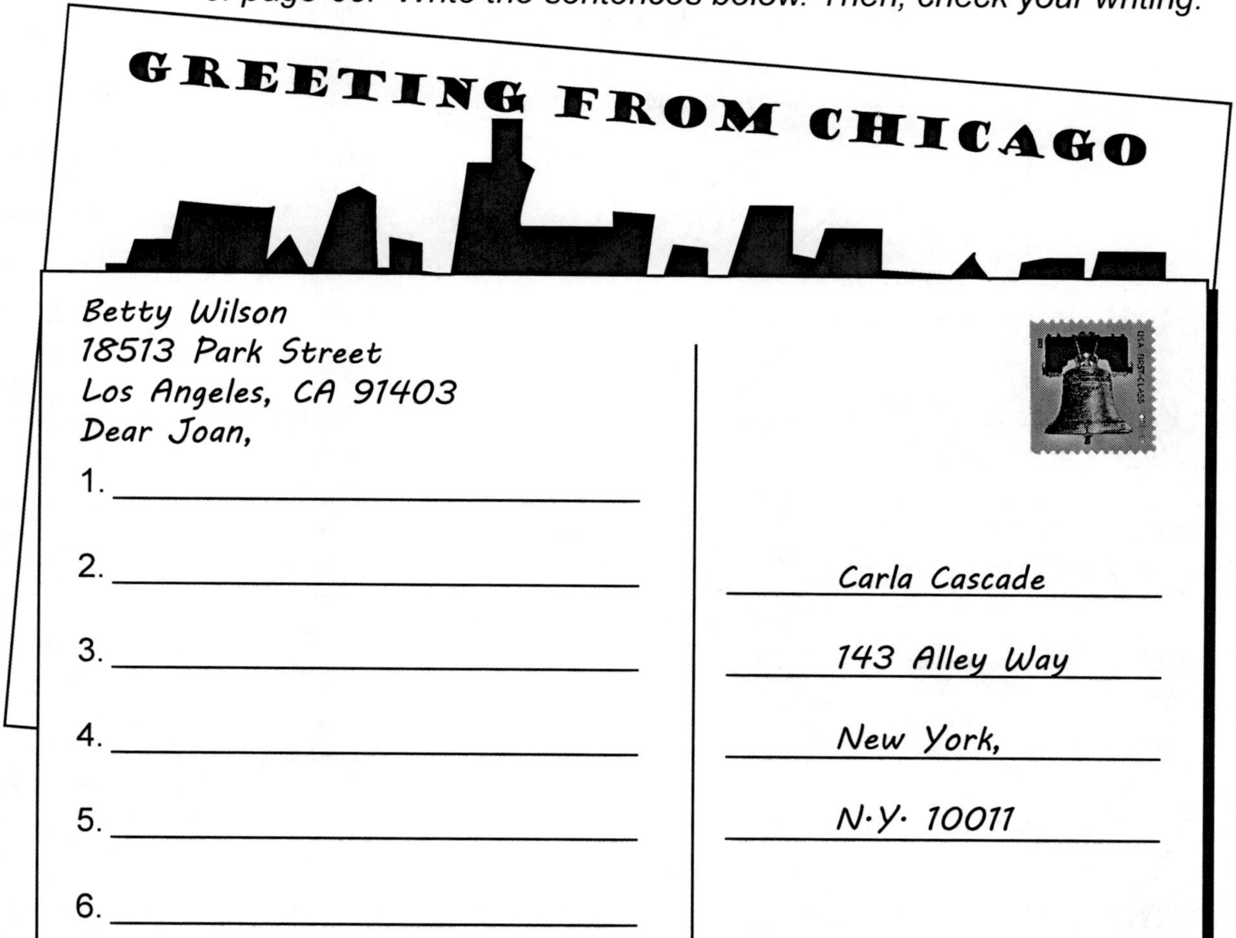

Map Exercise *Write the number in front of the name of the state. See the example.*

19 Alabama
___ Alaska
___ Arizona
___ Arkansas
___ California
___ Colorado
___ Connecticut
___ Delaware
___ Florida
___ Georgia
___ Hawaii
___ Idaho
___ Illinois
___ Indiana
___ Iowa
___ Kansas
___ Kentucky
___ Louisiana
___ Maine
___ Maryland
___ Massachusetts
___ Michigan
___ Minnesota
___ Mississippi
___ Missouri
___ Montana
___ Nebraska
___ Nevada
___ New Hampshire
___ New Jersey
___ New Mexico
___ New York
___ North Carolina
___ North Dakota
___ Ohio
___ Oklahoma
___ Oregon
___ Pennsylvania
___ Rhode Island
___ South Carolina
___ South Dakota
___ Tennessee
___ Texas
___ Utah
___ Vermont
___ Virginia
___ Washington
___ West Virginia
___ Wisconsin
___ Wyoming

Practice *Work with a partner. Talk about what city is in what state. See the example below.*

Student 1: What state is ..(city).. in?
Student 2: ..(city).. is in ..(state)...

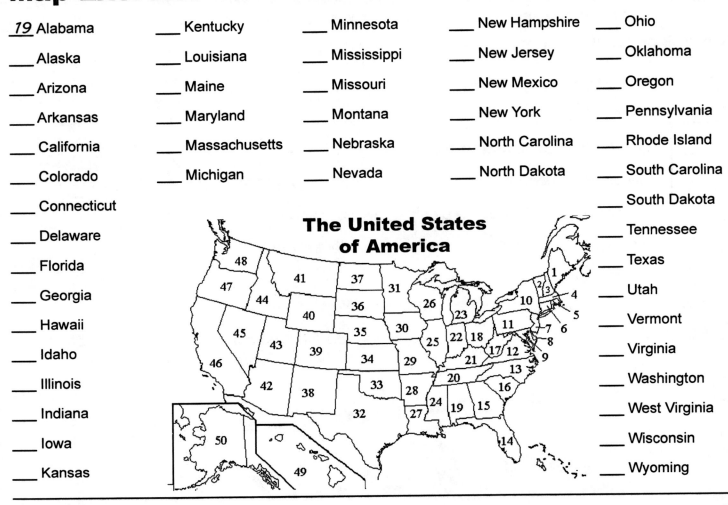

What state is Seattle in?
Seattle is in Washington.

Challenge *Plan a trip. Draw a route on the map to five major cities you want to visit. Then, discuss your route with some of your classmates. Use the expression* ***going to.*** *Example: I'm going to start in Los Angeles. First, I'm going to travel to San Francisco, second ...., then ...., next, ..., and finally ....*

Write *Address the envelope. Send it to Betty. Use her address on the previous page. Use your own return address. Then, answer Betty's questions from page 66. Write about your city.*

From:

____

____

____

____

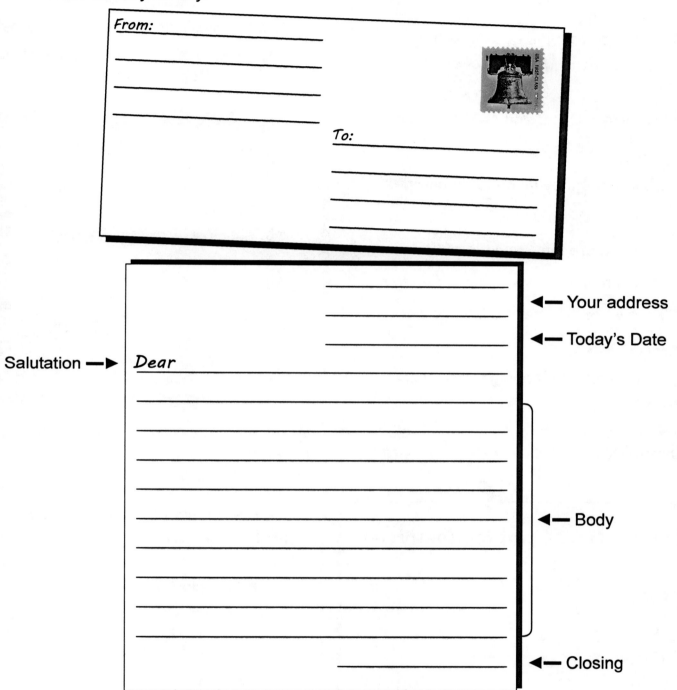

To:

____

____

____

____

______________________ ◄— Your address

____

______________________ ◄— Today's Date

Salutation —► *Dear* ______________________

______________________ ◄— Body

______________________ ◄— Closing

Dictation *(See page 66.) Read this dictation to your partner.*

1. I'm going to be in your city next month.
2. Please send me some information.
3. Where can I stay? How's the weather?
4. What kind of clothes will I need to bring?
5. What is there to see in your city?
6. Send me the information at the address above.

Practice *Fold this page along the dotted lines. Practice with a partner.*

Student 1

Ask your partner the questions below about David and Alice Morris' weekend trip to Mexico.

1. How are David and Alice Morris going to get to Ensenada?
2. What are they going to do on Friday?
3. Where will they stay?
4. Where are they going to eat?
5. How many days are they going to stay?
6. How are they getting back to Los Angeles?
7. When are they going to go back?

Fill in the "To Do" list for your partner. Listen carefully to the information your partner tells you.

My "TO DO" List for Tomorrow

6 a.m. ______________________________

8 a.m. ______________________________

10 a.m. ______________________________

12 noon ______________________________

2 p.m. ______________________________

4 p.m. ______________________________

6 p.m. ______________________________

8 p.m. ______________________________

10 p.m. ______________________________

FOLD HERE

FOLD HERE

Student 2

Listen to the questions. Find the answers below.

David and Alice Morris's Weekend Trip to Mexico

Friday
- *drive to Ensenada, Mexico*
- *stay at the Amigo Hotel*
- *eat at Casa Rosa Restaurant*

Saturday
- *take a tour in the morning*
- *go shopping in the afternoon*
- *go to a night club in the evening*

Sunday
- *eat breakfast at the port*
- *drive back to Los Angeles*
- *get ready for Monday*

Your partner will fill out your "To Do" list for tomorrow. Tell your partner what you plan to do at the following times.

Ask the question: ***What are you going to do ...?***

- 6:00 o'clock in the morning
- 8:00 o'clock in the morning
- 10:00 o'clock in the morning
- 12:00 noon
- 2:00 o'clock in the afternoon
- 4:00 o'clock in the afternoon
- 6:00 o'clock in the afternoon
- 8:00 o'clock in the evening
- 10:00 o'clock in the evening

Spelling Double Consonant Combinations

• The */l/* and */s/* sounds are usually spelled with double letters after a one-vowel letter (short vowel).

Examples:

fall

bell

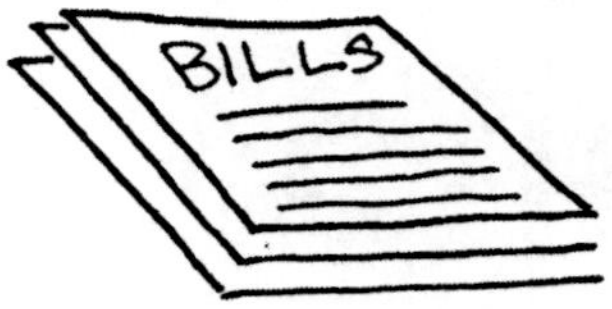

bill

full

glass

mess

miss

boss

• The following words are exceptions to this rule. Remember them.

is ***gas*** ***yes*** ***this*** ***us*** ***bus*** ***plus***

Write *Fill in the spaces with double* ***ss*** *or* ***ll****.*

1. I wi*ll*___ ca*ll*___ the bo*ss*___ and te___ him to fi___ a ___ the ta___ wine gla___es.
2. Do___s and ba___s se___we___ in the fa___.
3. Please clean off the me___ on the wa___ acro___ from the be___ in the ha___.

Challenge *The sound* ***/f/*** *also follows the rule for double consonants at the end of words. Find the words for the following items. Use your dictionary, computer, or smart phone.*

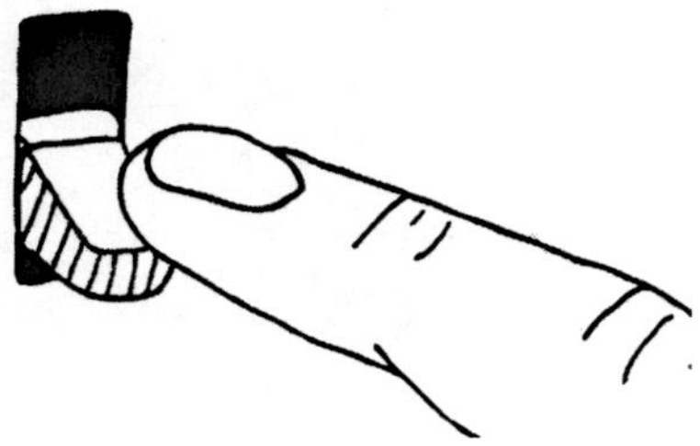

Please turn (1) _____ the light when you leave.

The company has a (2) _______ meeting every Monday morning.

David hit the ball (3) ______ the (4) _______.

CHAPTER 5

Where Were You About 11 O'clock?

SKILLS	• Reporting a Crime
	• Describing Emotions
	• Describing Levels of Difficulty
GRAMMAR	• Past Tense of the Verb *"to be" (was, were)*
VOCABULARY	• Office Equipment
	• Time Expressions (Past Tense)
	• Emotions
	• Descriptive Adjectives
PRONUNCIATION	• The */w/* and */v/* Sounds

Read & Listen

It's Monday evening at school. Helen Pavlos is speaking to Rita Lachance about yesterday's picnic.

Helen: Were you at the picnic yesterday?
Rita: Yes, I was.
Helen: How was it?
Rita: It was wonderful.
Helen: Where was it?
Rita: It was at the lake.
Helen: How was the weather?
Rita: It was fantastic. It was warm and sunny.
Helen: How long were you there?
Rita: We were there all day.
Helen: Who was there?
Rita: Everybody was there.
Helen: Were Maria and Wanda there?
Rita: Yes, they were, and their families were there, too. Why weren't you there?
Helen: I wasn't at the picnic because I was sick in bed with a cold.
Rita: That's too bad. Maybe next time.

Understand *Circle **True, False,** or **We don't know.***

1. Helen was at the picnic.	True	False	We don't know.
2. Helen's friends were at the picnic.	True	False	We don't know.
3. Helen was at home yesterday.	True	False	We don't know.
4. The weather at the picnic was good.	True	False	We don't know.
5. Everybody was sick yesterday.	True	False	We don't know.
6. Helen's husband was at home yesterday.	True	False	We don't know.

Write Underline ***was, were, wasn't,*** and ***weren't*** in the sentences above.

Grammar Past Tense - To Be

- We use ***"was"*** with ***I, he, she,*** and ***it.***
- We use ***"were"*** with ***you, we,*** and ***they.***

Examples:

Affirmative

I	***was***	at the picnic.
The picnic	***was***	wonderful.
It	***was***	at the lake.
It	***was***	fantastic.
We	***were***	there all day.
They	***were***	there, too.

Question

	Were	you at the picnic?
How	***was***	it?
Where	***was***	the picnic?
How	***was***	the weather?
Who	***was***	there?
Why	***were***	Anna and Mary there?

Negative

I	***wasn't***	there because I was sick.
Why	***weren't***	you there?

Short Answers

Yes, I	***was.***
Yes, they	***were.***
No, I	***wasn't.***
No, they	***weren't.***

Read *Make logical complete sentences with the words in the box.*

The picnic I Everybody Mary and Anna We They Helen It	was wasn't were weren't	sick at the picnic there wonderful in bed with a cold at the lake	yesterday. yesterday morning. yesterday afternoon. yesterday evening. all day.

Was Were	you Helen Mary and Anna Amir the picnic the weather	at the picnic at home sick in bed at the lake good with their family	yesterday?

Yes, No,	I he she it we they	was. wasn't. were. weren't.

Practice *Work with a partner. Use the the words and the pictures below. See the example.*

Student 1: How was the ....?
Student 2: It was ....

How was the picnic?
It was wonderful.

1. picnic / wonderful

2. lake / cold

3. food / delicious

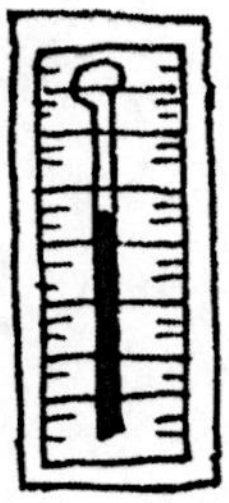
4. temperature / warm

5. area / clean

6. weather / fantastic

7. park / big

8. day / great

Practice *Work with a partner. Use the the words and the pictures below. See the example.*

Student 1: How was /were...........?
Student 2: He / She / They ....

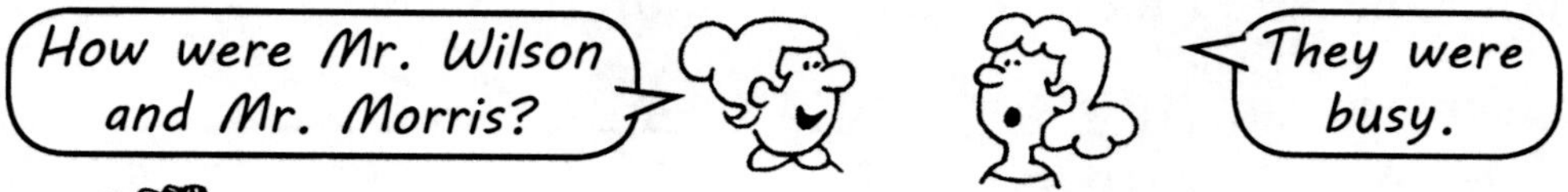
How were Mr. Wilson and Mr. Morris?
They were busy.

1. Mr. Wilson and Mr. Morris / busy

2. Martin Ngon / full

HEE
HEE
3. Yuri Tanaka / happy

4. Amir / sleepy

5. Anna and Manuel / tired

6. Theresa / afraid

7. Mary / worried

8. kids / quiet

Read & Listen

Practice

Work with a partner. Use the the words and the pictures below. See the example.

Student 1: Was / Were there ......?
Student 2: Yes / No, ...

1. potato salad
2. bananas
3. hamburgers
4. soup
5. cake
6. milk
7. hot dogs
8. potato chips
9. beer
10. cookies
11. juice
12. ice cream

Write

Fill in the spaces with questions The answers will help you write the questions.

Jen Yang and Helen are talking about the picnic

Helen: Hi, Jen. (1) *Were you at the picnic?*

Jen: Yes, I was at the picnic.

Helen: (2) ______________________________

Jen: The weather was very nice.

Helen: (3) ______________________________

Jen: All the students were there.

Helen: (4) ______________________________

Jen: Yes, David was there.

Helen: (5) ______________________________

Jen: No, Carmen wasn't there.

Helen: (6) ______________________________

Helen: I was sick all last week with a cold.

Jen: I'm sorry to hear that.

Read & Listen

It's Tuesday evening. Amir is asking Rita Lachance about yesterday's class.

Rita: Where were you yesterday?

Amir: I was at work, and I have to work overtime again tomorrow. How was the class yesterday?

Rita: It was OK. There was a surprise quiz.

Amir: There was? How was it?

Rita: It wasn't very easy. It was complicated and a little confusing.

Understand *Circle True, False, or We don't know.*

1. Amir wasn't in class on Monday.	True	False	We don't know.
2. Amir has to work overtime again tonight.	True	False	We don't know.
3. A quiz is a short test.	True	False	We don't know.
4. The quiz was difficult.	True	False	We don't know.

Practice *Work with a partner. Use the words and pictures above. See the example.*

Student 1: How was the quiz ....?
Student 2: It was ....

How was the quiz?
It was complicated.

1. complicated

2. confusing

3. easy

4. hard

5. simple

6. difficult

7. long

8. fair

Write *Match the questions with the anwers.*

1. Were the directions simple?
2. Was the quiz easy?
3. Was it long?
4. Were the grades high?
5. Was it unfair?

a. No, it was short.
b. No, it was fair.
c. No, they were low.
d. No, it was difficult.
e. No, they were complicated.

Write *Answer the questions in the questionnaire with the adjectives in the box.*

easy	hard	long	short	clear	confusing
fair	simple	complicated	unfair		difficult

QUESTIONNAIRE

1. How was your last test? ____________________
2. How was your homework? ____________________
3. How was your last quiz? ____________________
4. How is the registration process at your school? ____________________
5. How are the directions in this book? ____________________
6. How are the exercises in this book? ____________________
7. Are the chapters too long? ____________________
8. Was your last dictation easy? ____________________
9. Are the lessons too complicated? ____________________
10. How's your class?____________________
11. Are your tests fair or unfair? Why? ____________________

Read & Listen

The school principal is calling the police about a robbery at school.

Principal: Hello, Police Department? My name's Lanny Nelms. I'm the principal of the local school. I want to report a robbery.

Officer: Where was the robbery?

Principal: It was here in the school office.

Officer: When was it?

Principal: Last night.

Officer: Was there a security guard on duty?

Principal: No, there wasn't.

Officer: What can you tell me about the robbery?

Principal: All the office equipment was here last night, and now it isn't.

Officer: I'll send a police officer right there.

Understand *Circle **True, False,** or **We don't know.***

1. It's Wednesday.	True	False	We don't know.
2. The robbery was on Tuesday night.	True	False	We don't know.
3. The officer is at the school.	True	False	We don't know.
4. The office equipment was there yesterday.	True	False	We don't know.

Write *Fill in the spaces with **was, were, wasn't,** or **weren't.***

The students are talking about the robbery.

Rita: There (1) ___*was*___ a robbery last night.

Yuri: Oh, really? (2) _______ it at your home?

Rita: No, it (3) _______. It (4) _______ here, and the office equipment is missing.

Anna: What time (5)_______ the robbery?

Rita: I don't know. I think it (6) _______ very late.

Mary: (7) _______ the security guards here?

Rita: No, they (8) _______ here last night. They usually go home at ten o'clock.

Read

The Police officer is writing her report.

Officer: Do you have a picture of the office before the robbery?
Prinicpal: Yes, I do. Here's one.

Here's the office now.

Practice *Work with a partner. Use the two pictures above. See the example below.*

Student 1: What's the problem?
Student 2: There was / were ...(*item*)...... in the office before the robbery, but now there isn't /aren't.

Practice *Work with a partner. Give the location of the office equipment before the robbery. Use the picture on the previous page. See the example below.*

Student 1: Now tell me. Where was / were ..*(items)*...?

Student 2: It was / They were ..*(location)*......

Now tell me.
Where was the computer?
It was on the desk.

1. computer
2. file cabinet
3. clocks
4. tablet
5. printer
6. adding machine
7. cash register
8. calculators
9. pencil sharpener
10. staplers
11. safe
12. fax
13. desk lamps
14. *(Use your own word.)*

Write *Write the sentences in the correct order from the words below each line.*

There's a witness!

Witness: (1) I have some information about the robbery.
the robbery / have / about / I / some information /.

Officer: (2) ____________________
have / do / you / What kind / information / of / ?

Witness: (3) ____________________
a strange man / behind / the school / was / There /last night /.

Officer: (4) ____________________
time / he / What / there / was / ?

Witness: (5) ____________________
was / about / He / eleven / there/ p.m. / at

Officer: (6) ____________________
you / know / this / do / How / ?

Witness: (7) ____________________
see / I / can / from my bedroom window / the school / .

Officer: (8) ____________________
you / Will / that man / recognize / if you see him again / ?

Witness: (9) ____________________
know / I'll / Sure / him / , / .

Officer: (10) ____________________
for / Thanks / help / your / .

Read & Listen

The witness is looking at some pictures at the police station.

Write *Fill in the spaces with* ***was, were, wasn't*** *or* ***weren't****.*

Later that day...

Officer: OK, Max, where (1) ___were___ you about eleven o'clock last night?

Max: I (2) ________ with a sick friend.

Officer: (3) ________ you and your sick friend at home all night?

Max: Yes, we (4) ________. Why?

Officer: (5) ________ you and your sick friend near the school last night?

Max: No, we (6) ________. We (7) ________ at home.

Officer: A witness says you (8) ________ behind the school about 11 p.m.

Max: No! I (9) ________ there, I tell you. I (10) ________ at home!

Officer: Why is there office equipment in your apartment?

Max: OK! OK! OK! It (11) ________ me!

Practice

Fold this page along the dotted lines. Practice with a partner.

Student 1

Ask your partner the questions below about the picture to the right.

1. Where's the computer?
2. Is the computer in front of or next to the printer?
3. Is the pencil sharperner above or below the file cabinet?
4. Is the safe to the right or left of the desk?
5. Is the safe behind or between the file cabinet and the desk?
6. Where's the chair?

Listen to the questions from your partner and find the answers in the appointment book below.

Appointment Book

Date: *Monday*

1 p.m.	• *meet with the office*
2 p.m.	*staff in my office*
3 p.m.	• *write police report*
4 p.m.	*in my office*
5 p.m.	• *dinner with counselor*
6 p.m.	*at the snack bar*
7 p.m.	• *visit Mr. Wilson's class*
8 p.m.	• *visit Mr. Morris's class*
9.p.m.	• *meet with teachers*
10 p.m.	*in the teachers' room*

FOLD HERE

FOLD HERE

Student 2

Listen to the questions. Find the answers in the picture below.

Ask your partner these questions about the principal's schedule yesterday.

1. Where was the principal at 1 p.m.?
2. Where was the prinicpal at 5 p.m.?
3. Where was he at 3 p.m.?
4. Who was with the prinicpal at dinner time?
5. Was he in his office at 6 p.m.?
6. When was he in Mr. Wilson's class?
7. Where was he at 9 p.m.?
8. Was he in his office at 2 p.m.?

Pronunciation The /w/ and /v/ sounds.

• The */w/* and */v/* sounds are often confused by English language learners. The words ***"worry"*** and ***"very"*** are good examples of how the sounds are mispronounced.

• The */w/* sound is made when you put your lips forward and round them, and you need to put the back of your tongue against the back of the roof of your mouth.

• The */v/* sound is made using the lower lips and the upper teeth. The lower lips are slightly put behind or against the upper teeth. The sound is "voiced." That means that you let your vocal cords vibrate when pronouncing it.

Examples:

1. woman

2. world

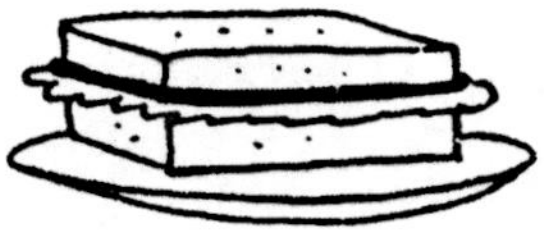

3. sandwich

4. wind

5. November

5

6. five

7

7. seven

8. evening

Practice *Practice pronouncing these words.*

vacuum	level	work	when	wait	wheel
volcano	vegetable	weather	warm	twelve	weak
envelope	van	week	word	with	housewife
television	violin	woman	vanilla	vent	vein
river	wine	seven	wake	went	vane
shovel	welcome	wait	where	will	vale
wave	warm	vase	five	won't	weird

Write *Fill in the spaces with **w** or **v**.*

1. Why __w__ere you __w__ith that __w__oman for fi__v__e __eeks on your __acation?
2. How __ill the __eather be on No__ember ele__enth and t__el__eth?
3. He __orks __ery __ell __ithout __isits from la__yers.
4. Those se__en __omen __ill __isit his __ife e__ery __ednesday.
5. __e __ant you to open the __est __indow in the e__ening.

CHAPTER 6

Thank You, But No Thank You.

SKILLS
- Describing Past Actions
- Reading a Time Card
- Reading a Personal Schedule

GRAMMAR
- Regular Verbs in the Past Tense

VOCABULARY
- Common Work-related Vocabulary
- Expressions of Time: *ago, last*

PRONUNCIATION
- The ***-ed*** Ending
- Rules for Adding the ***-ed*** Ending

Read & Listen

Amir Abbas is an auto mechanic. He is telling Vince Cartelli about his job.

Vince: Did you attend class last night?

Amir: No, I didn't. My boss asked me to work overtime in our new paint department at the garage. I stayed and earned a few extra dollars. I wanted to come to school, but I decided the work was important. I learned a new skill.

Vince: What kind of skill?

Amir: How to paint cars.

Vince: Oh, really?

Amir: Yes, I tried to paint my car last week, but I didn't do a very good job.

Vince: What happened?

Amir: I didn't use the right kind of paint, and I didn't mix it enough. When I picked up the can of paint, I dropped it and it spilled all over my car. I wiped off some paint, but it didn't help. My car looked terrible. All the guys at the garage laughed, and we joked about it all week.

Vince: What did you do?

Amir: I waited until the next day. The bad paint dried, and the guys showed me how to paint a car correctly. I repainted my car, and now it looks great. I improved a lot. Do you want me to paint your car?

Vince: Thank you, but no thank you!

Understand *Circle **True, False,** or **We don't know.***

1. Vince attended class last night.	True	False	We don't know.
2. Amir worked a few extra hours overtime.	True	False	We don't know.
3. Amir is learning how to paint cars.	True	False	We don't know.
4. Amir's car is new.	True	False	We don't know.
5. Vince wants Amir to paint his car.	True	False	We don't know.

Grammar Regular Verbs in the Past Tense

- We add the ***-ed*** ending to form the past tense of regular verbs in the affirmative only Do not use the ***-ed*** ending with verbs in the question and negative forms.
- We use ***did*** to signal the question.

Examples: ***Affirmative Statements***

My boss	***asked***	me to work overtime.
I	***wanted***	to come to school.
I	***decided***	the work was important.
I	***painted***	my car.
I	***picked up***	the can of paint.
I	***dropped***	it.
It	***spilled***	all over my car.
I	***tried***	to wipe off the paint.
The guys	***laughed***.	
We	***joked***	about it.
I	***waited***	until the next day.
The paint	***dried***.	
The guys	***showed***	me how to paint correctly.
I	***improved***	a lot.

- We use ***did not*** to signal negatives. ***Didn't*** is the contraction of ***did not***.

Examples: ***Negative Statements***

I	***didn't do***	a good job.
I	***didn't use***	the right paint.
I	***didn't mix***	it enough.

Questions

	Did	you	***attend***	class?
What	***did***	you	***do***?	
How	***did***	you	***spill***	it?

Short Answers: Did *you* ***attend*** *class?* ***Yes, I did.*** *or* ***No, I didn't.***

Read *Make logical complete sentences with the words in the box.*

Amir	used	the wrong paint.
The guys	joked	the right paint.
The boss	painted	about my mistake.
Vince	didn't use	his car.
I	didn't joke	Vince's car.
	didn't paint	paint.

Did	you	work	overtime?
	Amir	drop	the paint?
	Vince	paint	over the car?
	the boss	spill	a new skill?
	the guys	learn	about the problem?

Yes,	I	did.
No,	he	didn't.
	it	
	they	

Pronunciation The *-ed* ending

- We pronounce the ***-ed*** ending of the past tense in three different ways:

1. When the verb ends in a voiceless sound (except ***/t/***), ***-ed*** is pronounced ***/t/***.
2. When the verb ends in a voiced sound (except ***/d/***), ***-ed*** is pronounced ***/d/***.
3. When the verb ends in a ***/t/*** or ***/d/*** sound, ***-ed*** is pronounced ***/id/***.

Examples:

/t/

1. worked

2. washed

3. cooked

4. watched

/d/

5. opened

6. closed

7. cleaned

8. called

/id/

9. rested

10. visited

11. waited

12. painted

Read *Pronounce the words in the list below. Be careful with the endings. Write the sound that the -ed ending represents:* ***/t/, /d/,*** *or* ***/id/***. *See the examples below.*

1. stayed /d/	9. cleaned ___	17. listened ___	25. started ___	33. spilled ___
2. dressed /t/	10. helped ___	18. lived ___	26. thanked ___	34. painted ___
3. decided /id/	11. closed ___	19. looked ___	27. visited ___	35. joked ___
4. played ___	12. learned ___	20. loved ___	28. moved ___	36. watched ___
5. asked ___	13. opened ___	21. needed ___	29. waited ___	37. washed ___
6. ended ___	14. showed ___	22. practiced ___	30. wanted ___	38. cooked ___
7. called ___	15. danced ___	23. rained ___	31. washed ___	39. arrived ___
8. finished ___	16. liked ___	24. rested ___	32. poured ___	40. returned ___

Challenge *How many complete sentences can you make with the verbs in the list above?*

Read & Listen

1. He opened the can of paint.

2. He mixed the paint.

3. He picked up the can.

4. He poured the paint.

5. He dropped the can.

6. The paint spilled.

7. He wiped off the paint.

8. He cleaned the floor.

9. He waited until the next day

10. The paint dried.

11. He repainted the car.

12. The car looked great.

Practice

Work with a partner. Talk about the activities above. See the example below.

Student 1: What happened first?
Student 2: ....
Student 1: Then what happened?
Student 2: ....
Student 1: What happened next?
Student 2: ....

What happened first?
Amir opened the can.
Then what happened?
Then he mixed the paint.

Practice

Work with a partner. Ask and answer questions about the pictures above. Use short answers. See the example below.

Student 1: Did he ....?
Student 2: Yes he did. / No, he didn't.

Practice *Work with a partner. Use the phrases below. See the example below.*

Student 1: What did the guys show you how to do?
Student 2: They showed me how to ....

1. paint cars
2. mix paint
3. open a can
4. do a good job
5. work well
6. joke about problems
7. use paint
8. repaint a car
9. speak English
10. laugh
11. help people
12. *(Use your own words.)*

Practice *Work with a partner. Use the phrases below and use short answers. See the example below.*

Student 1: Did you ever learn how to .... when you lived at home?
Student 2: Yes, I did. *or* No, I didn't.

1. swim
2. drive a car
3. paint
4. cook
5. wash clothes
6. use a computer
7. use simple tools
8. clean the house
9. fix things
10. make a cake
11. make clothes
12. *(Use your own words.)*

Practice *Work with a partner. Ask about the items in the pictures below. Use the words in the box to answer. See the example below.*

Student 1: How does the .... look?
Student 2: It looks ....!

terrible	fantastic	good	OK
dirty	wonderful	bad	nice
damaged	old	new	great

1. new car

2. old car

3. used car

4. sports car

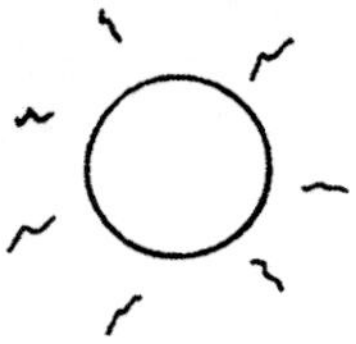
5. sun

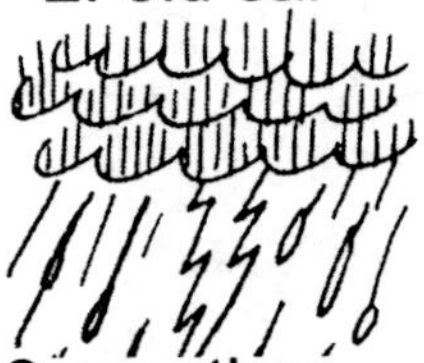
6. weather

7. coat

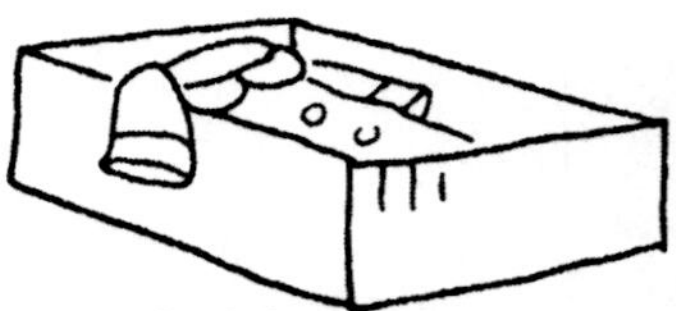
8. blouse

Write *Match the questions with the anwers.*

1. What did you mix?
2. How long did you work?
3. What did you learn?
4. What did you drop?
5. Whose car did you paint?
6. Who laughed?
7. What kind of paint did you use?
8. Who asked you to work overtime?

a. A new skill.
b. A few hours.
c. The guys.
d. The paint.
e. The wrong kind.
f. The boss.
g. The can.
h. Mine.

TIME CARD

Name Amir Abbas **DATES: From** 2/16 **to** 2/23

	Sun.	Mon.	Tues.	Wed.	Thur.	Fri.	Sat.	TOTAL
Regular Hours:	0	8	8	8	8	8	8	48
Overtime:	0	1	1.5	2	2	1.5	3	11
Total Hours:	0	9	9.5	10	10	9.5	11	59

Practice *Work with a partner. Ask and answer questions. Use the time card above. See the example below.*

Student 1: How many hours did Amir work on ....?
Student 2: He worked ....

How many hours did Amir work on Wednesday?
He worked eight hours, plus two hours overtime.

Practice *Work with a partner. Ask and answer questions. Use the time card above. Use short answers. See the example below.*

Student 1: Did Amir work overtime on ....?
Student 2: Yes, he did. *or* No, he didn't.

Did Amir work overtime on Sunday?
No, he didn't.

Read & Listen

Yuri and Amir are talking before class.

Amir: Hi, Yuri, what are you doing?

Yuri: I'm sending an e-mail to my cousin, Yoshi, in Japan.

Amir: Didn't she study here last semester?

Yuri: Yes, she did. Yoshi visited the United States last year. She was here because she wanted to improve her English. She's a translator and she needs English in her work. She arrived in June, and she stayed three months. We both studied English in a summer program at the College of the Desert in Palm Desert. We really enjoyed our classes. We lived with a family near campus. We traveled around the state on the weekends. She returned home in September, and I stayed here. I miss her very much.

Amir: Will she come back?

Yuri: I don't know. Maybe she will. She wants to come back next summer.

Understand *Circle* ***Yes, she did.*** *or* ***No, she didn't.***

1. Yuri studied English last summer.	Yes, she did.	No, she didn't.
2. Yuri lived in Japan.	Yes, she did.	No, she didn't.
3. Yoshi stayed here.	Yes, she did.	No, she didn't.
4. Yuri traveled around California.	Yes, she did.	No, she didn't.
5. Yuri returned to Japan with Yoshi.	Yes, she did.	No, she didn't.
6. Yuri lived in Palm Desert.	Yes, she did.	No, she didn't.

Write

1. Underline all verbs in the past tense in the sentences above.

2. Draw a circle all the verbs in the present tense in the sentences above.

3. Draw a box around all the verbs in the future tense in the sentences above.

Write *Help Amir ask Yuri questions. The answers will help you write the questions.*

Amir: (1) When did Yoshi arrive?
Yuri: Yoshi arrived in June.

Amir: (2) ______________________________
Yuri: Because she wanted to improve her English.

Amir: (3) ______________________________
Yuri: We studied English.

Amir: (4) ______________________________
Yuri: We studied at the College of the Desert in Palm Desert.

Amir: (5) ______________________________
Yuri: Our class started at nine o'clock in the morning.

Amir: (6) ______________________________
Yuri: It ended at three o'clock in the afternoon.

Amir: (7) ______________________________
Yuri: We traveled around the state.

Amir: (8) ______________________________
Yuri: Yoshi returned to Japan last September.

Amir: (9) ______________________________
Yuri: I stayed here because I want to improve my English.

Read & Listen

Amir and Yuri are talking about last month.

Yuri: I didn't answer Yoshi's e-mail last month, so I have to answer it now.

Amir: Why were you so busy? What did you do?

Yuri: I worked overtime. I cleaned my apartment. I visited some senior citizens at a nursing home. I played tennis. I washed my car and my cat. I moved to a new apartment, and I painted my living room.

Amir: Your cat? You washed your cat!

Yuri: Yes, I did. Never again!

Amir: I see. You were really, really busy.

Understand *Circle **True** or **False**.*

1. Senior citizens are people over 65 years old.	True	False
2. All senior citizens live in nursing homes.	True	False
3. Yuri learned how to drive a car.	True	False
4. Yuri knows how to play tennis.	True	False
5. Yuri doesn't know how to paint.	True	False
6. Yuri has a dog.	True	False

Write *Help Yuri answer the questions. Use short answers **Yes, I did.** or **No, I didn't.** See the example below.*

1. *Amir:* Did you paint the furniture?
2. *Amir:* Did you clean your apartment?
3. *Amir:* Did you wash your dog?
4. *Amir:* Did you work?
5. *Amir:* Did you visit some friends?
6. *Amir:* Did you fix your car?
7. *Amir:* Did you move?
8. *Amir:* Did you answer Yoshi's e-mail?

Yuri: No, I didn't.
Yuri: Yes, I did.
Yuri: ____________________
Yuri: ____________________
Yuri: ____________________
Yuri: ____________________
Yuri: ____________________
Yuri: ____________________

Read

Here's Yuri's calendar for last month.

FEBRUARY						
Sunday	Monday	Tuesday	Wednesday	Thursday	Friday	Saturday
1 walk in the park	2 work overtime	3 attend exercise class	4 answer some e-mails	5 clean apartment	6 cook dinner for friends	7 move to new apartment
8 call parents	9 Watch TV special	10 visit the library	11 start new book	12 finish work early	13 visit senior center	14 play tennis
15 visit the museum	16 no work	17 finish book	18 invite friends for dinner	19 rain, stay home	20 paint living room	21 shop for new dress
22 relax at home	23 work late	24 attend exercise class	25 work overtime	26 shop for food	27 visit senior center	28 play tennis

Practice

Work with a partner. Ask and answer questions in the past tense. Use the calendar above. See the example below.

Student 1: What did Yuri do on ...(date)......?
Student 2: She ....

Practice

Work with a partner. Ask and answer questions. Use the calendar above. Use short answers. See the example below.

Student 1: Did she ....?
Student 2: Yes, she did. *or* No, she didn't.

Did she watch TV on February ninth?
Yes, she did.

Practice *Work with a partner. Ask questions in the past tense with the phrases below. Answer in your own words. Notice how* ***"ago"*** *is used in the answers. See the example.*

When did you last visit a museum?
I visited a museum last year.
I last visited a museum about a month ago.

Student 1: What did you last ....?
Student 2: I .... ago. What about you?
Student 1: I .....(Use your own words.).........
or
I never ....

1. visit a museum
2. start to read a new book
3. answer n e-mail
4. wash windows
5. call your relatives
6. work late
7. move to this city
8. clean your apartment
9. invite people to your home
10. .(Use your own words.).........

Practice *Work with a partner. Ask questions in the past tense with the phrases below. Use original short answers. See the example below.*

Did you play tennis yesterday?

Student 1: Did you .... yesterday?
Student 2: Yes, I did. / No, I didn't.

1. play tennis
2. shop for food
3. wash clothes
4. watch T.V.
5. stay home
6. cook
7. work
8. relax
9. call a friend
10. practice English
11. finish your homework
12, ...

Practice *Work with a partner. Ask and answer original questions in the past tense. Use the words in the box below. See the example below.*

ask	dance	close	decide	open	talk
help	listen	learn	end	play	travel
rest	study	start	finish	use	return
laugh	enjoy	joke	live	walk	arrive

Student 1: When did you ....?
or
Where did you ....?
or
What did you ....?
or
Why did you ....?
or
How did you ....?
Student 2: I ....

Write *Fill in the spaces with* ***-ed, -d, did,*** *or* ***didn't.*** *Use an* ***"x"*** *for blank spaces. See the examples below.*

Yuri is asking Amir about his past.

Yuri: What about you, Amir? I don't know very much about you.

When (1) ___did___ you (2) immigrate_x_ to this country?

Amir: I (3) immigrated__ here a few months ago.

Yuri: Where (4) ___did___ you (5) live_x_ before?

Amir: I (6) lived__ in Egypt.

Yuri: (7) ______ you live alone?

Amir: No, I (8) _______. I (9) live___ with my relatives.

Yuri: (10) _______ you (11) live___ in Cairo?

Amir: Yes, I (12) _______.

Yuri: (13) _______ you (14) work___ in Cairo, too?

Amir: No, I (15) _______. I (16) work___ in a garage outside of the city.

Yuri: (17) _______ you (18) work___ every day?

Amir: I (19) work___ six days a week; I (20) _______ (21) work___ on Friday.

Yuri: (22) _______ you (23) like___ your job?

Amir: Yes, I (24) _______.

Yuri: (25) _______ you (26) like___ your house and relatives?

Amir: Of course, I (27) _______.

Yuri: Why (28) _______ you (29) move___ here?

Amir: I (30) move___ here because I (31) want___ to start a new life.

Spelling Rules for adding the *-ed* ending

• If the word ends in a silent **e**, only add ***-d***.

Examples: live → lived   joke → joked   like → liked

• If the word ends in a consonant + ***y*** pattern, change the ***y*** to ***i*** and add ***-ed***. If the ***y*** follows a vowel, simply add ***-ed***.

Examples:

y changes to ***i***	***y*** after a vowel
study → studied	play → played
marry → married	stay → stayed
dry → dried	enjoy → enjoyed

• When a word ends in a ***consonant-vowel-consonant*** pattern and the final vowel is stressed, the last consonant is doubled before adding ***-ed***. A final ***w***, ***x***, or ***y*** is never doubled.

Examples:

Consonant Doubled	***Not Doubled***
shop → shopped	fix → fixed
drop → dropped	need → needed
stop → stopped	pick → picked

Write

Fill in the spaces with the past tense of the verbs under the lines. Don't forget to make all necessary spelling changes.

I'm Amir Abbas. When I was in Egypt, I (1) lived (***live***) and (2) worked (***work***) in Cairo. I (3) _______ (***like***) Egypt, but I (4) _______ (***decide***) to come to this country to start a new life. I (5) _______ (***move***) here a few months ago, but my relatives (6) _______ (***stay***) in Egypt. When I (7) _______ (***arrive***) in Los Angeles, I (8) _______ (***apply***) for a job, and I was lucky because I (9) _______ (***start***) to work immediately. I (10) _______ (***register***) at school because I (11) _______ (***want***) to study English. I (12) _______ (***try***) to learn English quickly because I (13) _______ (***need***) it for my work. I (14) _______ (***practice***) every day, (15) _______ (***study***) very much, and I (16) _______ (***ask***) many questions. Today my English isn't too bad.

Write *Answer the questionnaire using in the past tense.*

QUESTIONNAIRE

1. What school did you attend last semester? ______________________
2. When did your last class end? ______________________
3. Did your English language skills improve in your last class? ______________________
4. What book or books did you use in your last class? ______________________
5. When did you register for this class? ______________________
6. When did you start this class? ______________________
7. Why did you decide to come to this school? ______________________

____

8. How did you learn about this school? ______________________
9. Did you study English before you arrived in this country? ______________________
10. What kind of school did you attend in your country? ______________________
11. What subjects did you study in your country? ______________________
12. Where did you live before you moved here? ______________________
13. Where did you work before you moved here? ______________________
14. Why did you move to this country? ______________________

CHAPTER 7

It's Nice To Be Back Home.

SKILLS	• Describing Past Actions
	• Identifying Major States and Cities
GRAMMAR	• Common Irregular Verbs
	• Preposition: *through*
VOCABULARY	• U.S. Cities, States, and Areas
WORD BUILDING	• The Prefix ***re-***

Read & Listen

Betty Wilson and Alice Morris are having lunch. Betty is telling Alice about her trip.

Alice: How was your trip?
Betty: It was wonderful.
Alice: Where did you go, and what did you do?
Betty: I went around the country, but I had an especially good time my last night in New York City.
Alice: What did you do there?
Betty: My sister and her husband live there, you know. Well, they took me to dinner at a famous restaurant. We ate a delicious meal, and we drank champagne. We had a great time. Then, my sister gave me a present.
Alice: What did she give you?
Betty: She bought tickets for a Broadway show. We finished dinner a little late, and we didn't want to be late for the show, so we took a taxi to the theater. We were very lucky because just as we got there, the show began.
Alice: What kind of show did you see?
Betty: We saw a musical, and we sat in the front row, too.
Alice: What musical was it?
Betty: I forgot the name, but it was a wonderful show.
Alice: What did you do afterward?
Betty: Nothing much. We went back to my sister's house. The next morning my brother-in-law drove me to the train station, and I left New York.

Understand *Circle **True, False,** or **We don't know.***

1. Betty had a good time in New York.	True	False	We don't know.
2. Betty went to dinner after the show.	True	False	We don't know.
3. She walked to the theater.	True	False	We don't know.
4. Betty's sister lives near the theater.	True	False	We don't know.
5. Betty took a train from New York.	True	False	We don't know.
6. Betty knows the name of the musical.	True	False	We don't know.

Grammar Irregular Verbs in the Past Tense

- We use the base form of the verb *(infinitive without **to**)* in the question and negative forms.

Examples: ***Base Form***

Question:	Did you	***go***	to San Francisco?
Negative:	No, I didn't	***go***	to San Francisco

- We use ***did*** to signal the question and ***didn't*** to signal the negative.
- We use the irregular forms only in the affirmative form.

Irregular Form

Affirmative: I ***went*** to New York.

Base Form		***Irregular Form***
go	→	went
have	→	had
take	→	took
eat	→	ate
drink	→	drank
buy	→	bought
get	→	got
forget	→	forgot
see	→	saw
sit	→	sat
begin	→	began
drive	→	drove
leave	→	left
give	→	gave

Read *Make logical complete sentences with the words in the box.*

Did	Betty Betty's sister she you they the show	eat drink begin sit leave get forget	the name of the show? in the front row? champagne? a delicious dinner? when they got there? to the theater on time? New York the next morning?

Yes, No,	I she it they we	did. didn't.

I Betty Betty's sister Her brother-in-law She They	went had saw bought took drove	some theater tickets. Betty to the train station. to a famous restaurant. a Broadway show. a taxi to the theater. a present for Betty.

Read

1. Her sister bought theater tickets.

2. They went to a famous restaurant.

3. They ate a meal and drank champagne.

4. Betty's sister gave her a present.

5. They took a taxi to the theater.

6. They got to the theater early.

7. They sat in the front row.

8. The show began on time.

9. They saw a musical.

10. Betty had a good time.

11. Her brother-in-law drove her to the station.

12. Betty left New York.

Practice

Work with a partner. Ask and answer questions about the pictures above. See the example below.

Student 1: What did .... do?
Student 2: He / She / They ....

What did Betty's sister do?
She bought some theater tickets.

Practice

Work with a partner. Ask and answer questions about the pictures above. See the example below.

Student 1: What / Where / When did ....?
Student 2: He / She / They....................

What did Betty see?
She saw a musical.

Practice

Work with a partner. Ask and answer questions about the pictures above. Use short answers. See the example below.

Student 1: Did ....?
Student 2: Yes .... did.
or
No, ... didn't.

Practice *Work with a partner. Ask questions in the past tense using the phrases below. Answer with original short answers. See the example below.*

Student 1: Did you ever ....?
Student 2: Yes, I did. / No, I didn't.

1. go to a famous restaurant
2. take a friend to dinner
3. eat a delicious meal
4. drink champagne
5. get a nice present
6. go to a Broadway musical
7. sit in the front row of the theater
8. go to New York
9. take a train
10. forget the show's name

Practice *Work with a partner. Ask and answer questions with the phrases below. Then, use your own words. See the example below.*

Student 1: When did you ....?
Student 2: I .... ago / last ....

1. eat in a restaurant
2. drive or take a bus to school
3. have a good time
4. arrive at a movie or show late
5. begin this course
6. leave your country
7. see ....
8. give ....
9. go to ....
10. forget ....
11. eat ....
12. buy ....

Write *Fill in the spaces with the correct form of the underlined verbs in the past tense. See the examples.*

1. __Did__ you eat well in New York?
2. ________ you take taxis in New York?
3. ________ you go to museums?
4. ________ you give your sister a present.
5. ________ you see any movies?
6. ________ you drive a car in New York?
7. ________ you leave early in the morning.
8. ________ you buy any presents?

Yes, I __ate__ very well.
Yes, I ________ taxis.
Yes, I ________ to a few.
Yes, I ________ her a sweater.
No, I ________ ________ any movies.
No, I ________ ________ there.
Yes, I ________ at 7 a.m.
Yes, I ________ a present for you!

Write *Fill in the spaces below with the words in the box. See the examples.*

Alice is asking more questions about Betty's trip.

did	didn't	go	went	eat	ate	drink	drank

Alice: When (1) ___did___ you ___go___ to the restaurant?

Betty: We (2) ___went___ at six o'clock in the evening.

Alice: How (3) ________ you ________ to the restaurant?

Betty: We (4) ________ in my brother-in-law's new car.

Alice: What time (5) ________ you ________ to the theater?

Betty: We (6) ________ to the theater at eight p.m., but we (7) ________ ________ by car. We took a taxi.

Alice: What kind of food (8) ___did___ you ___eat___ at the restaurant?

Betty: I (9) ___ate___ fish, and my sister and her husband (10) ________ chicken.

Alice: (11) ________ you ________ any dessert?

Betty: No, I (12) ________ ________ any dessert, but my brother-in-law (13) ________ some cake.

Betty: We (14) ___drank___ some very good champagne.

Alice: (15) ________ you ________ French champagne?

Betty: No, we (16) ________ ________French champagne We (17) ________ some very good champagne from California.

Alice: How much champagne did you (18) ________?

Betty: We (19) ________ only one bottle.

Write *Fill in the spaces below with the words in the box. See the examples.*

did	didn't	give	gave	see	saw	have	had

Alice: (1) Did your sister give you a present before or after dinner?

Betty: She (2) gave it to me after dinner.

Alice: What (3) ________ you ________ her?

Betty: I (4) ________ her a beautiful sweater.

Alice: (5) ________ you ________ your brother-in-law a sweater, too?

Betty: No, I (6) ________ ________ him a sweater; I (7) ________ him a shirt from New York.

Alice: What (8) did you see in New York?

Betty: I (9) saw the Statue of Liberty.

Alice: (10) ________ you ________ Central Park?

Betty: No, I (11) ________ ________ that, but I (12) ________ the Empire State Building.

Alice: What else (13) ________ you ________?

Betty: I (14) ________ Rockefeller Center.

Alice: (15) Did you have a really good time?

Betty: Yes, I (16) ________ a wonderful time.

Alice: (17) ________ you ________ time to see your other relatives?

Betty: No, I (18) ________ ________ enough time to see all of them. They live outside the city.

Read & Listen

Betty is telling Alice about her trip back on the train.

Alice: How was your trip back?

Betty: It was a very restful three-day trip. I did very little. I slept late in the morning, relaxed, read a good book, and wrote some letters.

Alice: What else did you do?

Betty: Sometimes I sat in the sightseeing car and looked at the scenery.

Alice: What did you see from the train?

Betty: I saw a lot of interesting places: cities, mountains, and deserts.

Alice: Did you speak to any people?

Betty: Sure. I met and spoke to a lot of nice passengers on the train. I had dinner with some people. And I made some new friends, too.

Alice: Are you glad to be back?

Betty: All in all, I like to travel, but it's nice to be home.

Understand *Circle **True, False,** or **We don't know.***

1. Betty was on the train for three days.	True	False	We don't know.
2. Betty wrote three letters on the train.	True	False	We don't know.
3. Betty slept and ate on the train.	True	False	We don't know.
4. Betty isn't glad to be back.	True	False	We don't know.
5. ***"All in all"*** means ***"in general."***	True	False	We don't know.

Grammar More Irregular Verbs in the Past Tense

Examples:	*Base Form*	➡	*Irregular Form*
	sleep	➡	slept
	read	➡	read *(pronounced like the color **red**)*
	write	➡	wrote
	sit	➡	sat
	speak	➡	spoke
	meet	➡	met
	do	➡	did
	make	➡	made

Read *Make logical complete sentences with the words in the box.*

I The passengers She Betty They	slept spoke to did made met read wrote	some nice people on the train. very little. a few new friends. late in the morning. Betty. letters. a book.

Did	Betty the passengers she Alice	write read sit speak go take	a train? with Betty? alone? a book? a letter? to people?

Yes, No,	she they	did. didn't.

Write *Review the past tense of the verb **to be**. Fill in the spaces with **was** or **were**.*

Alice: (1) Were you on a small train or a big train?

Betty: I (2) was on a very big train.

Alice: (3) ________ there a dining car?

Betty: (4) There________ sleeping and sightseeing cars, too.

Alice: (5) ________ there many people on the train?

Betty: Yes, there (6) ________ a lot of people.

Alice: (7) ________ there many kids?

No, there (8) ________n't many kids. There (9) ________ only about five.

Read & Listen

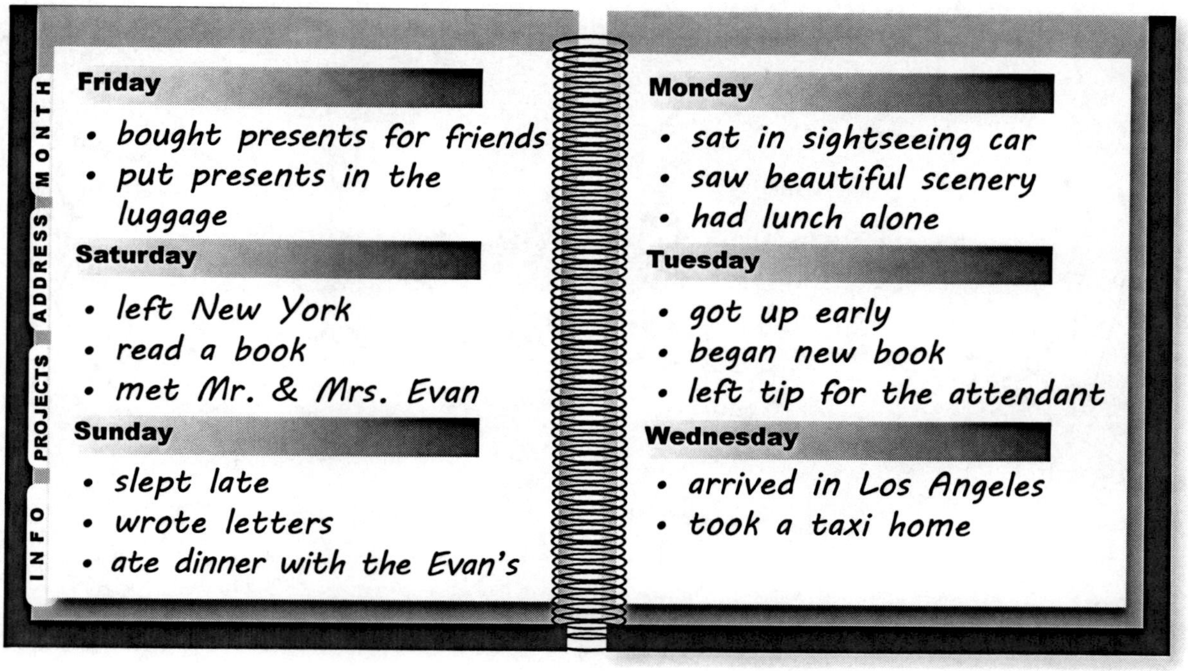

MONTH
ADDRESS
PROJECTS
INFO
Friday
• bought presents for friends
• put presents in the luggage

Practice

Work with a partner. Ask and answer questions with the past tense. Use the diary above. See the example below.

Student 1: What did Betty do on ...*(date)*......?
Student 2: She ....

What did Betty do on Saturday?

Practice

Work with a partner. Ask and answer questions. Use the diary above. See the example below.

Student 1: When did Betty ....?
Student 2: She .... on ...*(date)*......

When did Betty read a book?
She read a book on Saturday.

Practice

Work with a partner. Ask and answer questions. Use the diary above. Use short answers. See the example below.

Student 1: Did Betty ....?
Student 2: Yes, she did. *or* No, she didn't.

• left New York

• met Mr. & Mrs. Evan
Sunday
• slept late
• wrote letters
• ate dinner with the Evan's
Monday
• sat in sightseeing car
• saw beautiful scenery
• had lunch alone
Tuesday
• got up early
• began new book
• left tip for the attendant
Wednesday
• arrived in Los Angeles
• took a taxi home

Did Betty write a letter on Friday?

Read

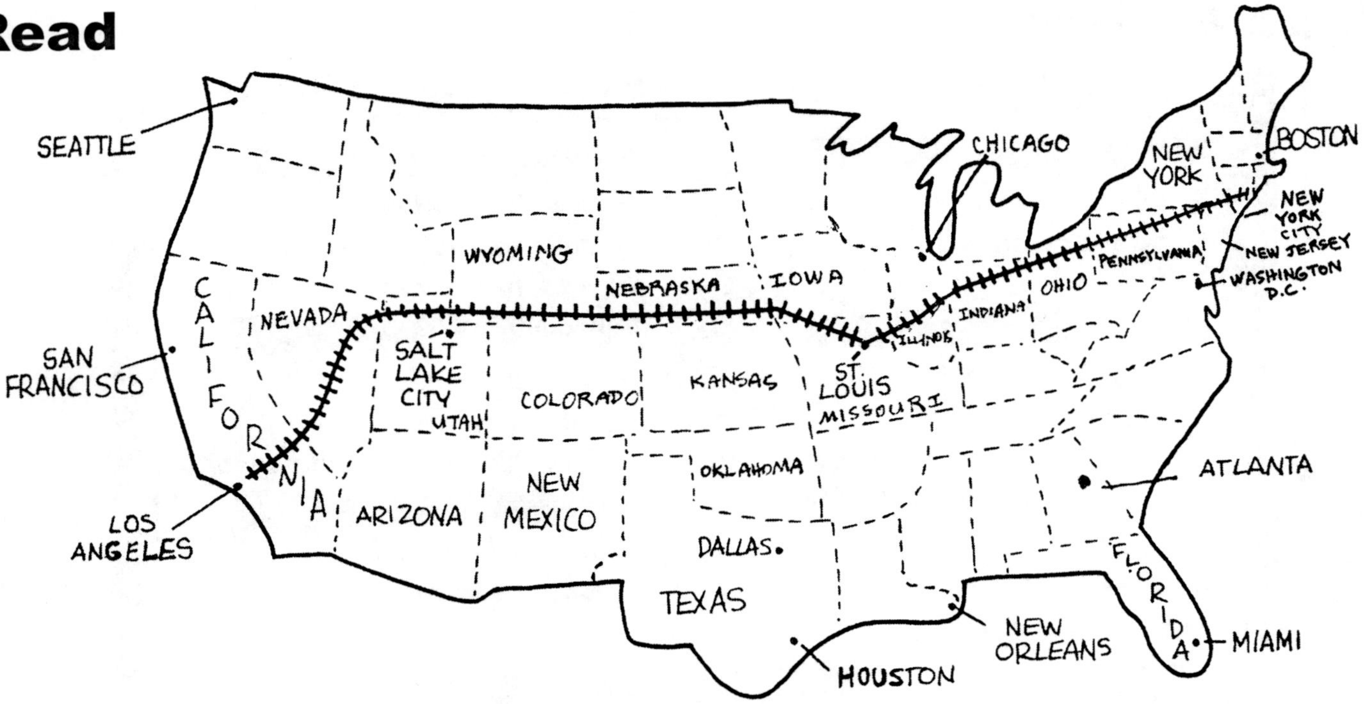

Practice *Work with a partner. Ask and answer questions about the train route with short answers. Use the map above. See the example below.*

Student 1: Did the train go through ....?
Student 2: Yes, it did. / No, it didn't.

Practice *Work with a partner. Ask and answer questions. Use the train route above. See the example below.*

Student 1: What states / cities did the train go through?
Student 2: It went through ....

Practice *Work with a partner. Ask and answer questions using the phrases below. See the example below.*

Student 1: What cities / states did you ....?
Student 2: I ....

1. visit
2. go to
3. see
4. drive through
5. live in
6. work in
7. study in
8. read about
9. leave
10. ....

Challenge *Fill in the missing names of the states in the map above.*

Write *Fill in the spaces below with the words in the box. See the examples.*

Alice is asking more questions about Betty's train trip.

did	didn't	sleep	slept	write	wrote	meet	met

Alice: (1) __Did__ you __sleep__ well on the train?

Betty: I (2) __didn't__ __sleep__ well the first night,

but I (3) ________ very well after that.

Alice: (4) ________ you ________ late every morning?

Betty: Yes, I (5) ________. And sometimes I

(6) ________ an hour in the afternoon, too.

Alice: (7) __Did__ you __write__ many letters?

Betty: Yes, I (8) __wrote__ a few letters.

Alice: (9) ________you ________ postcards, too?

Betty: No, I (10) ________ ________ any postcards;

I (11) ________ electronic cards from my

smart phone from the train. .

Alice: How many people (12) __did__ you __meet__?

Betty: I (13) __met__ a lot of people, but I (14) ________

an especially nice couple the first day.

Alice: How (15) ________ you ________ them?

Betty: I (16) ________ them in the dining car.

We (17) ________ for dinner every day after that.

Write *Unscramble the words below the lines. All the words are the past tense of* ***to be*** *or irregular verbs.*

Betty is sending her sister an e-mail.

Dear Sis,

Thank you again for the dinner and the Broadway show. I (1) ___had___ a
dah

wonderful time. I'm glad I (2) ________ the train back home. It (3) ________
koto **vega**

me time to relax. I (4) ________ a lot, I (5) ________ a good book, and I
ptsle **dare**

(6) ________ some letters. (7) ________ some interesting people and I
otwer **tem**

(8) ________ some beautiful scenery.
was

I (9) ________ lunch with my friend, Alice Morris, yesterday. She asked
adh

me a million questions about my trip. Maybe you know her. I (10) ________
otfrog

if you (11) ________ her when you (12) ________ here last year.
etm **erwe**

We (13) ________ about my trip, and I (14) ________ her a present.
ospek **vgea**

I (15) ________ her a nice blouse in New York. Do you remember when
hgbuto

when you (16) ________ to the store with me to buy it? Alice (17) ________
tnew **swa**

very surprised to get a present.

Paul and the kids will be home soon, and dinner will be ready in a few minutes, so I have to stop here. Take care, and please write soon.

Love, Betty

Practice

Fold this page along the dotted lines. Practice with a partner.

Student 1

Ask your partner the questions below. Use the words in the box to complete the questions.

1. Where did you .... yesterday?
2. What did you ....yesterday?
3. What time did you .... yesterday?
4. How long did you ....yesterday?
5. Why did you .... yesterday?
6. When did you ....?
7. How did you ....?
8. Who did you ....?

go	drink	see	leave
write	have	begin	sit
give	speak	take	eat
get	buy	forget	drive
sleep	read	meet	do

Listen to your partner's questions. Use the expressions of time in the box below to answer the questions.

every day	yesterday	tomorrow
sometimes	often	never
seldom	usually	always
last week	next week	every week
last month	next month	every month
last year	next year	every year
ago	in	on

FOLD HERE

Student 2

Listen to your partner's questions. Answer them with the words in the box below.

went	had	took	drank
began	got	saw	sat
forgot	left	gave	slept
wrote	spoke	met	ate
bought	drove	read	did

Ask your partner the questions with ***"When."*** *Use the words in the box to complete the questions.*

1. When did you ....?
2. When do you ....?
3. When will you ....?
4. When are you going to ....?
5. When do you have to ....?

see	have	eat	live
wash	look	buy	take
get	call	fix	visit
go	give	begin	help
cook	start	drink	forget
sit	listen	watch	end

FOLD HERE

Word Building The Prefix *re-*

• We use the prefix ***re-*** with verbs to mean ***again*** or ***to restore to a previous condition***.

Examples:

1. paint

2. repaint

3. write

4. rewrite

5. wash

6. rewash

7. build

8 rebuild

Write *Rewrite the following sentences. Use the prefix **re-**.*

1. Amir painted his car again. *Amir repainted his car.*
2. Betty read the book again. ______________________
3. Amir told her the story again. ______________________
4. The students took the test again. ______________________
5. Betty wrote the letter again. ______________________
6. Yuri visited the senior citizens center again. ______________________
7. Betty's sister invited her again. ______________________

Write *Fill in the spaces with the underlined verbs beginning with **re-**. Use the past tense. Pay special attention to irregular verbs in the past tense.*

1. Paul wanted to wash the clothes again, so he *rewashed* them.

2‘ José didn't make his bed correctly the first time, so he ____________ it.

3. Amir didn't mix the paint enough the first time, so he ____________ it.

4. The students didn't learn the lesson the first time, so they ____________ it.

5. They didn't do the exercise correctly the first time, so they ____________ it.

CHAPTER 8

The Past, Present, and Future

• Review Chapter

• Test

Read & Listen

Mr. Wilson is introducing a reporter to Manuel Perez.

Hi, Manuel. This is a news reporter. She wants to write a story about a typical ESL student. Can she interview you?
Sure, please sit down and join me.

Write *Write short answers to the reporter's questions.*

1. Can I ask you a few questions? — Sure, you can.
2. Are you an ESL student? — Yes, I am.
3. Did you know English in your country? — No, ________
4. Is it hard for you to learn English? — Of course, ________
5. Do you practice outside of class? — Yes, ________
6. Do you speak English at home? — No, ________
7. Is English necessary for your work? — Yes, ________
8. Is your English improving? — Yes, ________

Write *Fill in the spaces with the correct word.*

1. Are you married? — Yes, am.
2. Do you have children? — Yes, I do.
3. ________ it difficult to begin a new life here? — Yes, it was.
4. ________ you have any relatives in this city? — Yes, I do.
5. ________ they help you at first? — Yes, they did.
6. ________ you working now? — Yes, I am.
7. ________ it easy to find a job? — No, it wasn't.
8. ________ you stay in this country? — Yes, I will.

Write *Help Manuel ask the reporter some questions, too. Asl questions about the underlined phrases. The answers will help you form the questions.*

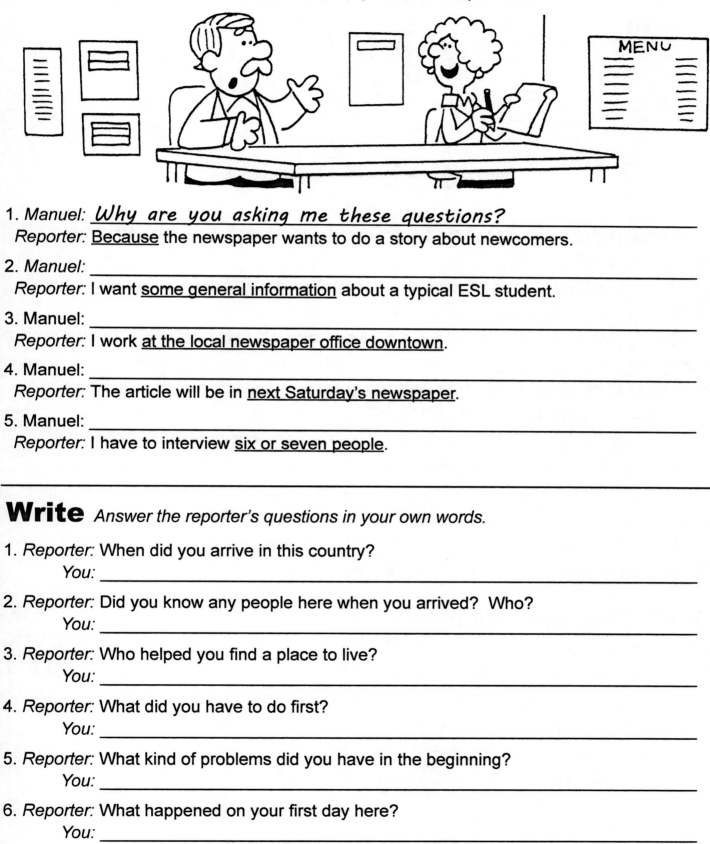

1. *Manuel:* *Why are you asking me these questions?*
   Reporter: Because the newspaper wants to do a story about newcomers.
2. *Manuel:* ____________________
   Reporter: I want some general information about a typical ESL student.
3. Manuel: ____________________
   Reporter: I work at the local newspaper office downtown.
4. Manuel: ____________________
   Reporter: The article will be in next Saturday's newspaper.
5. Manuel: ____________________
   Reporter: I have to interview six or seven people.

Write *Answer the reporter's questions in your own words.*

1. *Reporter:* When did you arrive in this country?
   You: ____________________
2. *Reporter:* Did you know any people here when you arrived? Who?
   You: ____________________
3. *Reporter:* Who helped you find a place to live?
   You: ____________________
4. *Reporter:* What did you have to do first?
   You: ____________________
5. *Reporter:* What kind of problems did you have in the beginning?
   You: ____________________
6. *Reporter:* What happened on your first day here?
   You: ____________________

Write *Fill in the spaces with the prepositions **in, on, to,** or **at.***

Manuel is describing his first day here.

Our first day (1) _in_ the United States was very busy. I remember the date. We arrived (2) _in_ Los Angeles (3) _on_ April 6th (4) _at_ 7 o'clock (5) ____ the morning. I think it was (6) ____ a Thursday. My cousin met us (7) ____ the airport, and he drove us (8) ____ his apartment. We were very tired, so we went (9) ____ bed (10) ____ noon and got up (11) ____ five (12) ____ the afternoon. (13) ____ the evening, some old friends from our country visited us. We were happy (14) ____ see them again after so many years. They spoke (15) ____ us about our new city. They told us many interesting facts -- especially about the weather here. They said we arrived (16) ____ a typical day. They said the weather changes very little during the year. It's cool (17) ____ the morning and (18) ____ night, but it's generally warm (19) ____ the afternoon. It's hot (20) ____ the summer and not very cold (21) ____ the winter. It rains (22) ____ the winter and (23) ____ the spring. Beautiful weather comes (24) ____ November when it's clear. We learned a lot from them. They left (25) ____ 11:30 (26) ____ night. Then, we went (27) ____ bed (28) ____ midnight. It was a very long and wonderful first day (29) ____ our new home. I'll never forget that day.

Write *Match the questions with their answers.*

1. When did you arrive?
2. Who met you at the airport?
3. How did you get to your cousin's apartment?
4. What did you and your friends talk about?
5. How was the weather on that day?
6. What time did you go to bed on that day?

a. A cousin.
b. The weather.
c. On April sixth.
d. Typical.
e. About midnight.
f. By car.

Read

Manuel is teling the reporter about the first six months.

APRIL	MAY	JUNE
• arrived in the U.S.A. • enrolled kids in school • stayed with cousin	• moved to an apartment • looked for a job • applied at many companies • enrolled in adult school	• got a social security card • got a job • went to summer school • took driving lessons
JULY	**AUGUST**	**SEPTEMBER**
• bought a used car • Anna learned to drive • worked overtime	• bought used furniture • visited San Francisco • Anna began to work	• new semester began • got a small raise at work

Practice

Work with a partner. Ask and answer questions about the calendar above. See the examples below.

Student 1: What did Manuel and Anna do in ....?
Student 2: They ....

(month)

Practice

Work with a partner. Ask and answer questions about the calendar above. See the examples below.

Student 1: When did ....?
Student 2: He / She / They ....

Read

What did you have to do when you first arrived?
We had to find an apartment, look for a job, enroll the kids in school, begin to study English, buy some furniture, get a social security card, and work for low wages.

Practice

Work with a partner. Answer questions with original sentences. Use the past tense of ***have to: had to.*** *See the example below.*

Student 1: What did you have to do when you arrived here?
Student 2: I had to ....

What did you have to do when you arrived here?
I had to enroll in school.

Practice

Work with a partner. Answer the questions with short answers. See the example below.

Student 1: Did you have to .... when you arrived here?
Student 2: Yes, I did. / No, I didn't.

Did you have to find a place to stay when you arrived here?
Yes, I did.

Write

What did you have to do the first few months here? Write a list below.

THINGS I HAD TO DO

1. *I had to enroll in school.*
2. ______
3. ______
4. ______
5. ______
6. ______
7. ______
8. ______

Read

Manuel is giving some advice.

Manuel: We were very lucky to have relatives here. It was nice to be with them again and they helped me find a job. I was also lucky to meet some nice people here at school.

Reporter: Do you have any advice for newcomers?

Manuel: Yes, I do. Don't forget the past, enjoy the present, and plan for the future,

Write

Help Manuel give some comments and advice for newcomers.

When a newcomer first comes here...

1. It's hard to *begin a new life.* ______________________
2. It's also hard to ______________________
3. It's expensive to ______________________
4. It's not very easy to ______________________
5. It's necessary to ______________________
6. It's important to ______________________
7. It's impossible to ______________________
8. It's interesting to ______________________
9. But it's possible to ______________________

Read & Listen

The reporter meets some of the other students.

Practice

Work with a partner. Answer questions with original sentences. Use some of the answers above. See the example below.

Student 1: What will you do in the future?
Student 2: I'll .... What about you?
Student 1: I'll ....

Write

*What **will** you and **won't** you do in the future? Make a list.*

MY FUTURE PLANS

1.	*I will...*	*I won't...*
2.		
3.		
4.		
5.		

Write *Pretend you're a reporter and interview another student in your class. Ask the questions below. Then write the information on the lines.*

INTERVIEW QUESTIONS

1. Who are you interviewing? Name: ____________________

2. Where's he / she from? ____________________

3. Does he / she have friends or family here? Who? ____________________

4' What's his / her occupation? ____________________

5. When did he / she arrive here? ____________________

6. Who helped him / her when he / she arrived? ____________________

7. Where does he / she live? ____________________

8. Does he / she work? ____________________

9. If he / she works, where? ____________________

10. How were his / her first few months? ____________________

11. What were his / her problems at first? ____________________

____

12. What kind of advice does he / she have for newcomers? ____________________

____

13. What will he / she do in the future? ____________________

____

14. What does he / she like about this area? ____________________

____

15. What doesn't he / she like about this place? ____________________

____

16, What does he / she miss about his or her country? ____________________

____

Write *Write a story about the person you interviewed. Use he information on the previous page.*

is a student in my class.

Challenge *Read your story to the students in your class.*

Challenge *Interview an English-speaking friend or neighbor. Write a story. Read it to your classmates.*

Read

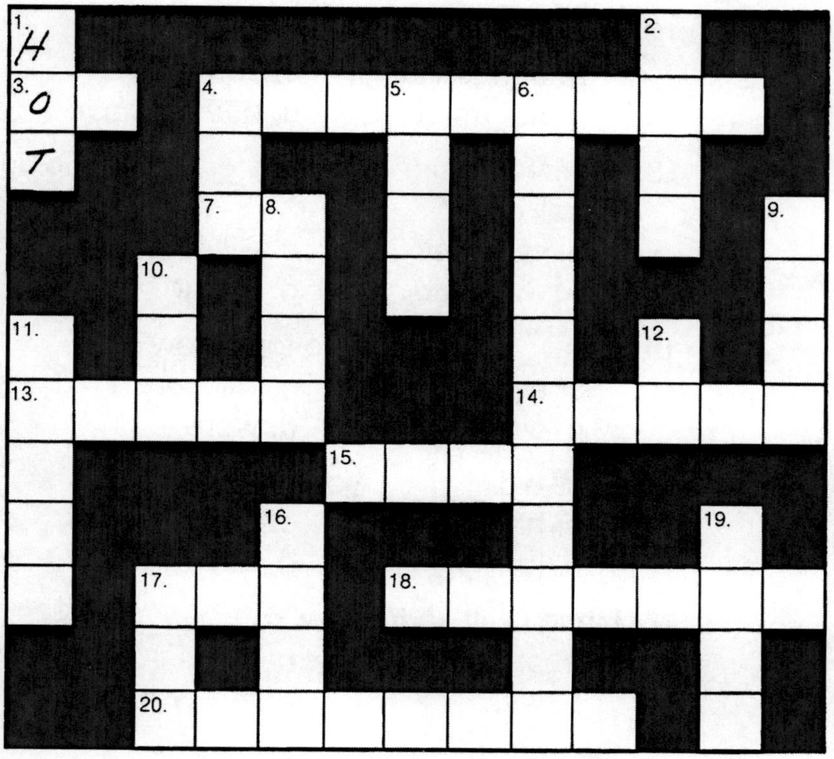

DOWN ↓

1. Open the window because it's .... in here.
2. How .... does it cost?
4. A .... car usually uses a lot of gas.
5. Let's not buy a new car; let's buy a .... car.
6. Not expensive.
8. The ceiling is .... my head.
9. How .... people are there in this room?
10. She's not ....; she's very thin.
11. ..... Birthday!
12. Don't sit down; please stand .....
16. I work .... 8 a.m. to 5 p.m.
17. He lives very .... from here.
19. Please .... down. You're driving too fast.

ACROSS →

3. It's dark in here. Please turn .... the light.
4. It's a .... day today!
7. I .... to school every day.
13. I usually go home .... work.
14. Please give me more water; this glass is ....
15. Please sit ....
17. I bought this present .... you.
18. This machine isn't noisy. It runs very ....
20. I'm sorry, but I don't .... your last name. I forgot it.

Test *Circle the correct answer.*

1. What floor is the office _____ ?
   a. in c. to
   b. on d. at

2. Alberto Duran lives in Los Angeles; he ___________ in Santa Monica.
   a. live c. doesn't lives
   b. don't live d. doesn't live

3. Do Alberto and Alfonso live together? No, _____.
   a. he doesn't c. they doesn't
   b. he don't d. they don't

4. That's Mr. Wilson. He's my teacher. The students like _____ very much.
   a. her c. his
   b. him d. he's

5. How ______ do you work overtime?
   a. often c. never
   b. always d. sometimes

6. I take a bus ______ .
   a. twice day c. twice in a day
   b. twice a day d. twice in day

7. It's hard ______ a good job.
   a. find c. to find
   b. to finding d. for find

8. The young man isn't ______ to work here.
   a. old enough c. too old enough
   b. enough old d. to young

9. If you want to go to college, you ______ to study hard.
   a. must c. have
   b. mustn't d. has

10. Before you leave, you _____ take out the garbage.
    a. has c. must
    b. have d. must to

11. He can't go to college ____good grades.
    a. with not c. not have
    b. without d. if not

12. I _____to work on Sunday.
    a. don't must c. don't have
    b. not must d. doesn't have

13. Nancy and her daughter _____ shopping tomorrow.
    a. will goes c. will to goes
    b. will to go d. will go

14. What ______ you do tomorrow?
    a. are c. will not
    b. will d. were

15. How old ______ you?
    a. have c. is
    b. has d. are

16. Nancy will go to New York _____ bus.
    a. at c. by
    b. with d. in

17. When's the picnic _____ be?
    a. going c. will
    b. going to d. go to

18. The students _____ to bring the food.
    a. will c. is going
    b. won't d. are going

19. Where _____ you yesterday?
    a. was c. were
    b. where d. wear

20. I ____ at the picnic because I was sick in bed with a cold.
    a. was c. weren't
    b. were d. wasn't

21. _____was a robbery at the school last night.
    a. The c. They
    b. There d. Their

22. Amir _____ a few hours overtime last week.
    a. works c. worked
    b. work d. will work

23, When _____ Yoshi study in the United States?
a. is
b. will
c. do
d. are

24. What _____ yesterday?
a. do you did
b. did you do
c. did you did
d. do you do

25. Where _____ before you moved here?
a. did you live
b. lived you
c. did you lived
d. do you live

26. When I moved here, I _____ to learn English quickly.
a. tried
b. tryd
c. tryed
d. treid

27. When Nancy was in New York, her sister _____ her theater tickets.
a. will buy
b. bought
c. buyed
d. buys

28. Betty Wilson _____to New York last month.
a. go
b. went
c. was go
d, goes

29. Did you _____ a taxi to the theater?
a. taked
b. tooked
c. take
d. took

30. Did you drink French champagne? No, we _____ French champagne.
a. not drink
b. not drank
c. didn't drink
d. didn't drank

31. Did you have a good time there? Yes, _____.
a. I do
b. I did
c. I have
d. I has

32. Did the train go _____ St. Louis?
a. at
b. through
c. between
d. across

33. How many people did you _____ on the train?
a. meet
b. met
c. meeted
d. meat

34. Nancy _____ some letters on the train.
a. write
b. wrote
c. writed
d. writing

35. What will you do _____?
a. tomorrow
b. yesterday
c. next day
d. last week

36. When did you return? I returned two _____.
a. days ago
b. days before
c. ago days
d. days past

37. I'll fix the sink _____.
a. a week ago
b. last week
c. next week
d. next day

38. Did Amir paint his car again? Yes, he _____ it yesterday.
a. repainted
b. paint
c. repaint
d. will paint

39. Do you plan to stay here? Yes, _____.
a. I do
b. I am
c. I did
d. I have

40. Is your English improving? Yes, _____.
a. it is
b. I am
c. it will
d. I will

CHAPTER 9

Please Follow the Directions Carefully.

SKILLS	• Understanding Written Directions
GRAMMAR	• More Regular Verbs in the Past Tense
VOCABULARY	• Commonly Used Technical Words
WORD BUILDING	• The Suffix ***-al***

Read & Listen

Joanne Yates is visiting Rita Lachance.

Rita: Come in.
Joanne: What's up?
Rita: I bought two bookcases yesterday, but there's a problem.
Joanne: What's the problem?
Rita: They're unassembled, and I don't know if I can put them together. I'm not very good with tools.
Joanne: Maybe I can help. Where are the instructions?
Rita: Here they are.

INSTRUCTIONS TO ASSEMBLE BOOKCASE

Tools needed: screwdriver and hammer.
Follow the steps below carefully.

1. Remove the pieces from the box.
2. Make sure all pieces are included. This kit includes screws, nails, and seven pieces of wood: top board, bottom board, two side boards, back board, and two shelves.
3. Place all pieces on the floor.
4. Position the sides and match the letters on the ends of the boards. (See picture.)
5. Place screws in the holes and attach sides.
6. Tighten all screws.
7. Nail the large board to the back side of the bookcase.
8. Lift bookcase upright.
9. Insert and adjust shelves.

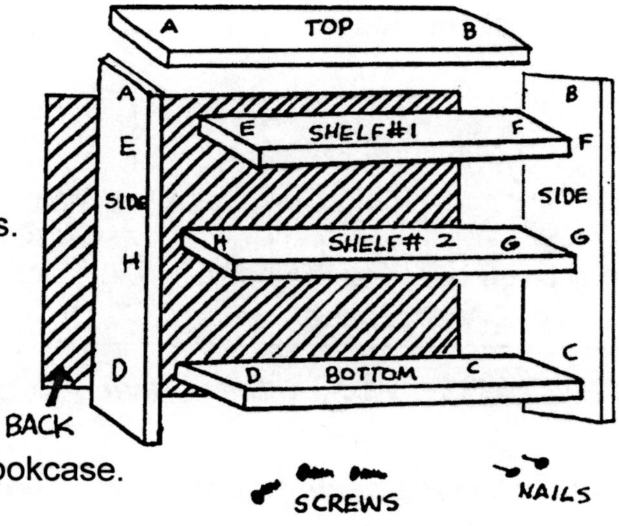

Understand *Circle **True, False,** or **We don't know.***

1. ***"What's up?"*** means ***"What are you doing?"***	True	False	We don't know.
2. ***"Assemble"*** means ***"put together."***	True	False	We don't know.
3. ***"Make sure"*** means ***"check."***	True	False	We don't know.
4. Joanne doesn't want to help Rita.	True	False	We don't know.
5. They need tools to assemble the bookcase.	True	False	We don't know.

Grammar More Regular Verbs in the Past Tense

• Most common verbs in English are irregular, but most other verbs are regular. To form the past tense, simply add the ***-d*** or ***-ed*** ending. (See Chapter 6.)

Examples:	***Present Tense***	***Past Tense***
	remove	removed
	check	checked
	place	placed

Read

1. Remove pieces from box.

2. Check all parts.

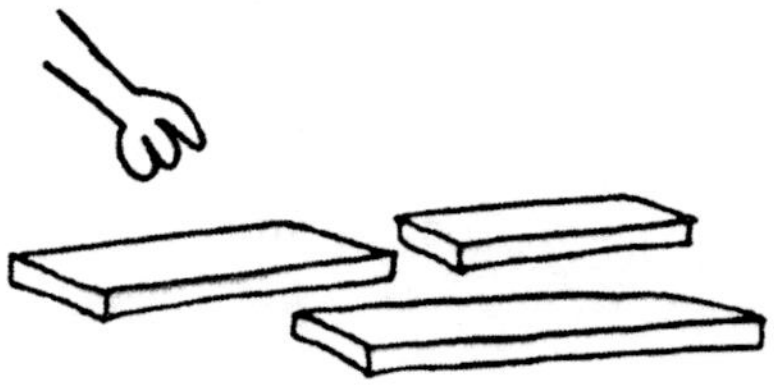

3. Place pieces on the floor.

4. Position pieces.

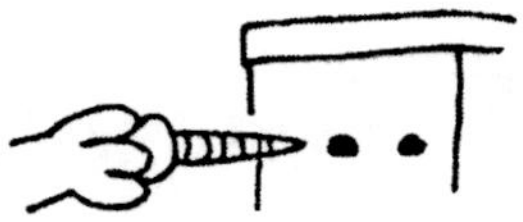

5. Place screws in the holes.

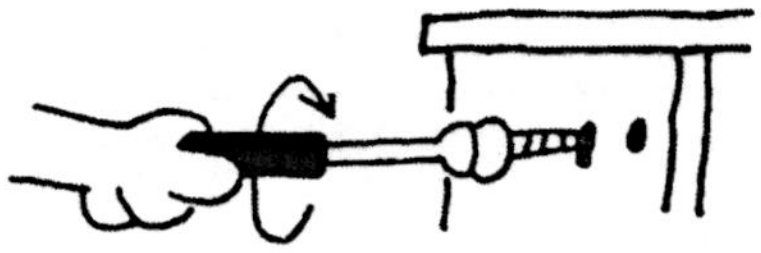

6. Tighten screws.

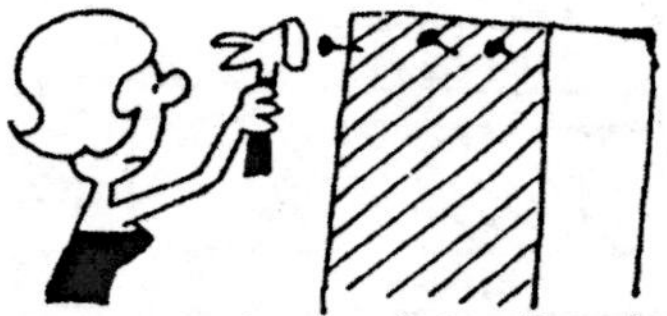

7. Nail large board to the back of the bookcase.

8. Lift bookcase upright.

9. Insert and adjust shelves.

Practice *Work with a partner. Ask and answer questions in the past tense. See the example below.*

Student 1: What a beautiful bookcase! What did they do to make it?
Student 2: First, they ....
Student 1: What did they do next?
Student 2: Next, they ....

What a beautiful bookcase! What did they do to make it?
What did they do next?
First, they removed the pieces from the box.
Next, they checked the parts.

Write *Fill in the spaces below with the past tense of the verbs in the box.*

Joanne and Rita are looking at one of the assembled bookcases.

follow	adjust	nail	attach
include	position	remove	check
place	tighten	insert	lift

Rita: Wow! That was fast!

Joanne: It was easy.

Rita: How did we do that?

Joanne: We (1) followed the directions carefully. We (2) ________ the pieces from the box. We (3) ________ all the pieces. The kit (4) ________ all the necessary parts. We (5) ________ all the parts on the floor and (6) ________ them in the right places. We (7) ________the boards together and (8) ________ all the screws. Then, we (9) ________ the large board on the back side and (10) ________ the bookcase upright. Finally, we (11) ________ the shelves and (12) ________ them.

Rita: Now let me try to assemble the second bookcase.

Write *Label the pieces for her. Use the words in the box.*

bottom shelf	shelf	side	back
top shelf	nails	screws	box

1. side
2. ________
3. ________
4. ________
5. ________
6. ________
7. ________
8. ________

Read

Rita has another problem.

Rita: Before you go, can you help me check my living room lamp? It doesn't work.
Joanne: Did you check the light bulb?
Rita: No, I didn't. I don't like to work with electrical equipment.
Joanne: Let's begin with the light bulb.
First, let's turn off the lamp.
OK. Now unplug the cord.
Remove the lamp shade.
Unscrew the light bulb. Check the bulb.
Get a new bulb. Is the old one burned out?
Rita: Yes, it is.
Joanne: Screw the new bulb in the socket.
Place the shade back on the lamp.
Plug the cord in the outlet.
Now turn on the switch.
Rita: It works!
Joanne: It was only a burned-out bulb. Here. You can throw it away.
Rita: That looks very easy.
Joanne: It is. You can do it yourself next time.

Understand *Circle **True, False,** or **We don't know.***

1. Rita fixed the lamp.	True	False	We don't know.
2. The living room lamp had a broken plug.	True	False	We don't know.
3. The living room lamp had a burned-out bulb.	True	False	We don't know.
4. Joanne is an electrician.	True	False	We don't know.
5. Joanne likes to fix things.	True	False	We don't know.

Read

1. Turn off the lamp.

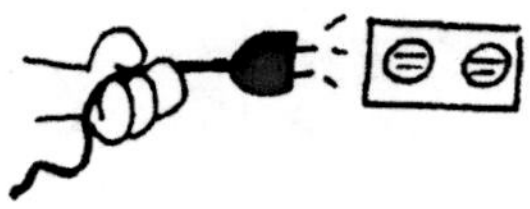

2.Unplug the cord.

3. Remove the shade.

4. Unscrew the bulb.

5. Get a new bulb.

6. Screw in the new bulb.

7. Place the shade back the lamp.

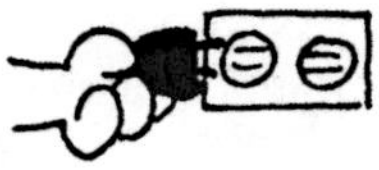

8. Plug in the cord.

9. Turn on the switch.

Practice

Work with a partner. Talk about what Joanne did in the past tense. See the example below.

Student 1: What did Joanne do first?
Student 2: She................................
Student 1: Then what did she do?
Student 2: Next, she ....

Practice

Work with a partner. Use ***had to*** *or* ***didn't have to*** *in the answers. See the example below.*

Student 1: Did she have to ....?
Student 2: Yes, she had to .... it.
or
No, she didn't have to .... it.

Write *Fill in the spaces below with the past tense of the verbs in the box.*

Rita is trying to repeat the directions.

turn on	get	screw	turn off
remove	plug	unscrew	check
turn off	unplug		

Rita: Let me see if I can repeat that. First, you (1) turn off the lamp. Then, you (2) __________ the cord. You (3) __________ the shade, and (4) __________ the light bulb. You (5) __________ the bulb because it was burned out. You (6) __________ a new bulb, (7) __________ it in, (8) __________ the shade back on the lamp, (9) __________ the cord in the outlet, and (10) __________ the lamp. Right?

Joanne: That's right. Next time, you can replace a burned-out bulb.

Rita: What's the name of this thing again?

Joanne: That's a plug.

Write *Help Rita learn the names of the parts. Match the words in the box with the pictures.*

plug	cord
switch	outlet
socket	light bulb

1. __________

2. __________

3. __________

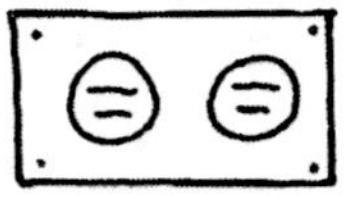

4. __________

5. __________

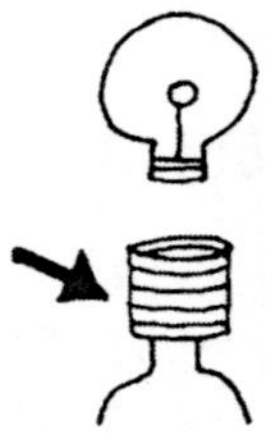

6. __________

Write *Write sentences about what Joanne is doing. Use the present continuous tense. See example below.*

1. *She's turning off the lamp.*

____

____

____

____

____

____

____

____

____

____

Challenge *Place the pictures in the correct order.*

Write *Fill in the spaces with the words in the box.*

Now Rita is replacing a dirty filter in the heater.

replace	turn on	turn off	throw away
remove	close	open	

Let me see. Where do I begin?

1. First, I *turn* *off* the heater.
2. Then, I have to __________ the heater cover.
3. I __________ the dirty filter.
4. I __________ it with the new filter.
5. I have to __________ the cover.
6. Then I __________ __________ the heater.
7. And I __________ the dirty filter.

Challenge *How many machines and appliances can you name that use electrical plugs?*

Read & Listen

A man is asking Rita for help at the supermarket.

Man: Excuse me, ma'am, can you help me use this machine?
I have to make a photocopy of this paper.
Rita: Sure, let me read the instructions to you.

INSTRUCTIONS

1. Deposit money.
2. Open lid.
3. Place paper on the glass surface.
4. Close lid.
5. Select size of copy.
6. Press button to start.
7. Wait for light.
8. Open lid.
9. Remove original paper and copy.

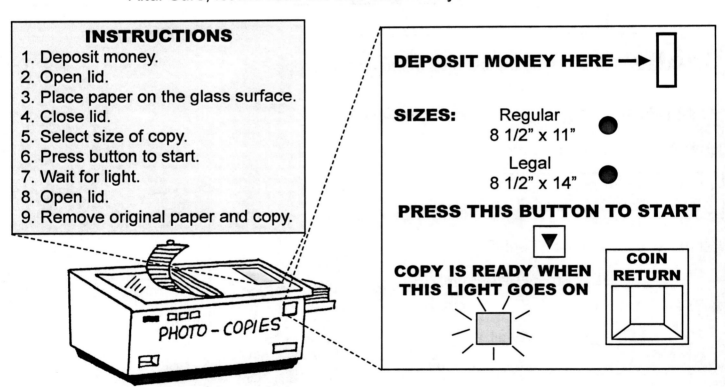

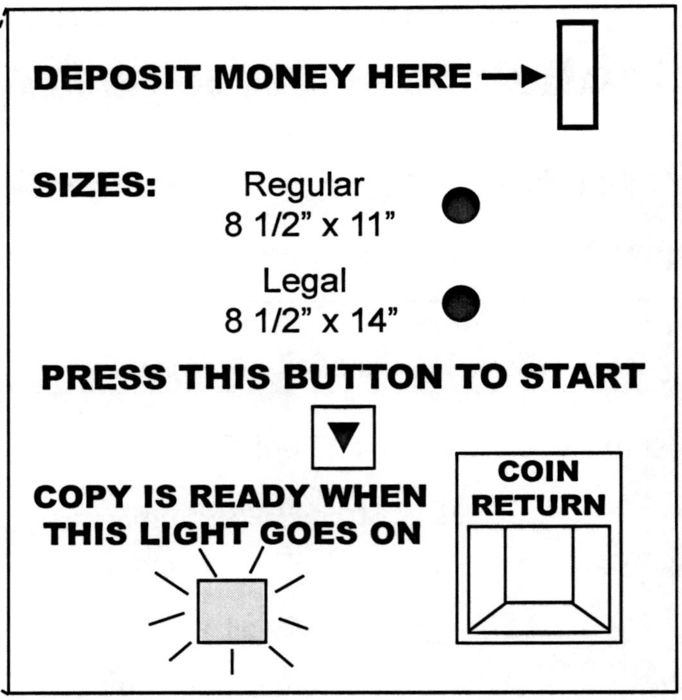

Understand *Circle **True, False,** or **We don't know.***

1. The man knows how to use the machine.	True	False	We don't know.
2. ***"Select"*** means ***"choose."***	True	False	We don't know.
3. A copy costs ten cents.	True	False	We don't know.
4. ***"Legal size"*** means ***"a small size."***	True	False	We don't know.
5. A page from this book is legal size.	True	False	We don't know.

Read

1. Deposit the money.

2. Open the lid.

3. Place paper on glass surface.

4. Close the lid.

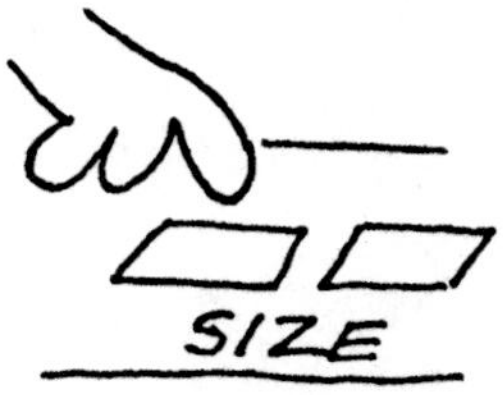

5. Select the size.

6. Press the button to start.

7. Wait for light to go on.

8. Open the lid.

9. Remove the original copy.

Practice

Work with a partner. Ask and answer questions using the present continuous tense. See the example below.

Student 1: What is Rita doing?
Student 2: She's ....

What's Rita doing?
She's depositing the money.

Write

Explain Rita's steps above. Use the past tense. See example below.

1. First, she deposited the money.
2. Then, she __________
3. Next, __________
4. __________
5. __________
6. __________
7. __________
8. __________
9. __________

Read *Put the instructions below in the correct order.*

TO OPERATE COFFEE MACHINE:

_____ Lift the plastic door.

_____ Press the button to start.

__1__ Deposit the money.

_____ Remove the cup.

_____ Select an item.

TO OPERATE MICROWAVE OVEN:

_____ Remove the hot food.

_____ Close the door.

_____ Press the button to start.

_____ Wait for the red light telling that food is ready.

_____ Place the cold food in oven.

__1__ Open the door.

_____ Select the time and temperature.

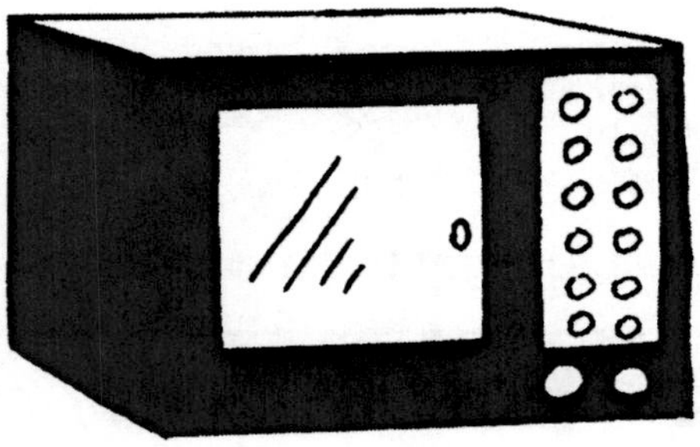

TO OPERATE COIN-OPERATED WASHING MACHINE:

_____ Wait for the machine to finish.

_____ Close the lid.

_____ Push the button in to start.

__1__ Open the lid.

_____ Remove the clean clothes.

_____ Place the dirty clothes and detergent in washer.

_____ Select the water temperature.

_____ Deposit the money.

Note: *In many written instructions the definite article **"the"** is not used.*
Example: Deposit money. Deposit <u>the</u> money.
Open lid. Open <u>the</u> lid.

Write *Fill out the questionnaire.*

QUESTIONNAIRE

1. What kind of machines can you operate?

a. ____________ e. ____________
b. ____________ f. ____________
c. ____________ g. ____________
d. ____________ h. ____________

2. What kind of tools can you use?

a. ____________ e. ____________
b. ____________ f. ____________
c. ____________ g. ____________
d. ____________ h. ____________

3. How well do you follow directions correctly? ____________
4. Can you lift heavy boxes? ____________
5. Do you know how to work with electrical equipment? ____________
6. Do you have any mechanical skills? ____________
7. Do you like to build things? ____________
8. Do you like to fix things? ____________
9. Who fixes broken things in your home? ____________

Write *Explain how to replace a battery in a smoke alarm. Use some of the words in the box.*

take down	battery
smoke	replace
alarm	install
ceiling	press
open	test
compartment	button
check	put back

1. ____________
2. ____________
3. ____________
4. ____________
5. ____________
6. ____________
7. ____________
8. ____________
9. ____________

Challenge *Read the directions you wrote above and compare them with other students in your class.*

Practice *Fold this page along the dotted lines. Practice with a partner.*

Student 1

Ask your partner the questions below about the picture to the right.

1. Is there a bookcase in the picture?
2. What's on the top of it?
3. What's on the first shelf?
4. What's to the left of it?
5. What's on the second shelf?
6. What's to the right of it?
7. Is there a plant in the picture?
8. Is the TV on or off?
9. What else is in the picture?

Listen to the questions from your partner and find the answers in the picture below.

FOLD HERE

FOLD HERE

Student 2

Listen to the questions. Find the answers in the picture below.

Ask your partner these questions about the picture to your left.

1. Is there a lamp in your picture?
2. Where is it?
3. Does the lamp have a plug?
4. Is the plug in an outlet?
5. What is next to the lamp?
6. Is there a bulb in the lamp?
7. What's wrong with the bulb?
8. Where is the lamp shade?
9. Is there anything else in the picture?

Word Building The Suffix *-al*

• We use ***-al*** to form adjectives from nouns, with the meaning "relating to, of the kind of, having the form or character of: nature + -al = natural (having the character of *nature*).

Examples:

1. A mechanic uses mechanic<u>al</u> skills.

2. A dentist works on dent<u>al</u> problems.

Write *Make adjectives from the following nouns.*

1. nation ___national___
2. practice ________________
3. origin ________________
4. profession ________________
5. instrument ________________
6. magic ________________
7. classic ________________
8. occupation ________________

Write *Fill in the spaces with adjectives ending in the suffix **-al**.*

1. A ***technician*** has ___technical___ skills.
2. A ***politician*** works with ________________ problems.
3. A ***person*** can have many ________________ problems.
4. ***Musicians*** usually have ________________ skills.
5. An ***electrician*** usually knows about ________________ problems.

Write *Write original sentences with the following adjectives.*

1. physical: ________________________________
2. special: ________________________________
3. general: ________________________________
4. official: ________________________________
5. medical: ________________________________

CHAPTER 10

Isn't That Women's Work?

SKILLS	• Identifying Daily Activities
	• Making a Household Work Schedule
GRAMMAR	• Expressions with ***do***, ***make***, and ***get***
VOCABULARY	• Household Chores
	• Daily Activities
WORD BUILDING	• The Suffix ***-ing*** Used as a Noun (Gerund)
SPELLING	• Rules for adding ***-ing*** to a Verb

Read & Listen

It's Saturday morning and Paul Wilson is vacuuming. The door bell rings. David Morris is at the door.

David: Are you ready for our tennis game?

Paul: I'll be ready in a minute.

David: What are you doing?

Paul: I'm doing some housework. Let me turn off this vacuum cleaner. I can't hear you. It makes too much noise.

David: Isn't that women's work?

Paul: We all share the housework in this family. Betty does the laundry, the ironing, and the bathrooms. I do the gardening, and the kids help me with the cleaning. I do the vacuuming and the windows, and Theresa does the dusting and the dishes. Steve helps, too. The kids do a pretty good job. They even make their beds.

David: Who does the shopping?

Paul: We all do the shopping on Friday.

David: And the cooking? Who does that?

Paul: Betty and I both do. I usually make breakfast and she makes dinner. She doesn't let me make dinner. She says I make a mess in the kitchen. We sometimes let Theresa make a meal, but we make sure one of us is in the kitchen with her. What do you do, David? Don't you help your wife do any housework?

David: Well, oh, ah, hum, let's play tennis.

Paul: Oh, I see.

Understand *Circle **True, False,** or **We don't know.***

1. Paul likes to do housework.	True	False	We don't know.
2. Betty does the gardening.	True	False	We don't know.
3. The family does the shopping together.	True	False	We don't know.
4. David Morris helps his wife do housework.	True	False	We don't know.
5. ***"Even"*** means ***"also."***	True	False	We don't know.
6. ***"I see."*** means ***"I understand."***	True	False	We don't know.

Grammar *"do"* and *"make"*

• We often use expressions with ***do*** and ***make*** to describe household duties. ***Do*** means perform an activity. ***Make*** usually means produce something.

Examples:

Expressions with **do**		*Meaning*
do the housework	=	work in the house
do the dishes	=	wash the dishes
do the cooking	=	cook
do the work	=	work
do a good job	=	work well
do the laundry	=	wash and dry clothes
do the ironing	=	iron the clothes
do the bathrooms	=	clean the bathrooms

Expressions with **do**		*Meaning*
do the shopping	=	shop for food
do the cleaning	=	clean the house
do the dusting	=	dust the furniture
do the vacuuming	=	vacuum the carpets
do the floors	=	clean the floor
do the gardening	=	work in the yard
do the windows	=	clean the windows
do nothing	=	perform no work

Expressions with **make**		*Meaning*
make the beds	=	arrange the bedding (sheets, blankets, pillows)
make the meals	=	prepare/cook food or meals (breakfast, lunch, dinner)
make a mess	=	create a mess
make noise	=	produce noise
make a mistake	=	do incorrectly
make sure	=	check

Read *Make logical complete sentences with the words in the boxes.*

Roy Nancy Theresa They The family The kids The vacuum cleaner I	do does make makes	the housework. the vacuuming. the shopping. the cooking. their beds. breakfast. noise. laundry and ironing.

Do Does	Roy Nancy Patty the family the vacuum they you	do make	breakfast? noise? the dusting? a good job? the gardening? bathrooms? dishes?

Yes, No,	I he she it they	do. does. don't. doesn't

Write *Match the questions with the answers. See example below.*

1. Who does the dusting?
2. Who does the cooking?
3. Who does the bathrooms?
4. Who does the shopping?
5. Who does the dishes?
6. Who does the laundry?
7. Who does the gardening?
8. Who does the windows?

a. I wash the windows.
b. Betty washes the clothes.
c. Theresa dusts the furniture.
d. I work in the yard.
e. Theresa washes them after we eat.
f. We all buy the food.
g. Betty and I make the meals.
h. Betty scrubs the bathtub.

Write *Match the questions with the answers. See example below.*

1. Who makes the beds?
2. Who makes dinner?
3. Who makes breakfast?
4. What makes noise?
5. Who makes mistakes?
6. Who makes a mess?
7. Who makes sure Theresa's OK in the kitchen?

a. Betty cooks the evening meal.
b. I prepare the morning meal.
c. Betty or I check on her.
d. The vacuum is loud.
e. I'm always neat and clean.
f. The kids straighten the sheets, blankets, and pillows.
g. I never do anything wrong.

Read

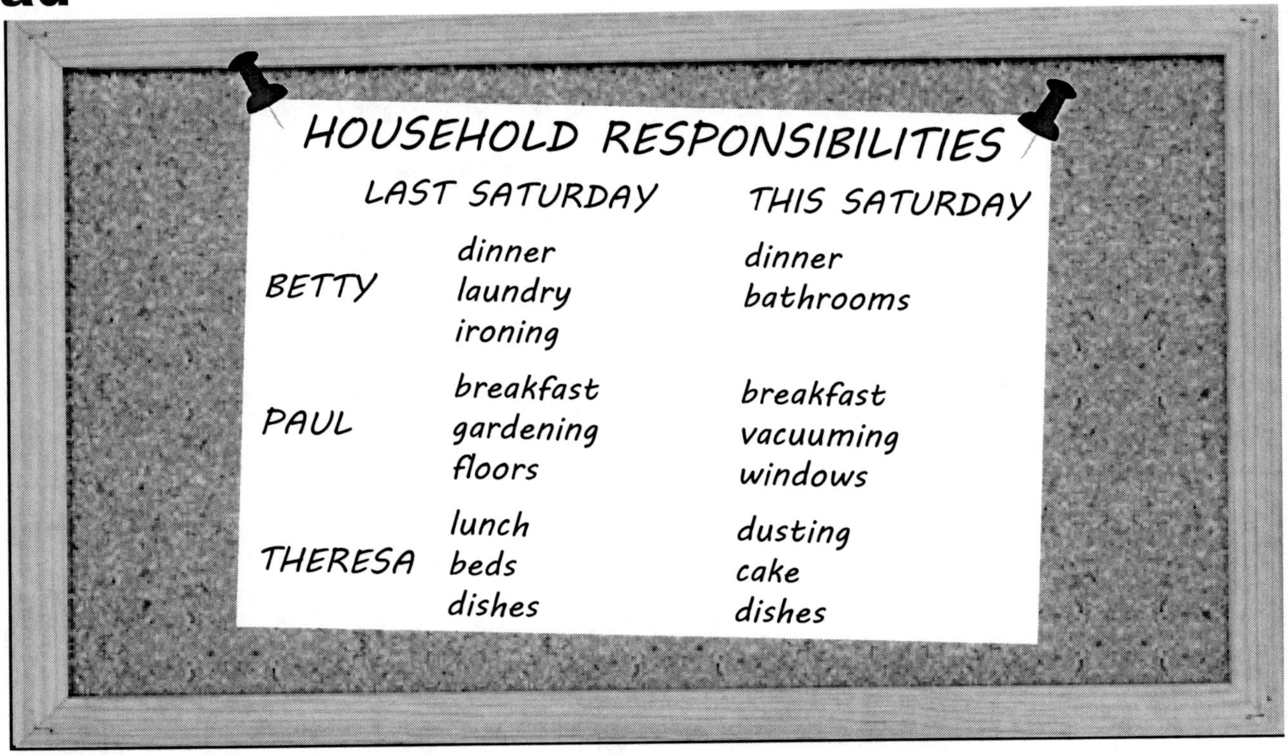

Practice *Work with a partner. Talk about the chores above. Use the present tense. See the example below.*

Student 1: Who does / makes ....?
Student 2: .... does / makes ....

Practice *Work with a partner. Talk about the chores above. Use the past tense. See the example below.*

Student 1: Who did / made ....?
Student 2: .... did / made ....

Who made lunch last Saturday?
Theresa made lunch last Saturday.

Practice *Work with a partner. Talk about the chores above. Use the future tense. See the example below.*

Student 1: When will .... do / make ....?
Student 2: .... will do / will make ....

When will Theresa make a cake?
She will make a cake on Saturday.

Practice *Work with a partner. Talk about your family's chores. See the example below.*

Student 1: Who does / makes ...... in your family?
Student 2: ....do / does / make / makes ....

Who does the cooking in your family?
I do the cooking.

1. the cooking
2. the laundry
3. dinner
4. ironing
5. housework
6. cleaning
7. vacuuming
8. breakfast
9. the dishes
10. shopping
11. noise
12. mess

Practice *Work with a partner. Ask and answer the questions about what you know how to do. Use the phrases below Use short answers. See the example.*

Student 1: Do you know how to do / make ....?
Student 2: Yes, I do. / No, I don't.

1. coffee
2. a cake
3. the beds
4. the dishes
5. the ironing
6. the laundry
7. the bathroom
8. the cooking
9. the gardening
10. a good meal
11. a good job
12. *(Use your own words.)*

Write List your personal or family household responsibilities below. Use expressions with ***do*** and ***make***.

WEEKLY HOUSEHOLD RESPONSIBILITIES

	Duties
Name: ____________________	1. ____________________ 2. ____________________ 3. ____________________
Name: ____________________	1. ____________________ 2. ____________________ 3. ____________________
Name: ____________________	1. ____________________ 2. ____________________ 3. ____________________
Name: ____________________	1. ____________________ 2. ____________________ 3. ____________________

Write

Replace the phrases under the lines with expressions from the box. Change the verbs to the past tense.

do a good job	do the bathroom	do the housework	make a mess
do the work	do the cleaning	do the ironing	do the shopping
do the dishes	do the cooking	do the gardening	do the laundry

Paul and David are playing tennis.

Paul: Who (1) ______________________ in your home when you were a child?
worked in the house

David: My mom and three sisters (2) ______________ and they (3) ________________, too.
worked ***worked well***

My mother (4) __________________ and (5) ____________________, too. My big sister,
cooked ***shopped for food***

Susan, (6) ______________________ and she also (7) ______________________________.
washed the clothes ***ironed the clothes***

My sister, Pauline, (8) ______________________ and (9) __________________________
cleaned the house ***cleaned the bathrooms***

My little sister, Rina, (10) ____________________
washed the dishes

Paul: What did you do?

David: I (11) ________________________ with my dad.
worked in the yard

Paul: Is that all?

David: No, I often (12) ______________________, too.
created a mess

Discussion

Talk about the questions below.

1. Is it OK for men to do housework? Why or why not?
2. Do the men do housework in your home? What kind?
3. How much time do you spend doing housework every week?
4. How many hours did your mother spend doing housework when you were a child? Why?
5. Why did women stay home and do housework in the past?
6. Why do many women work outside the home today?
7. Are there different occupations for men and women? Why or why not?
8. What is "women's work" and what is "men's work" in your culture?
9. Do men and women get the same pay for the same kind of work? Why or why not?
10. Are men and women equal? Why or why not?

Read & Listen

Paul and David are returning from their tennis game.

Paul: My hands are full. Can you get the door for me?

David: Sure.

Paul: Let's sit down. I'll get us some cold drinks. I really get thirsty and a little tired after a tennis game with you.

David: Sorry, but I can't stay. I have to go.* I have to do a lot of things today. I have to get a haircut, get some money from the ATM** at the bank, get some new shoes, get the mail, and get ready for a dinner party tonight.

The telephone rings. Paul answers it.

(A minute later.)

Paul: David, this call is for you. It's your wife.

David: What does she want?

Betty: She wants you to get home NOW!

Understand *Circle **True, False,** or **We don't know.***

1. Paul has to do a lot of things today.	True	False	We don't know.
2. Paul is tired.	True	False	We don't know.
3. David is thirsty.	True	False	We don't know.
4. David can stay at Paul's house.	True	False	We don't know.
5. David's wife wants him to come home.	True	False	We don't know.

* *A popular variation of **have to** is **have got to**, usually pronounced **'v gotta**.*

** *ATM = Automatic Money Machine*

Grammar Expressions with *"get"*

- The verb ***get*** has many different meanings.
- The past tense is irregular: ***got***.

Examples:

Expressions with "get"		***Meaning***
get the door or telephone	=	open the door / answer the telephone
get a cold drink (or object)	=	go, pick up, and return with it
get tired, thirsty	=	become tired, thirsty
get a haircut	=	when a person cuts your hair
get money (or an object)	=	receive money
get some shoes (or object)	=	buy some shoes
get the mail	=	open a mailbox and take the mail
get ready for a party (or event)	=	prepare for a party
get home/get to a place	=	come home / arrive at a place
get up	=	rise (usually in the morning)
get dressed	=	put on clothes

Read *Make logical complete sentences with the words in the box.*

Betty Paul David I	got will get get gets	the mail a haircut a check home ready tor work food hungry up dressed	soon. every day. in the afternoon. yesterday. in the morning. at 10 p.m. on Saturday. every month.

Write *Match the questions with their answers.*

1. When will you get a haircut?
2. Can I get you some juice?
3. What will you get at the store?
4. When will you get home?
5. What kind of mail do you get?
6. Are you getting thirsty?

a. I'll buy some shoes.
b. I don't receive many letters; I receive bills.
c. The barber will cut my hair at 2 o'clock.
d. No, I'm not, but I'm getting a little hungry.
e. I'll arrive at about 4 p.m.
f. No, thanks. I'm not thirsty.

Practice

Work with a partner. Ask and answer questions about the pictures below. Use ***get*** *in the present continuous tense. See the example below.*

Student 1: What is Rita doing?
Student 2: She's ....

Practice

Work with a partner. Ask questions with ***become*** *and the answer with* ***get****. Then, answer in your own words. See the example below.*

Student 1: When do you usually become..........?
Student 2: I usually get ....

1. tired
2. thirsty
3. hungry
4. nervous
5. sleepy
6. sick
7. angry
8. hot
9. cold
10. ....

Practice

Work with a partner. Ask questions with ***bring*** *and the answer with* ***get****. See the example below.*

Student 1: Can you bring me ....?
Student 2: Sure, I'll get you a .... right away.

1. a cold drink
2. some coffee
3. a sandwich
4. a chair
5. some food
6. a magazine
7. some water
8. a pillow
9. e-mails
10. ....

Practice *Work with a partner. Ask questions with* ***get*** *and the answer with* ***buy****. Use the past tense. See the example below.*

Student 1: What did you get?
Student 2: I bought ....

What did you get?
I bought new shoes.

1. new shoes
2. some socks
3. some clothes
4. some wine for dinner
5. a cake for dessert
6. tennis balls
7. a new tennis racket
8. some flowers

Practice *Work with a partner. Ask questions with* ***receive*** *and the answer with* ***get****. See the example below.*

Student 1: What did you receive in the mail?
Student 2: I got ....

What did you receive in the mail?
I got some bills.

1. some bills
2. a check
3. a few letters
4. a package
5. a present
6. a large envelope
7. a magazine
8. nothing

Write Unscramble the questions, and then answer the questions with ***get.***

QUESTIONNAIRE

1. Question: *What do you get your guests when they visit you?*
you / get / when /they visit you / your guests / do / What / ?
Answer: ____________________

2. Question: ____________________
get / Do / enough money / your bills / you / to pay / ?
Answer: ____________________

3. Question: ____________________
sick / you / How often /do / get / ?
Answer: ____________________

4. Question: ____________________
to work / What time / you / get / or school / do / ?
Answer: ____________________

5. Question: ____________________
at the supermarket / What / get / you / do / every week / usually / ?
Answer: ____________________

Write *Replace the words under the lines with expressions using **get**. Make sure that the verbs are in the past tense.*

David and Alice Morris are at a dinner party. They're speaking to a guest.

Guest: How was your day today, David?

David: Don't ask. It was very busy. I (1) got up (***rose****) late this morning. I had breakfast and (2) ________ (***prepare***) for my tennis game with Paul Wilson. I (3) ________ (***went***) to his house at 10 a.m. We left his place about ten minutes later. When we (4) ________ (***came***) to the tennis courts, they were all full, so we (5) ________ (***bought***) some drinks and waited for an empty court. We played for two hours, then Paul wanted to stop because he (6) ________ (***became tired***). In the afternoon I went to the bank for some money, but I (7) ________ (***didn't receive***) any because the ATM machine was broken. Then, I went to the shoe store and (8) ________ (***bought***) some new shoes with my credit card. Next, I walked to the barber and (9) ________ (***received a hair cut***). Then, I drove to the post office and (10) ________ (***picked up the mail***). When I (11) ________ (***came home***), I (12) ________ (***prepared***) for this dinner party. We left the house and drove here. We (13) ________ (***came***) here a few minutes ago. You (14) ________ (***brought****) us a drink, and here we are.

Guest: Relax and have a good time. The night is young.

* ***Rose*** is the past tense of ***rise***, and ***brought*** is the past tense of ***bring***.

Write *Write a story about last weekend. Describe what you did. Use some of the expressions in the box. Make sure you use the past tense.*

do the housework	do the dishes	do the shopping	make noise
do the dusting	do the gardening	make breakfast	get up
do the cooking	do the laundry	do the cleaning	get ready for
do the vacuuming	do the bathrooms	make dinner	get home
do the work	do the ironing	make a mistake	get (buy)
do a good job	make the beds	make a mess	get (receive)

Last Weekend

Challenge *Read your story to the other students in the class.*

Word Building The Suffix *-ing* Used as a Noun (Gerund)

- We use the suffix ***-ing*** in the present continuous tense.

  Example: I'm reading this sentence now.

- We can also use words with the suffix ***-ing*** as nouns (gerunds)
- Gerunds can be used after some specific verbs and expressions such as: *love, like, enjoy, be crazy about, can't stand,* and *hate.*

Examples:

1. Buying food is necessary.

2. Swimming is fun.

3. Paul does the vacuuming.

4. They do the shopping together.

5. We like eating out at a restaurant.

6. She hates working.

Spelling Rules for Adding *-ing* to a Verb

- When a verb ends in a consonant-vowel-consonant pattern and the final vowel is stressed, the last consonant is doubled before adding ***-ing***. A final ***w***, ***x***, or ***y*** is never doubled.

Examples:

Consonant Doubled			***Not Doubled***		
swim	→	swimming	show	→	showing
sit	→	sitting	fix	→	fixing
run	→	running	say	→	saying

Write *Fill in the spaces below with your own words. Use gerunds. See the example.*

1. I like dancing. ______________

2. I don't like ______ ______________

3. I hate __________ ______________

4. I love __________ ______________

5. ______________ ________ is fun.

6. ______________ ______ is difficult.

7. ______________ is expensive.

8. ______________ is easy.

9. ______________ is important.

CHAPTER 11

Everything Went Wrong!

SKILLS • Describing a Series of Events

GRAMMAR • Intransitive Verbs with Prepositions of Direction

• Two-word Verbs

VOCABULARY • Common Separable and Non-Separable Two-Word Verbs

PRONUNCIATION • The **/ər/** Sound

Read & Listen

Carmen Martinez is at a restaurant with her friend, George. She's describing her day.

George: How was your day, Carmen?

Carmen: Everything went wrong today! I woke up at eight-thirty and got up quickly because I was late for work. I took a shower, put on my work clothes, and went to the kitchen for a fast breakfast. I wasn't very careful, so I dropped a cup of coffee on the floor and made a big mess. I cleaned it up and threw away the broken pieces. Then, I went out of the house, and ran to the bus stop. I opened my handbag, looked for some money for a bus ticket, and took out some change, but it wasn't enough. I went back home, got some more money, and ran back to the bus stop. I got on the bus, but it was the wrong bus, so I got off and walked to work. I got to work two hours late. When I arrived, I took off my coat, punched in, set up my equipment, turned on the machine, picked up my tools, and began to work. A few minutes later, I looked around and saw nobody. Finally, I turned off my machine, put down my tools, sat down, and remembered it was Saturday--my day off!

Understand *Circle **True, False,** or **We don't know.***

1. Carmen works on Saturday.	True	False	We don't know.
2. The bus ticket costs two dollars and fifty cents.	True	False	We don't know.
3. She drove to work.	True	False	We don't know.
4. She got to work on time.	True	False	We don't know.
5. ***"A day off"*** means ***"a day you don't have to work."***	True	False	We don't know.

Grammar Intransitive Verbs with Prepositions of Direction

- Here are some common prepositions:

up 

down 

around 

out  or 

in  or 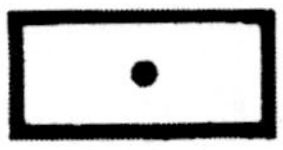

back 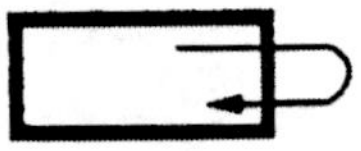

- We often use particles (words that took like prepositions) with intransitive verbs such as ***go, come, run, drive, look*** and ***sit.***

Examples:

Carmen	woke	up	at 8:30.
She	got	up	quickly.
She	went	out	of the house.
She	went	back	home.
She	ran	back	to the bus stop.
She	looked	around.	
She	sat	down.	

Read *Make logical complete sentences with the words in the boxes.*

I Carmen	went ran woke got looked sat came	up around back down out	to the bus stop. home. the room of the house. early. quickly. at 8:30.

Read *Make logical questions with the words in the boxes. Then, answer them in your own words.*

When Where What	do did will	you	get wake sit look come run	back? up? down? out? around?

Read

1. wake up

2. get up

3. go out

4. go back home

5. run back to the bus stop

6. punch in

7. look around

8. sit down

Practice

Work with a partner. Talk about the pictures above. Use the past tense. See the example below.

Student 1: What did Carmen do first ....?
Student 2: She ....
Student 1: Then, what did she do ....?
Student 2: She ....

Practice

Work with a partner. Talk about the pictures above. Use the past tense and the prepositions **before** *and* **after***. See the example below.*

Student 1: Did Carmen .... before or after she ....?
Student 2: She .... before / after she ....

Grammar Non-separable Two-Word Verbs

• In non-separable two-word verbs, the verb and the particle stay together, and the object follows both parts.

Examples:	*Verb*	*Particle*	*Object*
	Carmen	***got on***	the bus.
	She	***got off***	the bus.
	She	***looked for***	some money.
	She didn't	***get in***	a car.
	She didn't	***get out of***	a car.

Read *Make logical complete sentences with the words in the boxes.*

I Carmen	got didn't get looked didn't look	for on off in out of	money a bus. a train. a car. her friends. an airplane. a job.

Read

1. look for some money

2. get on the bus

3. get off the bus

4. get on the bus

5. get off the bus

6. look for a letter

Practice *Work with a partner. Talk about the pictures above. Use the past tense. See the example below.*

Student 1: What did Carmen do at .(time)?
Student 2: She ....

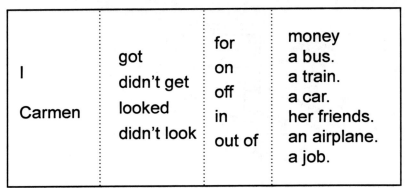

When did Carmen do at 9 a.m.?
She looked for some money.

Grammar Separable Two-Word Verbs

- In separable two-word verbs, the two parts (verb and particle) can be separated by an object, but when pronouns are used, they must go between the two parts.

Examples:

			Object	
She	turned	off	***the machine***.	
She	turned		***the machine***	off.
She	turned		***it***	off.

- It is incorrect to say. ***"She turned off it."***
- Here are some common particles and their general meanings:

Particles		*Meanings*
on	=	in operation, working, attached
off	=	not in operation, not working, unattached
up	=	completed, entirely, thoroughly
away	=	moving from you to a distance

Examples:

	Verbs	*Particles*	
Carmen	***put***	***on***	her work clothes.
She	***cleaned***	***up***	a mess.
She	***threw***	***away***	the broken pieces.
She	***took***	***out***	some change.
She	***took***	***off***	her coat.
She	***set***	***up***	her equipment.
She	***turned***	***on***	the machine.
She	***picked***	***up***	the tools.
She	***turned***	***off***	the machine.
She	***put***	***down***	the tools.

Read *Make logical sentences with the words in the box.*

Did Carmen	put turn take pick clean throw set	away down up on off out	the tools? the machine? her coat? money? a mess? the pieces? the equipment?

Yes, she	put turned took picked cleaned threw set	it them	away. down. up. on. off. out.

Practice *Work with a partner. Follow the commands using the phrases below. Use nouns in the answers. Do not separate the two-word verbs. See the example below.*

Student 1: Please ....?
Student 2: Do what?
Student 1: Please ....?

1. turn on the machine
2. turn off the machine
3. pick up the tools
4. put down the tools
5. put on the safety glasses
6. take off the glasses
7. clean up the mess
8. throw away the cups
9. set up the equipment
10. give back the money

Practice *Work with a partner. Repeat the same exercise. This time separate the two-word verbs. See the example below.*

Student 1: Please ....?
Student 2: Do what?
Student 1: Please .... the ....?

1. turn on the machine
2. turn off the machine
3. pick up the tools
4. put down the tools
5. put on the safety glasses
6. take off the glasses
7. clean up the mess
8. throw away the cups
9. set up the equipment
10. give back the money

Practice *Work with a partner. This time replace the noun with the pronouns **it** or **them**. Notice that the two parts of the two-word verbs are separated. See the example below.*

Student 1: Please ....?
Student 2: What do you want me to do?
Student 1: I want you to .... it / them.

1. throw the broken pieces away
2. turn the TV on
3. turn the radio off
4. pick your clothes up
5. put that bottle down
6. put your sweater on
7. take that watch off
8. clean your room up
9. set the game up
10. give the money back

Practice

Work with a partner. Use the two-word verbs below and you supply your own nouns. Use pronouns. See the example below.

Student 1: Can I .... the ....?
Student 2: Sure, you can .... it /them.

Can I put on the watch?
Sure, you can put it on.

1. put on ...
2. put down ...
3. pick up ...
4. tum on ...
5. throw away ...
6. take off ...
7. take out ...
8. clean up ...
9. set up ...
10. give back ...

Write

Fill in the spaces below with the words in the box. Then, match the questions to the answers. See the example below.

up	***away***	***down***	***on***	***for***	***back***

1. When did you wake __up__?
2. What did you put ________?
3. What did you clean ________?
4. What did you throw ________?
5. What did you look ________?
6. What did you turn ________?
7. What did you get________?
8. What did you set ________?
9. What did you pick ________?

a. A mess.
b. Some money.
c. At 8:30.
d. A machine.
e. The wrong bus.
f. The tools.
g. My work clothes.
h. The broken pieces.
i. My equipment.

Practice

Work with a partner. Use the present tense. Answer in your own words. See the example below.

Student 1: When do you usually ....?
Student 2: I usually ....

When do yo usually wake up?
I usually wake up at 7 a.m.

1. wake up
2. get up
3. put on your clothes
4. get on the bus
5. get off the bus
6. take off your shoes
7. turn on the T.V.
8. turn off the T.V.
9. throw away the garbage
10. look for money
11. go back home
12. set up your equipment

Write *Fill in the spaces below with the words in the box. Then, act out the commands in front of the class.*

in	***out***	***off***	***back***	***on***	***up***	***down***	***for***	***around***	***away***

1. Take your watch __off__, and put it __down__ on the table. Now, pick it __up__, give it to a student, and then take it __back__. Stand _____, go to the trash can, but don't throw your watch ______. Put it _____ and go ______ to your seat.

2. Stand ______, go to the door, open it, look ______ the hall, but don't go ______ . Close the door. Go to the light switch and turn it ______. Now, turn the light ______ again. Go ______ to your seat and sit ______.

3. Take ______ your wallet or purse. Open it and look ______ some money. Take a coin and stand ______. Walk to the teacher's desk and give the coin to the teacher. Take it ______ and put it ______ your pocket. Turn ______ and go ______ to your seat.

4. Stand ______. Walk ______ the room and look ______ a pair of glasses. Pick ______ the glasses and put them ______ . Take them ______ and give them ______. Walk ______ to your seat and sit ______.

Challenge *Write a series of commands and practice them in class. Use the examples above as models.*

____

____

____

____

____

____

____

____

____

____

Write *Fill in the spaces with the correct form of the past tense.*

Carmen's friend, George, is telling her about his day.

Carmen: And how was your day?

George: I (1) woke up (**wake up**) late today, too. My alarm clock (2) ____________ (**doesn't ring**).

I (3) ____________ (**get up**), (4) ____________ (**take**) a shower, and (5) ____________ (**put on**) my work clothes quickly. I (6) ____________ (**go**) to the kitchen for some coffee, but there (7) ____________ (**isn't**) any. I (8) ____________ (**get in**) my car, (9) ____________ (**turn on**) the radio to listen to the morning news, but it (10) ____________ (**doesn't work**). Suddenly, my car (11) ____________ (**stops**) because it (12) ____________ (**doesn't have**) any gas. I (13) ____________ (**get out**) of the car and I (14) ____________ (**begin**) to push it. A few people (15) ____________ (**help**) me push it to a gas station. Then I (16) ____________ (**realize**) that I (17) ____________ (**don't have**) my wallet, The gas station attendant (18) ____________ (**is**) very nice, and he (19) ____________ (**gives**) me a little gas to get to work. Finally, when I (20) ____________ (**arrive**) at work, the parking lot (21) ____________ (**is**) full, so I (22) ____________ (**have to**) park on the street. And yes, you (23) ____________ (**guess**) it. I (24) ____________ (**get**) a parking ticket! It (25) ____________ (**is**) a terrible day!

Practice *Fold this page along the dotted lines. Practice with a partner.*

Student 1

Ask your partner the questions below about the pictures to the right.

1. What items do you see?
2. What items can you turn on?
3. What items can you put on?
4. Is it possible to pick up all the items?
5. What items can you get on?
6. What items can you put down,
   turn off, turn on, clean up, throw away,
   and take out?

Listen to the questions from your partner and find the answers in the picture below.

FOLD HERE

Student 2

Listen to the questions. Find the answers in the pictures below.

Ask your partner these questions about the picture to your left.

1. Can you go up the mountain?
2. Is it possible to go around the lake?
3. What can you go around?
4. Is it possible to go across the street?
5. Is the train going in the tunnel?
6. Is it safe to walk across the train tracks?
7. What can you go up?
8. What can you go in?
9. What can you walk out of?
10. What do you always look for?

FOLD HERE

Pronunciation *The /ər/ Sound*

- We pronounce many vowels before ***r*** like the ***/ər/*** sound in the word ***her***.
- ***/ər/*** represents the sound of any of the vowels followed by ***r*** when stressed.
- The ***/ər/*** sound is difficult because there is no phonetic way to remember the many ways to make this sound. The /ər/ sound in English is tricky because there are several different ways to spell this sound and in some languages, this sound doesn't exist. The /ər / sound can be made in the following ways. See the list below:

Examples:

1. shirt

2. thirsty

3. work

4. collar

5. Saturday

6. nurse

7. mother

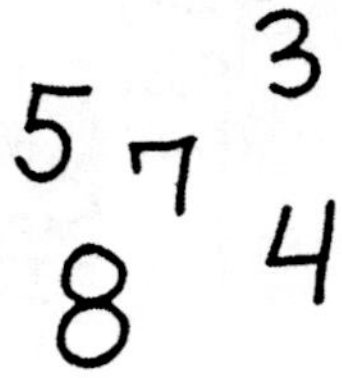

8. numbers

Listen *Listen to the three words in each set below. Circle the word that has the **/ər/** sound.*

1. skirt	read	haircut	6. Thursday	drive	more
2. hire	first	run	7. fruit	November	fire
3. car	truck	teacher	8. were	carry	write
4. wrong	doctor	dark	9. dark	street	dollar
5. third	rain	your	10. learn	program	rest

Write *Fill in the spaces with the letters **or**, **ir**, **er**, or **ur**.*

1. I saw a pict_ur_e of h_er_ moth___ and fath___ at ch___ch on Novemb___ th___d.
2. The store cl___k showed the two g___ls some new summ___ s___ts.
3. The n___se w___ked for the doct ___ on Th___sdays and Sat___days for a few doll___s.
4. The th___sty farm___ changed his d___ty sh___t before dinn___.

CHAPTER 12

The Super Store

SKILLS	• Reading a Shopping Directory
	• Understanding U.S. Measurements
	• Reading a Simple Recipe
	• Reading an Ad
	• Comparing Prices and Determining Savings
GRAMMAR	• The Prepositions ***"of"***
VOCABULARY	• Common Shopping Items
	• Containers and Measurements
WORD BUILDING	• The Suffix ***-ish***

Read & Listen

The Wilson family is doing the weekly shopping. Dad is pushing the shopping cart.

Paul: Do you have the shopping list?
Betty: Yes, here it is. I brought some coupons, too.
Paul: Good. Do we need any sugar?
Betty: Yes, we do. Get a bag.
Paul: Where's the sugar?
Betty: I don't know. Let's ask the clerk over there.

Paul: Excuse me, sir, can you tell me where I can find the sugar?
Clerk: It's in Grocery Section.
Paul: Thanks.
Clerk: You're welcome.
Betty: You get the sugar, and I'll meet you at the check out stands.

The Wilson's are waiting in line. A customer and the cashier are talking.

Customer: Here are some coupons.
Cashier: That's $164.72 minus $5.25 for the coupons.
Customer: How much is the total?
Cashier: It's $159.47.
Customer: Here's $160.00.
Cashier: And here's your receipt and your change. Have a good day.
Customer: You have a better day. You're working!
Cashier: *(Smiling)* Thanks.

Understand *Circle **True, False,** or **We don't know.***

1. It's the weekend.	True	False	We don't know.
2. Betty uses a shopping list.	True	False	We don't know.
3. The Wilsons don't have any sugar at home.	True	False	We don't know.
4. Betty paid $64.72.	True	False	We don't know.
5. The customer saved $5.25.	True	False	We don't know.
6. The customer got 54 cents in change.	True	False	We don't know.

STORE DIRECTORY

Item	Section	Item	Section	Item	Section
Apparel	1	Cosmetics	13	Jewelry	25
Auto Care	2	Crafts	14	Juices and Sodas	26
Baby	3	Dairy Products	15	Lawn & Garden	27
Bakery / Deli	4	Delicatessen	16	Liquor	28
Baking (Flour, Oil)	4	Detergents and Soap	17	Paper & Cleaning	29
Books & Magazines	5	Fresh Meat	18	Pet Food	30
Candy	6	Fresh Produce	19	Pharmacy	31
Canned Fish and Meal	7	Frozen Foods	20	Plants and Flowers	33
Canned Fruit& Vegetables	8	Grocery	21	Shoes	34
Cards & Party Supplies	9	Health & Beauty	22	Sporting Goods	34
Cereals	10	Home & Office	23	Sugar	4
Coffee and Tea	11	Houseware Items	24	Toys	35
Cookies and Crackers	12	Ice Cream	20	Waxes and Polish	36

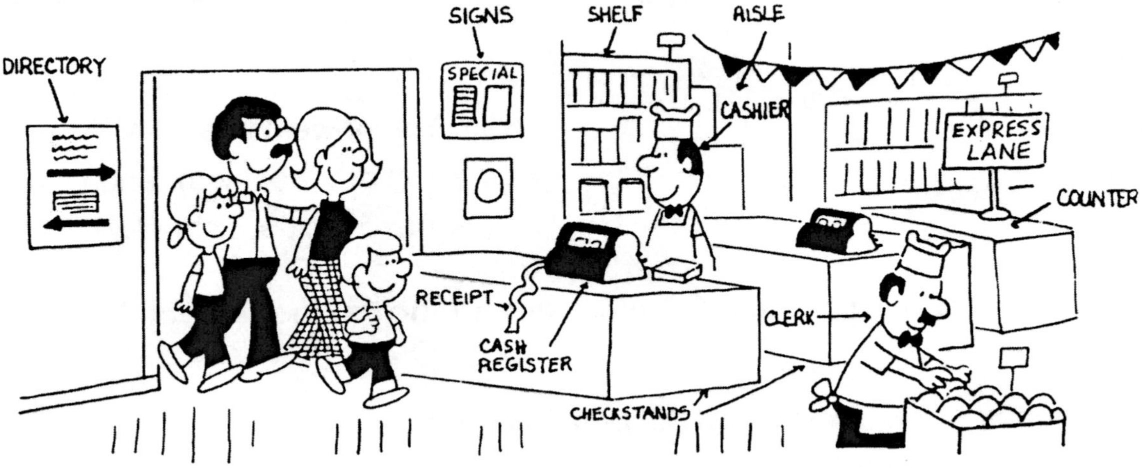

Practice *Work with a partner. Talk about the directory above. See the example below.*

Student 1: Where is / are ....?
Student 2: It is / They are ....

Practice *Work with a partner. Use the directory above. See the example below.*

Student 1: What's in Section ....?
Student 2: .... is / are in Section ....

Write *Match the questions with the pictures. Write the letters of the pictures in the blanks after the questions. See the example below.*

1. Where are the canned vegetables? d
2. Where's the detergent? ___
3. Where's the produce? ___
4. Where are the frozen vegetables? ___
5. Where's the bakery? ___
6. Where are the dairy products? ___
7. Where are the houseware items? ___
8. Where are the paper goods? ___
9. Where can I find a light bulb? ___
10. I'm looking for an extension cord. ___

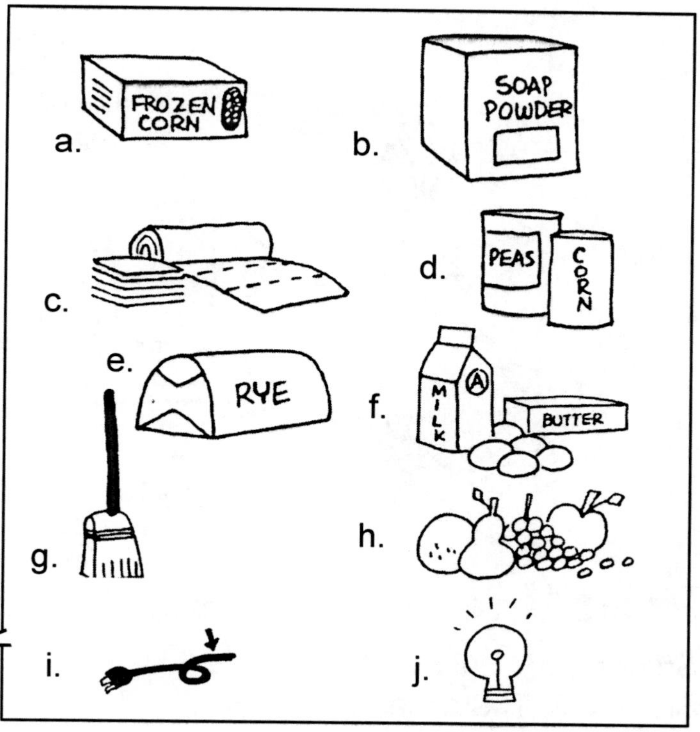

Where is / are ....?

1. The paper goods are in Section 29. b
2. The pet food is in Section 30. ___
3. Fresh produce is in Section 19. ___
4. Meat is in Section 18. ___
5. Canned fish is in Section 7. ___
6. Frozen food is in Section 20. ___
7. Cookies are in Section 12. ___
8. Liquor is in Section 28. ___
9. Hand tools are in Section 24. ___
10. Toys are in Section 35. ___
11. Shoes are in Section 34. ___
12. Jewelry is in Section 25. ___

Read

Paul is putting the items on the counter.

Practice *Work with a partner. Use the picture above. See the example below.*

Student 1: What's on the counter?
Student 2: There's a .... of ....

What's on the counter?
There's a jar of coffee.

Practice *Work with a partner. Talk about the containers in the picture above. See the example below.*

Student 1: What's in the ....?
Student 2: Some .

What's in the carton?
Some milk.

Practice *Work with a partner. Talk about the pictures above. See the example below.*

Student 1: What kind of container does / containers do .... come in?
Student 2: It comes in a .... / They come in a ....

What kind of container does milk come in?
It comes in a carton.

Grammar The Preposition *of*

- We use the preposition ***of*** to show that one thing contains something else. It shows belonging to, relating to, or connected with.

Examples:

a six-pack	***of***	soda
a carton	***of***	milk
a sack	***of***	flour
a bottle	***of***	cooking oil

- ***Of*** is often unstressed and pronounced **/əv/**.

Read *Make logical sentences with the words in the box.*

Please get me a	tube	of	napkins.
	carton		potatoes.
	sack		ice cream.
	bottle		toothpaste.
	jar		wine.
	bag		beer.
	box		jam.
	six-pack		potato chips.
	can		cereal.
	package		eggs.

Practice *Work with a partner. Talk about the pictures below. See the example.*

Student 1: How many .... of .... are there?
Student 2: There is ..... / There are .....

How many boxes of detergent are there?
There are two boxes of detergent.

1.

2.

3.

4.

5.

6.

7.

8.

Challenge *What kind of products come in the following containters. Make a list.*

1. cans ___soda___ ___juice___ __________ __________
2. boxes __________ __________ __________ __________
3. jars __________ __________ __________ __________
4. cartons __________ __________ __________ __________
5. bottles __________ __________ __________ __________

Read

Paul and the kids are placing some more items on the counter.

Practice

Work with a partner. Use the picture above. See the example below.

Student 1: What's on the counter?
Student 2: There is / are .... of ....

Practice

Work with a partner. Use the picture above. See the example below.

Student 1: How much / many .... is / are there?
Student 2: There is / are .... of ....

Challenge

What comes in the following measurements. Make a list.

1. slices ___soda___ ___juice___ ________ ________
2. rolls ________ ________ ________ ________
3. pieces ________ ________ ________ ________
4. bunches ________ ________ ________ ________

Read *Liquid Measurement*

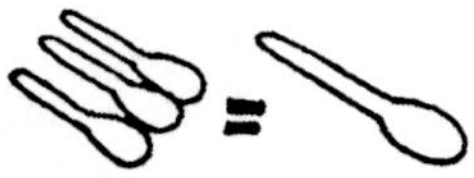

3 teaspoons (tps.) =
1 tablespoon (Tb.)

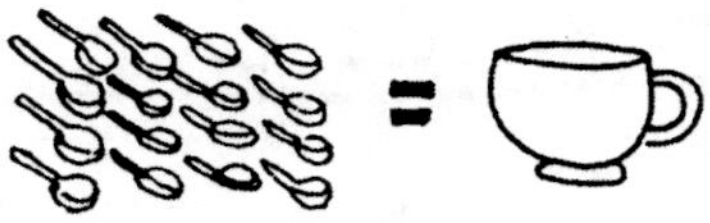

16 tablespoons = 1 cup

2 cups = 1 pint (pt.)

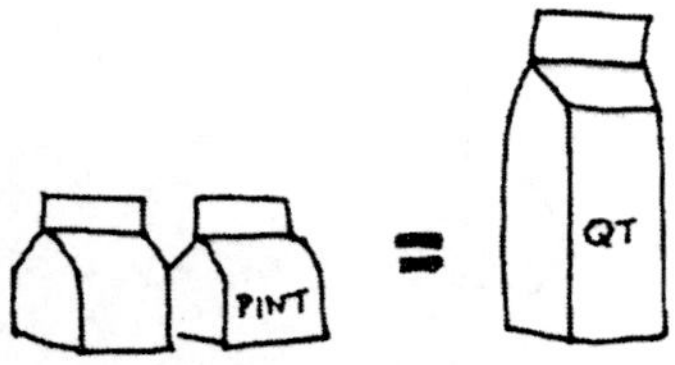

2 pints = 1 quart

4 quarts (qt.) - 1 gallon (gal.)

Read *Weight*

16 ounces (oz.) =
1 pound (lb.)

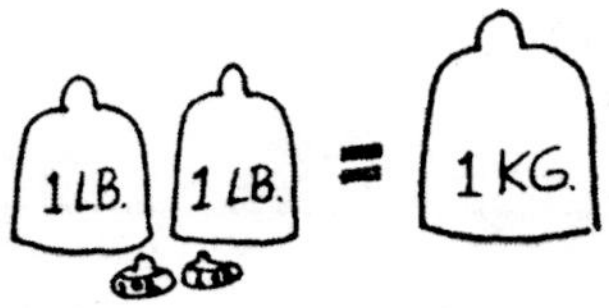

2.2 pounds (lbs.) =
1 kilogram

SPOONS AND CUPS	LIQUID OUNCES	LIQUID GRAMS
1 tsp, (teaspoon)	1/6	5
1 Tb. (tablespoon)	1/2	15
1 cup (16 Tb.)	5	227
2 cups (1 pint)	16 (1 pound)	454
4 cups (1 quart)	32	907
6 2/3 Tb	3 1/2	100
1 cup + 1 Tb	8 1/2	250
4 1/3 cups	2.2 pounds	1 kilo

Practice *Work with a partner. Use the information above. See the example below.*

Student 1: How many .... are there in a ....?
Student 2: There are .... in a ....

How many ounces are there in a pound?
There are 16 ounces in a pound.

Challenge *In what liquid measurement or weight can you find the items below?*

1. sugar ____________________
2. milk ____________________
3. cream ____________________
4. potatoes ____________________
5. juice ____________________
6. flour ____________________
7. butter ____________________
8. apples ____________________
9. coffee ____________________
10. cereal ____________________

Challenge *How many pounds do you weigh? I weigh __________ pounds.*

RECIPE FOR FROZEN FRUIT YOGURT DESSERT

Frozen fruit yogurt makes a delicious dessert in the summer months. Just follow these easy directions.

- 2 cups of frozen unsweetened strawberries
- 1 cup of yogurt
- 2 tablespoons of sugar
- 2 teaspoons of vanilla
- 1 tablespoon of orange juice

Place frozen strawberries in blender and mix.
Do not mix the strawberries too much.
Add yogurt, sugar, vanilla, and orange juice.
Mix a very short time.
Serve immediately.
Makes 4 servings.

Practice *Work with a partner. Talk about the recipe above. See the example below.*

Student 1: How many .... of ...... do you use?
Student 2: .... of ....

Practice *Work with a partner. Talk about the recipe above. See the example below.*

Student 1: How much .... do you use?
Student 2: We use ....

How much sugar do you use?
We use two tablespoons of sugar.

Practice *Work with a partner. Talk about the recipe above. See the example below.*

Student 1: How do you make this recipe?
Student 2: First, ... Then, ...

Group Discussion *Describe your favorite recipe in English.*

Read & Listen

Betty wants to buy some salami in the delicatessen section of the store.

Betty: Please give me some salami. How do you sell it?
Clerk: We sell it by the pound.
Betty: OK. Give me a quarter pound of salami.
Clerk: Will that be all?
Betty: No, give me a half-pound of potato salad, too.

Understand *Circle **True, False,** or **We don't know.***

1. Betty wants to buy a few slices of salami.	True	False	We don't know.
2. Betty wants to buy 4 oz. of salami.	True	False	We don't know.
3. Betty wants to buy 100 grams of potato salad.	True	False	We don't know.
4. The salami and the potato salad weigh 12 ounces.	True	False	We don't know.

Practice *Work with a partner. Talk about the foods below. Use the preposition **by** with the words in the box. See the example below.*

Student 1: How do you sell ....?
Student 2: By the ....

How do you sell salami?
By the pound.

bunch	head	pound	slice	ounce
quart	loaf	pint	piece	roll

1. salami

2. grapes

3. carrots

4. turkey

5. cheese

BREAD
6. bread

CREAM
7. cream

8. cake

Practice *Work with a partner. Use the words and pictures from the exercises above. Use short answers. **Yes, it is.** or **No, it isn't.** See the example below.*

Student 1: Is it possible to buy .... by the ....?
Student 2: Yes, it is. / No, it isn't.

Is it possible to buy chicken by the ounce?
No, it isn't.

Read

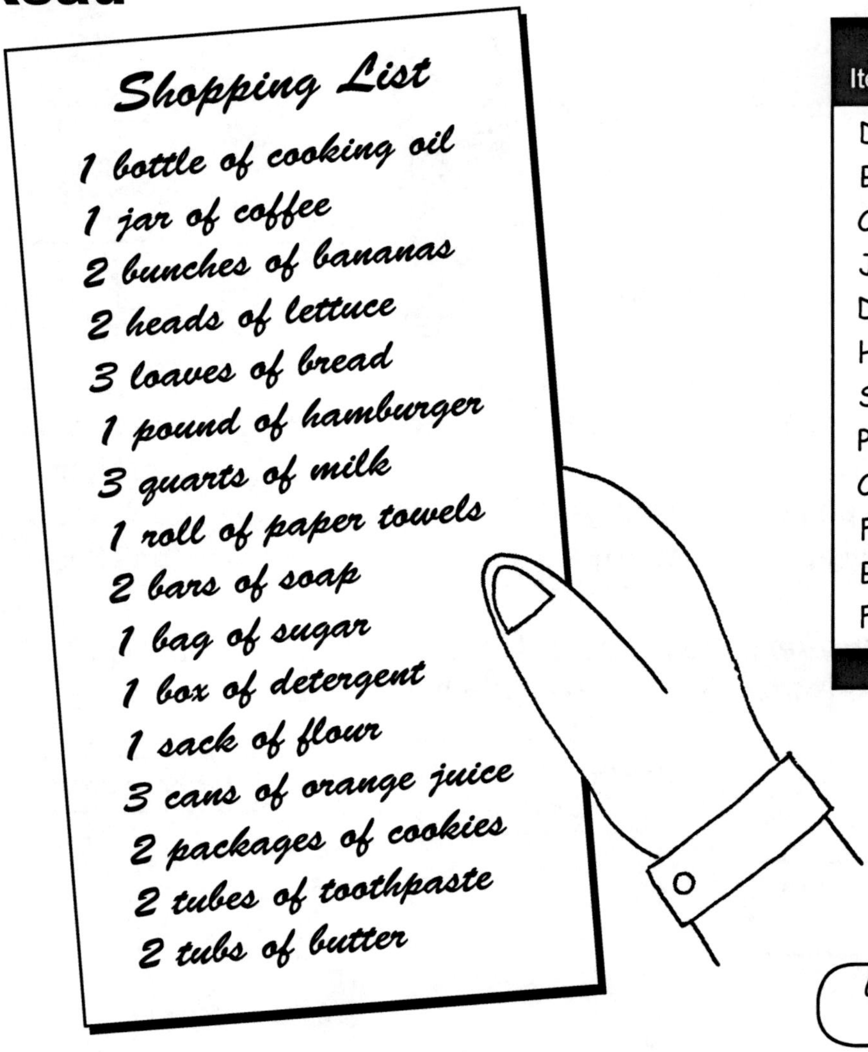

DIRECTORY

Item	Section
Dairy Products	15
Baking (Flour, Oil)	4
Coffee and Tea	11
Juices and Sodas	26
Detergents and Soap	17
Health & Beauty	22
Sugar	4
Paper & Cleaning	29
Cookies and Crackers	12
Fresh Meat	18
Bakery / Deli	4
Fresh Produce	19

Practice

Work with a partner. Talk about the two lists above. See the example.

Where's the soap?
It's in Section 17.
How many bars do you want?
Give me two bars of soap.

Student 1: Where is / are the ....?
Student 2: It's / They're in Section ....
Student 1: How many .... do you want?
Student 2: Give me .... of ....

Write

Make a shopping list for your next visit to your favorite store.

1. ______________________
2. ______________________
3. ______________________
4. ______________________
5. ______________________
6. ______________________
7. ______________________
8. ______________________
9. ______________________
10. ______________________
11. ______________________
12. ______________________
13. ______________________
14. ______________________
15. ______________________

Group Discussion

Compare your lists to the lists of your classmates.

Read

MEGA STORE MEGA ADS

ITEM	SIZE	PRICE
SHAMPOO	8 oz. bottle	$3.99
DETERGENT	49 oz. box	5.25
PAPER NAPKINS	360 in pkg.	2.49
DEODORANT	2 1/2 oz. bottle	5.99
COFFEE	1 lb. can	7.71
FROZEN ORANGE JUICE	12 oz. can	1.89
LARGE EGGS	1 dozen ctn.	3.79
CABBAGE	3 heads	1.00
SLICED CHEESE	5 oz. pkg.	4.99
SAUSAGE	8 oz. pkg.	2.53
APPLES	3 lbs. bag	2.98
GROUND BEEF	1 lb. pkg.	6.79
CHICKEN	1 lb.	5.69

COUPON
CHICKEN SOUP
50 cents off
8 oz. can
Expires Jan. 31

COUPON
REAL BUTTER
SAVE $1.00
Was $4, Now $3
1 lb. pkg.

COUPON
HOT DOG
PURE BEEF
2 LBS. PKG.
BUY 1, GET 1 FREE

Abbreviations:
lb. - pound
oz. - ounce
ctn. - carton
pkg. - package

COUPON
BOTTLED WATER
CASE OF 12
ONLY $2.99
TODAY ONLY

COUPON
ICED TEA
8 oz. bottle
.99 cents
While supplies last

Practice

Work with a partner. Ask and answer questions about the ads and coupons above. See the example below.

Student 1: How much do / does .... cost?
Student 2: .... cost / costs $ ....

Write *Complete the dialog with your own words.*

Betty: (1) Can you tell me where the milk is? ______

Clerk: (2) ______

Betty: I looked there. I saw only small cartons of milk. I want a large size.

Clerk: Did you look near the eggs?

Betty: (3) ______

Clerk: Wait here. I'll get you a large carton of milk. What size do you want?

Betty: (4) ______

Clerk: Here you are. Is this half gallon size OK?

Betty: (5) ______

Clerk: (6) ______

Betty: (7) ______

Challenge *Work with a partner. Write a short dialog. You are at a store, and you want to know the price of a product and where to find it in the market.*

You: ______

Clerk: ______

You: ______

Clerk: ______

You: ______

Clerk: ______

You: ______

Clerk: ______

Clerk: ______

Challenge *Practice your dialog with another student, and then present it in front of the class.*

Dictation

Listen to the teacher or your partner read the dictation at the bottom of the next page. Write the sentences below. Then, check your writing.

Dear Honey,

1. ______________________________
2. ______________________________
3. ______________________________
4. ______________________________
5. ______________________________
6. ______________________________

Love, Betty

Write

Write a note to a person in your home. Tell him or her to go to your favorite store and buy what you need for the next few days.

Dear ______________________________

I can't do the shopping today. Please go ______________________________

____

____

____

____

____

____

____

____

See you when I get home. ______________________________

Practice

Fold this page along the dotted lines. Practice with a partner.

Student 1

Ask your partner the questions below about the pictures to the right.

1. How much do two bottles of wine cost?
2. How many rolls of paper towels can you buy for 98 cents?
3. How much does one package of frozen vegetables cost?
4. How much do four pounds of apples cost?
5. Can you buy 3 bottles of wine for $6.00?
6. How much were frozen vegetables yesterday?
7. Can you buy 4 bottles of wine for $10.00?

Listen to the questions from your partner and find the answers in the picture below.

Abbreviations
per. = each item
reg. = regular price
lb. = pound

FOLD HERE

Student 2

Listen to the questions. Find the answers in the pictures below.

Ask your partner these questions about the picture to your left.

1. Is bread on sale?
2. How many oranges can you buy for $3.00?
3. How much does tomato juice cost without a coupon?
4. How much do five bars of soap cost?
5. How much does a loaf of bread cost?
6. Is soap on sale?

FOLD HERE

Dictation

(From the previous page) Read this dictation to your partner.

1. I'll be home a little late tonight.
2. Please go to the supermarket and get a few things for dinner
3. Get a quart of milk, a loaf of bread, and a jar of coffee.
4. Use the coupon for the coffee.
5. Don't buy any ice cream. Remember your diet!
6. See you about 6:30 this evening.

Word Building The Suffix *-ish*

• We use the suffix ***-ish*** form adjectives from nouns (or from other adjectives) and to express several meanings: 1. nationality, 2. having a certain quality or characteristic, and 3. similarity or belonging to.

Examples:

1. He's English.

2. He's very childish.

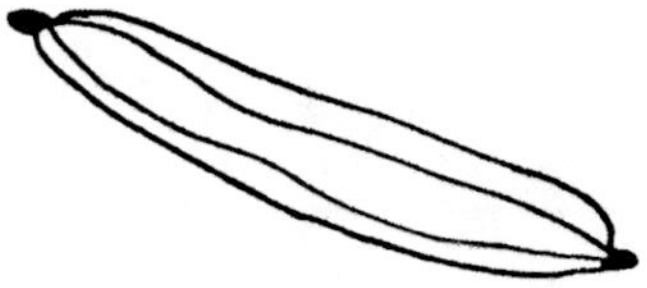

3. Bananas have a yellowish color.

Prounciation *Pronounce the following words and use them in a sentence.*

Nationality	
Danish	Finnish
English	Swedish
Polish	Turkish
Spanish	Irish

Color	
whitish	orangish
blackish	yellowish
grayish	greenish
bluish	purplish
reddish	lemonish

Apperance	
blondish	longish
oldish	smallish
youngish	squarish
roundish	biggish

Behavior	
babyish	selfish
boyish	coolish
girlish	slowish
childish	ticklish
foolish	devilish

Pronunciation *Practice saying the sentences aloud.*

1. That blondish Danish man is childish, selfish and foolish.
2. The new rose is smallish, roundish, and has a yellowish and lemonish color.
3. The oldish Polish woman was smallish, ticklish, and a little devilish.

Write *Describe the colors of the following fruits and vegetables. Use the suffix **-ish**.*

celery

1. *Celery has a greenish color.*

strawberries

2. ____________________

grapes

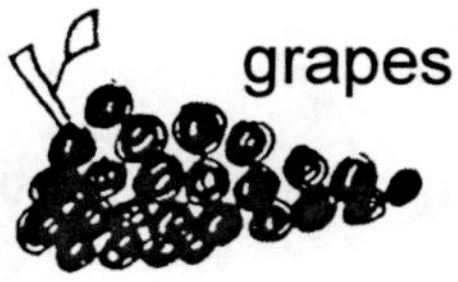

3. ____________________

apples

4. ____________________

tomatos

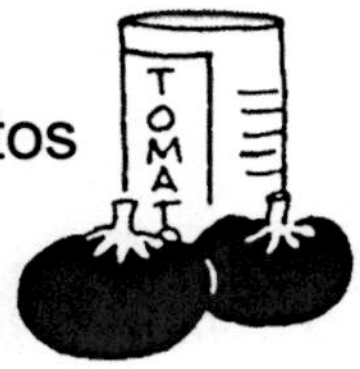

5. ____________________

pears

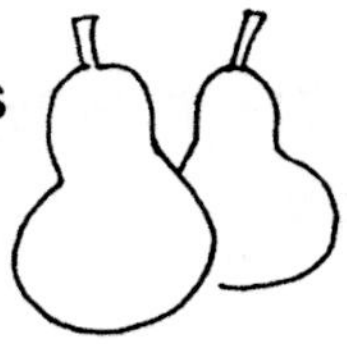

6. ____________________

potatos

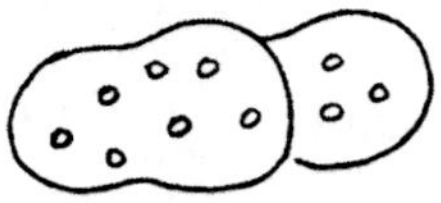

7. ____________________

watermelon

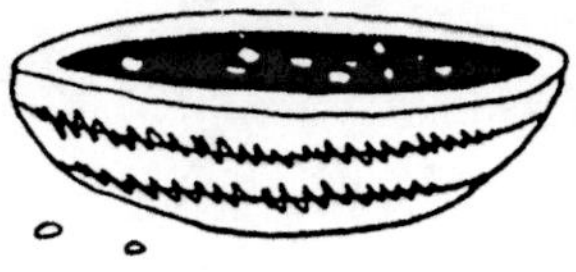

8. ____________________

CHAPTER 13

Where Does It Hurt?

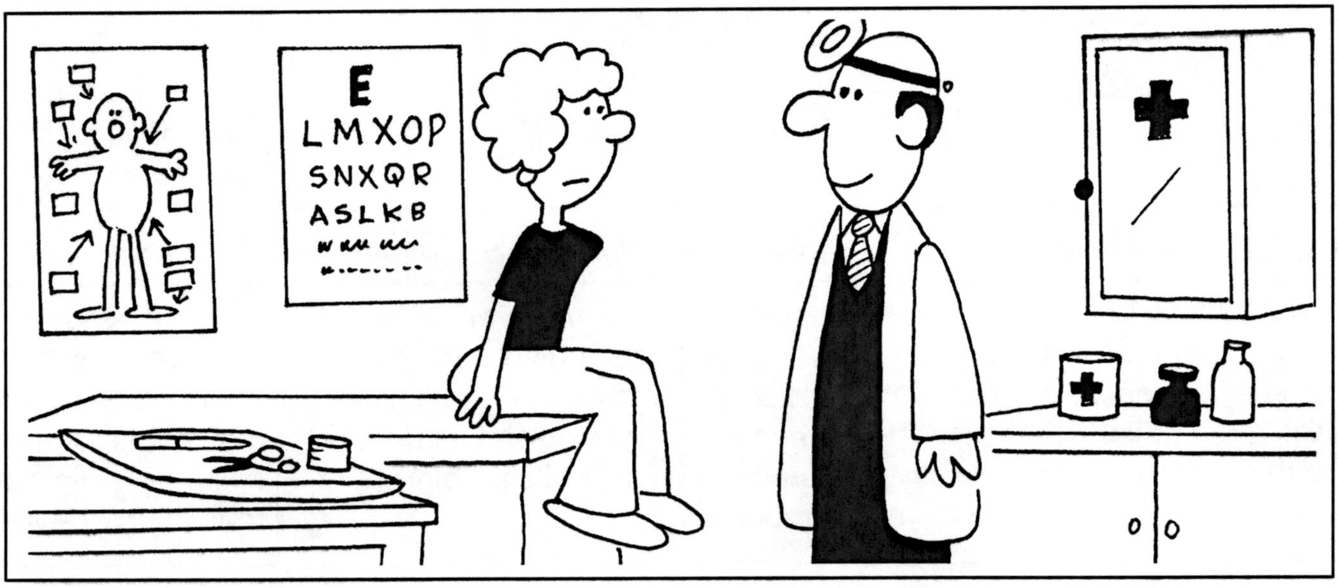

SKILLS
- Making a Medical Appointment
- Describing Medical Problems
- Filling Out Medical Forms

GRAMMAR
- ***would like***
- ***that*** with clause
- More Irregular Verbs
- ***say*** and ***tell***

VOCABULARY
- General Medical Terms
- Parts of the Body
- Symptoms and Illnesses

SPELLING
- The Silent ***gh***

Read & Listen

Alice Morris is calling her doctor to make an appointment.

A few minutes later.

Receptionist: Thank you for waiting. How may I help you?

Alice: Yes, I would like to make an appointment with Dr. Snow.

Receptionist: What's the problem?

Alice: I'd like to have a general physical examination and I'd like him to look at my left hand. It hurts a little when I open and close it.

Receptionist: Dr. Snow is booked up all this week. Can you come in next Tuesday at 10:00 a.m.?

Alice: That's fine.

Receptionist: Would you like me to call you if there is a cancellation?

Alice: Yes, please do.

Understand *Circle **True, False,** or **We don't know.***

1. Alice doesn't feel very well.	True	False	We don't know.
2. ***"Can you hold?"*** means ***"Can you wait?"***	True	False	We don't know.
3. ***"Booked up"*** means ***"The doctor is reading."***	True	False	We don't know.
4. Alice's appointment is next Tuesday.	True	False	We don't know.
5. Dr. Snow is a woman.	True	False	We don't know.
6. The receptionist will call Alice if a patient can not keep an appointment.	True	False	We don't know.

Grammar *would like*

- The expression ***would like*** means ***want***, but it is more polite.
- The contraction of ***would like*** is ***'d like***.

Examples: ***Affirmative***

I	***would like***	to make an appointment.
You	***'d like***	to have a physical examination.
She	***'d like***	the doctor to see her left hand.

Negative

I	***wouldn't like***	to have a late appointment.

Question

Would you like me to call you?

Read *Make logical complete sentences with the words in the box.*

I He She They	would 'd wouldn't	like	to make an appointment, to see the doctor. to cancel my appointment. to have a physical examination. to speak to the doctor. you to call me. the doctor to look at my hand.

Practice *Work with a partner. Use the phrases below. See the example below.*

Student 1: What would you like?
Student 2: I'd like to make an appointment with ....
or
I'd like to see a ....
or
I'd like to speak with ....

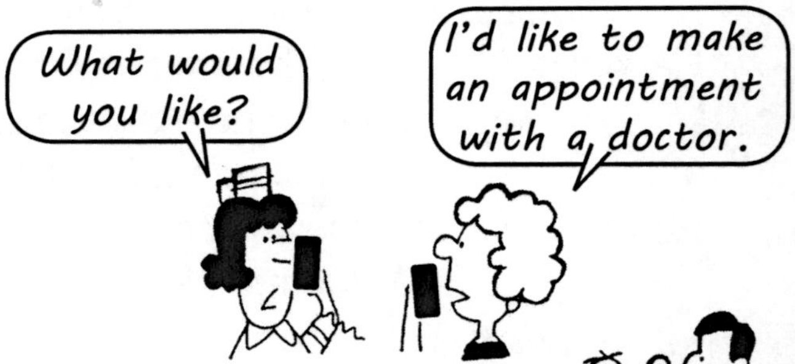
What would you like?
I'd like to make an appointment with a doctor.

1. a doctor

2. a dentist

3. an eye doctor (ophthalmologist)

4. an ear, nose, and throat doctor

MD

5. a pediatrician (for children)

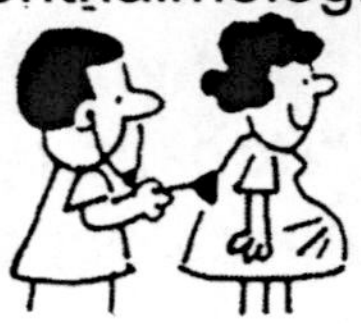

6. an obstetrician (for women)

Read

Alice is at the hospital.

PLEASE PRINT

Name: *Morris* (Last) *Alice* (First) *Louise* (Middle)

Address: *65 Hillside St. L.A. 90030* (Number Street City Zip Code) Telephone *555-1024*

Date of Birth: *April 7, 1966* (Month/Date/Year) Place of Birth: *Columbus, Ohio*

1, Do you have any medical insurance? *(Check one)* Yes √ No ___

2, Name of insurance provider: *Bluecare* Policy #: *6941003*

3. Whats the reason for this visit? *Physical Examination*

4. Are you taking any medicine now? *(Check one)* Yes ___ No √

If so, what kind of medicine? *none*

5. Are you allergic to any medicine? *(Check one)* Yes √ No ___

Ii so, what kind of medicine? *penicillin*

6. Do you have any pain at this time? *(Check one)* Yes √ No ___

If so, where? *my hand*

7.Are you in good health? *(Check one)* Yes √ No ___

8. Do you smoke drink or take drugs. *(Check one)* Yes ___ No √

If so, what kind and how often? ___

Today's Date: *May 4th* Signature: *Alice Morris*

Understand

Circle ***True, False,*** *or* ***We don't know.***

1 Alice has medical insurance.	True	False	We don't know.
2. Alice is 50 years old.	True	False	We don't know.
3, ***"If so"*** means ***"If the answer is yes."***	True	False	We don't know.
4. Alice is allergic to penicillin.	True	False	We don't know.
5. Alice smokes.	True	False	We don't know.

Read *Use your dictionary if necessary.*

The nurse forgot to give Alice a second form.

Excuse me, Ma'am, but I have to give you another form. Please fill it out, too.

HEALTH EXAMINATION RECORD

NAME: *Alice Morris* **DATE:** *5/5/16*

ADDRESS: *65 Hillside St. L.A. 90030* **PHONE:** *555-1024*

AGE: *50* **SEX** *(Circle one)* **Male** **(Female)** **BIRTHDATE:** *April 7, 1966*

MEDICAL HISTORY

Did you ever have one of the following? (Check √)

ILLNESSES	
Frequent fevers	☐
Frequent colds	☐
Frequent headaches	☐
Frequent sore throats	☐
Frequent upset stomach	☐
Allergies *cats & dust*	☐
Serious injuries	☐
Kidney trouble	☐
Tuberculosis	☐
Convulsions	☐
Diabetes	☐
Blood diseases	☐
High blood pressure	☐
Heart trouble	☐
Mental problems	☐
Liver trouble	☐
Nervousness	☐
Arthritis	☐

DESEASES	
Measles	√
Mumps	☐
Chicken Pox	√
Polio	☐
Scarlet Fever	☐
Whooping Cough	☐
Malaria	☐
Other ______	☐

IMMUNIZATIONS/TESTS	
Polio	√
Diphtheria	☐
Whooping Cough	☐
Tetanus	√
Smallpox	☐
Typhoid	☐
Tuberculin	√
Flu	√
Other ______	☐

SURGERIES	DATE
1. *Leg*	*1999*
2. ______	______
3. ______	______

MEDICATION YOU ARE TAKING NOW

1. *none*
2. ______
3. ______
4. ______

MEDICATION YOU ARE SENSITIVE TO

1. *penicillin*
2. ______
3. ______
4. ______

Practice *Work with a partner. Talk about Alice's health record above. Answer in short answers:* ***Yes, she did.*** *or* ***No, she didn't.*** *See the example below.*

Student 1: Did Alice ever have ....?
Student 2: Yes, she did. / No, she didn't.

Read

Anna Perez is also in the waiting room. She's asking Alice tor help.

Excuse me. I have to fill out this form. I don't understand all the medical words. Can you explain them to me?

I'll try.

Write
Match the questions and answers. Write the letters of the answers in the blanks after the questions.

1. What's a fever? __*f*__	a. It's being unable to move your joints.
2. What's an allergy? _____	b. It's being unable to keep food in your stomach.
3. What's an upset stomach? _____	c. It's a bad reaction to animals, medicine, or food.
4. What's diabetes? _____	d. It's the inability of your body to use sugar.
5. What's heart trouble? _____	e. It's pain in your head.
6. What is a headache? _____	f. It's a high body temperature,
7. What's an injury? _____	g. It's having a weak heart.
8. What's a sore throat? _____	h. It's a wound or other damage to the body.
9. What's arthritis? _____	i. It's pain in your throat.

Practice
Work with a partner. Talk about the pictures below. See the example.

Student 1: What the matter with the person in picture?
Student 2: He / She has

What's the matter with that person?

He has a headache.

1. a headache

2. a sore throat

3. a rash

4. a toothache

5. a broken leg

6. a stomach ache

7. the chills

8 a fever

Write *Fill out the form for yourself.*

PLEASE PRINT

Name: ______________________________
Last First Middle

Address: ______________________ Telephone: ______________
Number Street City

Date of Birth: ______________ Place of Birth: ______________
Month/Date/Year

1. Do you have any medical insurance? (check one) Yes ______ No ______
2. Name of medical insurance company: __________ Policy number #__________
3. What's the reason for this visit? ______________________
4. Are you taking any medicine now? (check one) Yes ______ No ______
   If so, what kind of medicine? ______________________
5. Are you allergic to any medicine? (check one) Yes ______ No ______
   If so, what kind of medicine? ______________________
6. Are you having any pain at this time? (check one) Yes ______ No ______
7. Are you in good health? (check one) Yes ______ No ______
8. Do you smoke, drink, or take drugs? (check one) Yes ______ No ______

AGE: ______ SEX: (circle one) Male Female

MEDICAL HISTORY

Did you ever have one of the following? (check ✓)

ILLNESSES	DISEASES	SURGERIES	DATE
Frequent fevers ______	Measles ______	1. ______	______
Frequent colds ______	Mumps ______	2. ______	______
Frequent headaches ______	Chicken Pox ______	3. ______	______
Frequent sore throats ______	Polio ______		
Frequent upset stomach ______	Scarlet Fever ______	MEDICATION YOU	
Allergies ______	Whooping Cough ______	ARE SENSITIVE TO	
Serious injuries ______	Other ______		
Kidney trouble ______			
Tuberculosis ______	IMMUNIZATIONS/TESTS	1. ______	
Convulsions ______		2. ______	
Diabetes ______	Polio ______	3. ______	
Blood diseases ______	Diphtheria ______		
High blood pressure ______	Whooping Cough ______	MEDICATION YOU	
Heart trouble ______	Tetanus ______	ARE TAKING NOW	
Mental problems ______	Smallpox ______		
Liver trouble ______	Typhoid ______	1. ______	
Nervousness ______	Tuberculin ______	2. ______	
Arthritis ______	Other ______	3. ______	

DATE: ______________ SIGNATURE: ______________________

Read & Listen

Alice is speaking to the doctor.

Doctor: What's the matter?
Alice: My left hand hurts. I have a pain in my wrist.
Doctor: When did you first notice the problem?
Alice: A few weeks ago.
Doctor: Let me examine it.

A few minutes later.

Doctor: It's probably arthritis. I can write you a prescription for some cream. Do you have any other problems?
Alice: No, I don't. I made this appointment for a general physical examination.
Doctor: When was your last exam?
Alice: Five years ago.
Doctor: I'll examine you here. Then take these papers to the laboratory for an X-ray, and urine and blood tests. When I get the test results, I'll call you.

Understand *Circle **True, False,** or **We don't know.***

1. Alice's right hand hurts.	True	False	We don't know.
2. Alice's problem began last month.	True	False	We don't know.
3. Alice has arthritis.	True	False	We don't know.
4. Arthritis is a disease.	True	False	We don't know.
5. Only doctors can write prescriptions.	True	False	We don't know.
6. The doctor will have the test results next week.	True	False	We don't know.

Read *Study the parts of the body.*

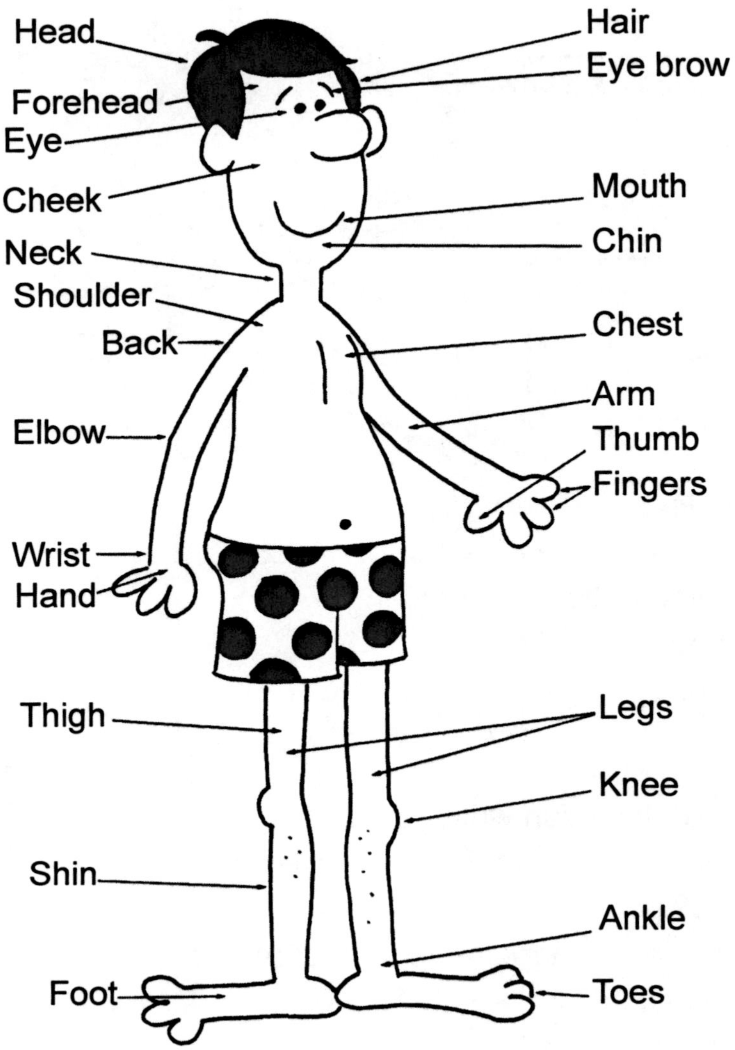

Practice *Work with a partner. Talk about the picture above. See the example below.*

Student 1: Where does it hurt?
Student 2: My .... hurts.

Practice *Work with a partner. Talk about the picture above. See the example below.*

Student 1: What's the matter?
Student 2: I have a pain in my ....

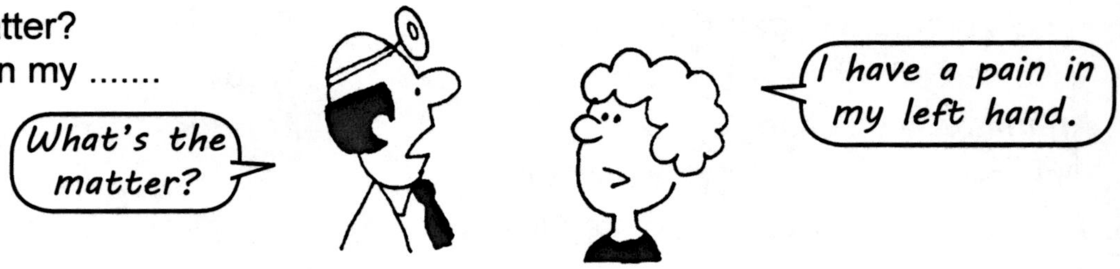

Read & Listen

Alice meets Anna in the elevator.

evator.

Directory
Room
Emergency Room 101
Laboratory 102
X-ray Lab 103
Surgery ....Basement
Intensive Care Unit 201
Maternity 210
Dietary Service 110
Pharmacy 112
Wards .... 3rd-5th Floors

Alice: Oh, hello again.
Anna: Hi. Can you tell me where the lab is?
Alice: : No, I can't. Let's look at the directory over there.
Anna: What do they do in the lab?
Alice: They take tests.

Challenge *Alphabetize the directory above in your notebook.*

Write *Match the questions and answers. Write the letters of the answers in the blanks after the question. See example.*

1 What do they do in the emergency room? ___
2. What happens in the X-ray lab? ___
3. What do they do in the intensive care unit? ___
4. What do they do in surgery? ___
5. What happens in maternity? ___
6. What do they do in dietary services? ___
7. What happens in the wards? ___
8. What do they do in the pharmacy? ___

a. They cook the patients' meals there.
b. Nurses take care of very sick patients.
c. They prepare medicine there.
d. Babies are born there.
e. A medical team gives quick help to serious accident victims or sudden illnesses.
f. They take pictures of the inside of your body.
g. The patients stay there.
h. Surgeons operate on patients there.

Read

It's the next day. Alice is telling Betty about her visit to the doctor's office.

Betty: I heard that you went to the doctor's office yesterday.

Alice: That's right.

Betty: Did you feel ill?

Alice: No, I felt fine except for a little arthritis in my left hand. I knew that it wasn't serious. I just thought that it was time for a general physical examination. The doctor understood my concern.

Betty: Well, what did the doctor say?

Alice: He said that my arthritis wasn't bad. He told me that I was OK.

Betty: Did he give you any medicine for your arthritis?

Alice: Yes, he wrote a prescription for some cream. He told me that I have to use it twice a day.

Betty: Are you using it?

Alice: I forgot to use it last night, but I remembered this morning.

Betty: Good. I'm glad that you're in good health.

Alice: So am I! So am I!

Understand *Circle **True, False,** or **We don't know.***

1. Betty's husband told her that Alice was at the hospital.	True	False	We don't know.
2. Alice has to take the medicine.	True	False	We don't know.
3. Alice uses the medicine in the morning and at night.	True	False	We don't know.
4. Alice is happy that she is in good health.	True	False	We don't know.

Write *Underline the word **that** in the dialog and sentences above.*

Grammar *that* with Clauses

• Many clauses begin with ***that*** and often follow verbs such as the following:

Present	***Past***	***Present***	***Past***
hear	heard	tell	told
say	said	write	wrote
feel	felt	forget	forgot
know	knew	understand	understood
think	thought	remember	remembered

Examples:

I	heard	***that***	you went to the doctor.
I	knew	***that***	it wasn't serious.
I	thought	***that***	it was time for a physical examination.
The doctor	told me	***that***	I was OK.
He	said	***that***	I had to use the medicine twice a day.

• The word ***that*** is often deleted.

Examples:

I	heard	~~that~~	you went to the doctor.
I	knew	~~that~~	it wasn't serious.

Read *Make logical complete sentences with the words in the box.*

I	understood	that	you	visited the doctor
The doctor	remembered		she	are taking medicine.
Alice	heard		Alice	wrote a prescription.
Betty	knew		it	wasn't serious.
	thought		I	was in good health.
	said		arthritis	had to use medicine.
	told			was OK.
	forgot			

Practice *Work with a partner. Ask and answer questions with the phrases below. See the example.*

Student 1: What do you know about ....?
Student 2: I think that it is / isn't serious.
or
I think that they are / aren't serious.

1. arthritis
2. headaches
3. a sore throat
4. an upset stomach
5. allergies
6. colds
7. diabetes
8. high blood pressure

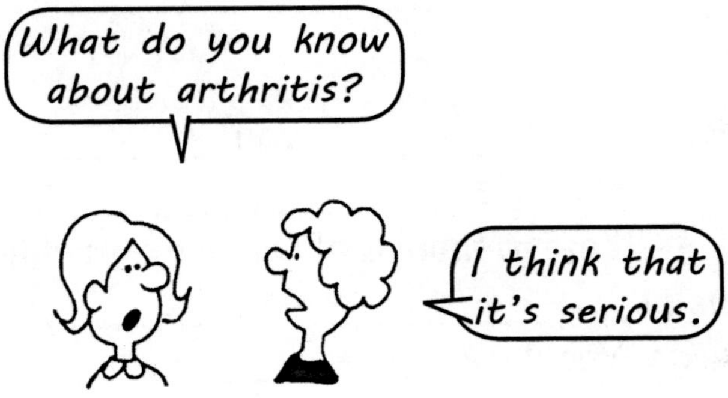
What do you know about arthritis?
I think that it's serious.

Write *Fill in the spaces below with the words in the box.*

Alice and Betty are talking.

did	didn't	know	knew	forget	forgot	think	thought

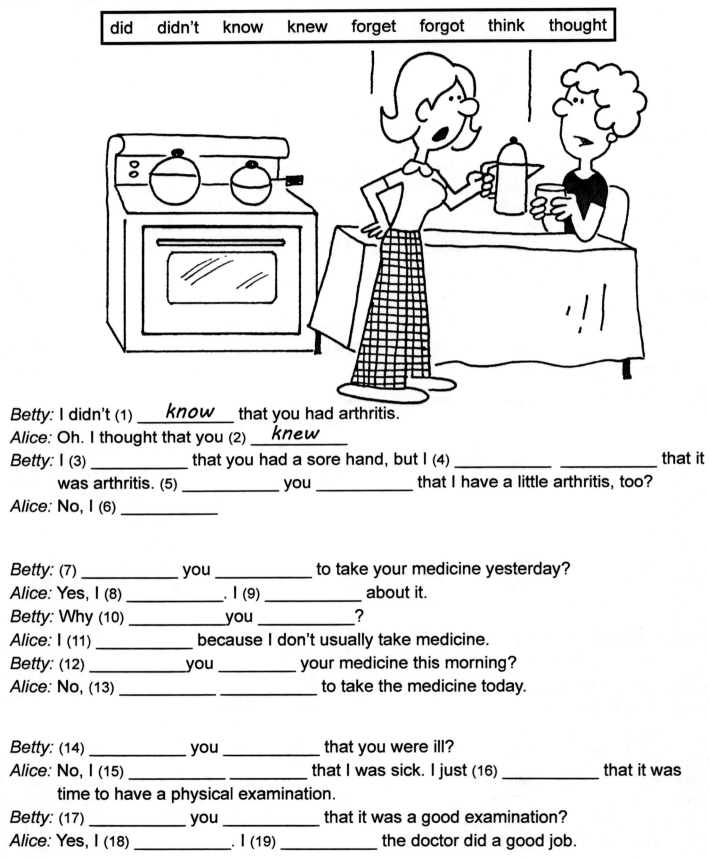

Betty: I didn't (1) ___know___ that you had arthritis.

Alice: Oh. I thought that you (2) ___knew___

Betty: I (3) __________ that you had a sore hand, but I (4) __________ __________ that it was arthritis. (5) __________ you __________ that I have a little arthritis, too?

Alice: No, I (6) __________

Betty: (7) __________ you __________ to take your medicine yesterday?

Alice: Yes, I (8) __________. I (9) __________ about it.

Betty: Why (10) __________you __________?

Alice: I (11) __________ because I don't usually take medicine.

Betty: (12) __________you __________ your medicine this morning?

Alice: No, (13) __________ __________ to take the medicine today.

Betty: (14) __________ you __________ that you were ill?

Alice: No, I (15) __________ __________ that I was sick. I just (16) __________ that it was time to have a physical examination.

Betty: (17) __________ you __________ that it was a good examination?

Alice: Yes, I (18) __________. I (19) __________ the doctor did a good job.

Write *Fill in the spaces below with the words in the box.*

did	didn't	understand	understood	hear	heard	feel	felt

Betty: (1) __Did__ you __understand__ the doctor's directions?

Alice: I course, I (2) __did__. I (3) ____________ everything.

Betty: (4) ______ you ____________ the medical forms?

Alice: Yes, I (5) __________, but a woman in the waiting room (6) _______ ________ all the items, so I helped her.

Alice: When (7) __did__ you __hear__ that I went to the hospital?

Betty: I (8) __heard__ it this morning.

Alice: How (9) ______ you __________ about it?

Betty: I (10) __________ it from my husband, Paul.

Alice: How (11) ______ he __________ it?

Betty: I don't know, but I think that he (12) __________ it from your husband.

Alice: (13) _____ you ________ that I was OK?

Betty: No, I (14) ______ __________ that. I only (15) ________ that you were at the hospital.

Betty: How (16) __did__ you __feel__ yesterday?

Alice: I (17) __felt__ fine.

Betty: (18) ______ your hand _________ OK, too?

Alice: No, it (19) __________. It (20) __________ a little sore.

Betty: How (21) _____ you ________ when you got your bill?

Alice: I (22) __________ terrible.

Read

The next day there was a message on Alice's telephone answering machine.

This is Dr. Snow at the Westend Hospital. I have the results of your tests. They show that you don't have any serious medical problems. I'm happy to tell you that you are in very good health.
I hope that your hand is better. I believe that it's a mild case of arthritis. I don't think that it's serious. Use the medicine and call when you need more.

Write

*What did you learn from the telephone message? Complete the sentences with **that** and clauses.*

1. The doctor said *that he got the results of the test.*
2. The tests showed ______________________________
3. The doctor told Alice ______________________________
4. The doctor hoped ______________________________
5. The doctor believes ______________________________
6. The doctor doesn't think ______________________________
7. We know ______________________________

Grammar *say* and *tell*

- The verbs ***say*** and ***tell*** have the same meaning, but they are used in different ways.
- They have irregular forms in the past tense: ***said*** and ***told***.
- We use ***tell*** when we ***tell somebody something***.
- We use ***say*** when we ***say something (to somebody)***.
- We also use ***tell*** in expressions such as ***tell a story, a lie,*** or ***a joke.***

Examples:		***Somebody***	***Something***
Alice	***said***	--	that her left hand hurt.
The doctor	***said***	--	that it wasn't serious.
Anna	***said***	--	that she didn't understand the words.
The doctor	***said,***	--	"Go to the lab."
Alice	***told***	the doctor	that her left hand hurt.
The doctor	***told***	Alice	that it wasn't serious.
Anna	***told***	Alice	that she didn't understand the words
The doctor	***told***	her	to go to the lab.

Read *Make logical complete sentences with the words in the box.*

I You He She It We They	said didn't say		about her visit to the doctor. that it wasn't serious. that I didn't understand. that I felt very well. "Go to the laboratory." "Call for more medicine." "May I help you?"
	told didn't tell	you him her them	

Practice *Work with a partner. Talk about the picture and cues below. See the example.*

Student 1: What did ....*name*..... say / tell you?
Student 2: He /She said / told me, "............."

Write *Fill in the spaces below with* ***say, said, tell,*** *or* ***told.***

It is a week late Alice is calling Betty.

Alice: I heard that you went to the doctor, too. How are you?

Betty: So-so.

Alice: What's the matter?

Betty: I think that I have a cold.

Alice: Did you see a doctor?

Betty: Yes, I did.

Alice: Well, what did he (1) __say__?

Betty: He (2) __said__, "Take two aspirins."

Alice: What did you (3) ______ the doctor?

Betty: I (4) ______ him that I had a sore throat, He (5) ______ me, "Drink a lot of liquids."

Alice: What else did he (6) ______ you?

Betty: He (7) ______, "Gargle with a pinch of salt and warm water." I (8) ______ the doctor that I felt terrible. He (9) ______ that it wasn't serious. He (10) ______ that it was only a cold. He (11) ______ me to go to bed and rest.

Alice: Is that all he (12) ______ you?

Betty: No, he (13) ______ me that my bill was $150!

Read Read the dialog above again, but delete ~~(cross-out)~~ the word ***that*** from the clauses.

Spelling The Silent *gh*

- The letter combination ***gh*** is often silent.
- It is usually silent after the long ***/ī/*** and ***/ô/*** sounds.
- It often appears in the past tense of irregular verbs.

Examples:

1.Turn on the light at night.

2.The fighers fought eight fights.

3.The catcher caught the high ball.

4. Is it right that you can only turn right?

5.The teacher taught bright students.

6. Betty bought tight shoes

7. Bob brought the right tools to work.

8. Ann's daughter is a delight.

Pronunciation *Practice saying the sentences aloud.*

1. The patient thought that she gave the doctor her right height and weight.
2. The strong light was bright at night.
3. The high school principal caught two boys in the hall. He brought them to the office because they fought.
4. They thought that they bought the right kind of light beer for the picnic.
5. I bought a bright-colored pair of shoes for my daughter.
6. He thought his flight was at eight at night.
7. My teacher taught me eight new words.
8. I might stay out late tonight to see the bright lights high in the night sky.
9. I thought it was a delightful sight to watch the mighty fighers fight a fair fight late last night.

Challenge *Gh sounds like the /f/ sound in a few English words. Look up the words in the sentence below in a dictionary or smart phone and practice their pronunciation.*

The day is rough enough. Don't laugh so hard that you cough.

CHAPTER 14

What Kind of Car Are You Looking For?

SKILLS	• Reading Road Signs
	• Requesting Information About the Price and Condition of a Car
	• Reading Car Ads
GRAMMAR	• How long does it ***take***?
VOCABULARY	• Common Road Signs
	• Parts of a Car
WORD BUILDING	• The Suffix ***-ward***

Read & Listen

Rita Lachance and Vince Cartelli are talking about Rita's driving test.

Rita: I'm nervous. I'm going to take my driving test today.

Vince: How long did it take you to learn to drive?

Rita: It took me a few months.

Vince: Are you ready for the tests?

Rita: I think so.

Vince: What do you have to do?

Rita: I have to pass a vision test, a driving test, and a test on traffic rules of the road.

Vince: How long will the tests take?

Rita: I think they'll take about an hour.

Vince: Where do you take the tests?

Rita: At the Department of Motor Vehicles.

Vince: Where's that?

Rita: On the corner of Fourth and A Streets. It takes only a few minutes to get there from here.

Vince: Do you know all the rules?

Rita: I think so. I studied them in a driver's manual.

Vince: What about the road signs? Do you understand them?

Rita: Take a minute and test me!

Understand *Circle **True, False,** or **We don't know.***

1. It took Rita about sixty days to learn to drive a car.	True	False	We don't know.
2. Rita is ready to take the test.	True	False	We don't know.
3. Rita will pass the test.	True	False	We don't know.
4. There are three kinds of tests.	True	False	We don't know.
5. The Department of Motor Vehicles isn't far.	True	False	We don't know.

Grammar *it takes*

- We use the expression ***it takes*** to describe the amount of time we need to do an action or to go a distance.
- We can use an indirect object after the expression ***it takes***.

Examples: Time

It	***took***	me	***a few months***	to learn to drive.
It'll	***take***		***about an hour***	to take the test.
It only	***takes***		***a few minutes***	to go there.

Read *Make logical complete sentences with the words in the box.*

It	takes took will take	me him her us them	a short time a few minutes an hour five days all day half an hour a long time	to drive to home. to get here. to go to work. to do the job. to take the test. to learn English. to eat dinner.

Practice *Work with a partner. Talk about the phrases below. Use the present tense. See the example below.*

Student 1: How long does it take to ....?
Student 2: It takes .... to ....

How long does it take to get to school?
It takes about 15 minutes to get to school.

1. get to school
2. do the homework
3. learn a language
4. learn English well
5. fly to your country from here
6. go home by bus
7. learn to drive
8. walk home from here
9. ...(Use your own words.)...

Practice *Work with a partner. Talk about the phrases below. Use the past tense. See the example below.*

Student 1: How long did it take you to ....?
Student 2: It took me .... to ....

It took me half an hour to get ready for school.

1. get ready this morning
2. come to this country
3. make breakfast this morning
4. make dinner last night
5. find an apartment
6. come to school
7. learn English
8. clean your house last week
9. do your food shopping last week
10. ...(Use your own words.)...

Read

Here are some road signs from the driver's manual.

1. No left turn

2. Two-way traffic

3. Railroad crossing

4. No U turns

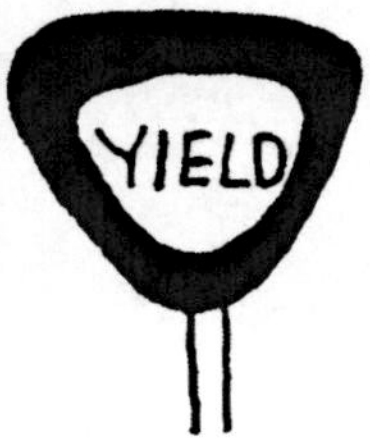

5. Yield

6. Merging traffic

7. Crossroad

8. Speed limit 35

9. Stop

10. One way

11. Do not enter

12. School crossing

13. Signal ahead

14. Side road

15. Fewer lanes ahead

16. Left turn

Write *Match the signs and the meanings.* Write the letters of the meanings in the spaces under the signs. See the example.*

1. *a*

2. ___

3. ___

4. ___

5. ___

6. ___

7. ___

8. ___

9. ___

10. ___

a. This sign means "stop."

b. This sign means that you can drive in only one direction.

c. This sign means that you cannot drive on this street.

d. This sign means that you must let other cars go first.

e. This sign means that you cannot turn right.

f. This sign means that there are railroad tracks ahead.

g. This sign means that there's an intersection ahead.

h. This sign means that there's a school ahead.

i. This sign means that you cannot drive over 50 miles per hour.

j. This sign means that two lanes become one.

---

* See the end of this chapter for more words and phrases used on road signs.

Read

SHAPE		Meaning
octagon *(8 sides)*	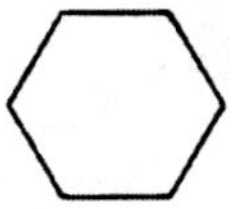	stop
triangle *(3 sides)*		yield
circle	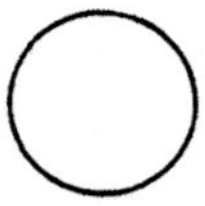	railroad crossing
diamond	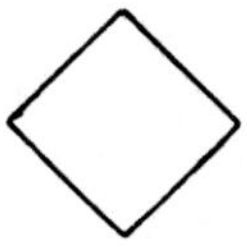	warning
square		traffic
flag	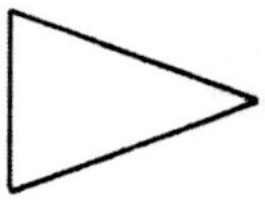	no passing
building		school

COLOR		MEANING
red	=	danger, stop
orange	=	construction
yellow	=	general warning
green	=	direction and distance
blue	=	service
white	=	traffic rules
brown	=	public recreation areas
black	=	night speed limit

Practice

Work with a partner. Talk about the colors of the road signs above. See the example below.

Student 1: What does .*(color)*.. mean?
Student 2: It means ....

Practice

Work with a partner. Talk about the shapes of the road signs above. Point to the shapes. See the example below.

Student 1: What does this shape mean?
Student 2: It means ....

Write *Fill in the spaces below with the words in the box. Use the map.*

one way	left	right	25	railroad crossing
yield	stopped	turned	2nd and A	do not enter

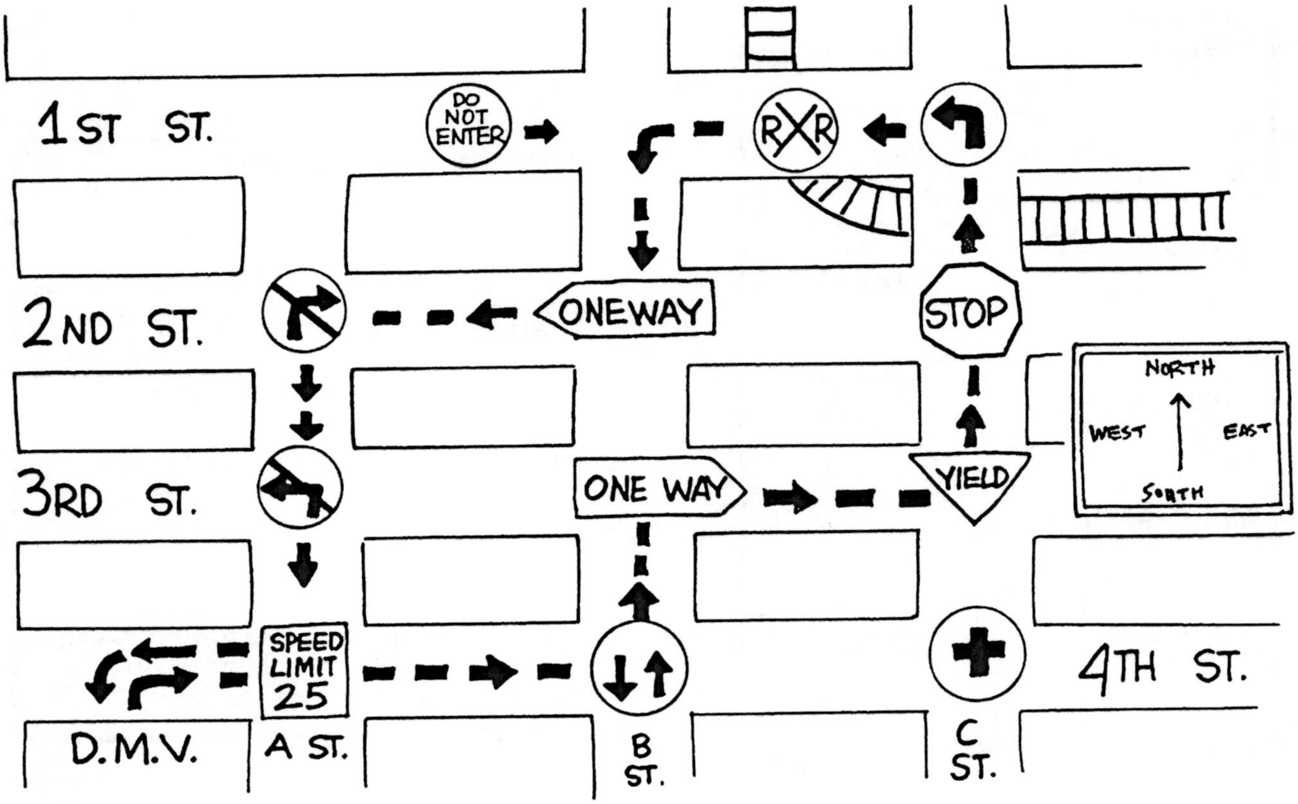

It's the following day. Rita is telling Vince about her driving test.

Rita: I passed my driving test. I did very well. Let me tell you all about it. We began at the Department of Motor Vehicles at the corner of 4th and A Streets. The sign at that corner said that the speed limit was (1) ___25___ mph. I drove east to 4th and B Streets and turned (2) __________ . I went one block and turned (3) ________ on 3rd Street. I drove one block. I saw a sign at the corner of 3rd and C Streets. It said (4) __________, so I drove slowly. Then, I (5) __________ north. I (6) __________ at the corner of 2nd and C Streets. After I turned west, I crossed a (7) ________ ________. I drove to 1st and B Streets. I saw a sign there. It said (8) __________, so I didn't continue on 1st Street. I turned south and went one block and turned west on 2nd Street because it's a (9) ________ ________ street. I drove one block, and then turned south at (10) __________ Streets. I drove past 3rd Street and arrived back at the Department of Motor Vehicles.

Read & Listen

Vince and Rita are talking about cars.

Now I want to buy a car.

Rita: I have my license. Now I want to buy a car.
Vince: What kind of car do you want?
Rita: I want a nice, small, beautiful, new, inexpensive car. And it has to get good mileage!
Vince: I'm sorry, but nobody has that kind of car. Do you want a domestic or foreign car?
Rita: It doesn't matter.
Vince: What kind of equipment do you want on the car?
Rita: Look at this. I made a list of equipment.

- air conditioning
- six cylinders
- leather interior
- good gas mileage
- good general condition
- two doors
- automatic transmission
- power brakes
- Radio and WiFi
- GPS*

Understand *Circle **True, False,** or **We don't know.***

1. Rita needs a car.	True	False	We don't know.
2. Rita wants to buy a foreign car.	True	False	We don't know.
3. Rita wants a car with power brakes.	True	False	We don't know.
4. She doesn't want power steering.	True	False	We don't know.

Practice *Work with a partner. Talk about Rita's list above. See the example below.*

Student 1: What kind of equipment does Rita want on the car?
Student 2: She wants ....

What kind of equipment does Rita want on the car?
She wants a car with a radio.

* Global Positioning System

Read *Use your dictionary or smart phone if necessary.*

HATCHBACK
power brakes
4 cylinder
good gas mileage
must sell $4000
call 213-0952

CONVERTIBLE
excellent condition
AM/FM radio
runs well $5000
call after 6 p.m.
494-9237

SEDAN
4 doors
air conditioning
automatic transmission
low mileage - $6000
943-5867

VAN
good condition
financing available
nice interior, clean
call weekends
818-9132

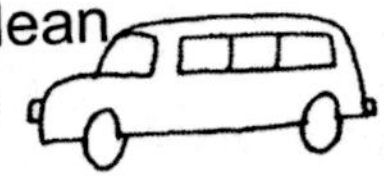

SPORTS CAR
power steering
standard transmission
stereo radio
great deal for only $4500
call 430-0261

PICKUP TRUCK
needs some work
rebuilt engine
new tires
best offer
call 804-9157

SPORTS UTILITY VEHICLE
40,000 miles
one owner
private party
call 653-09127

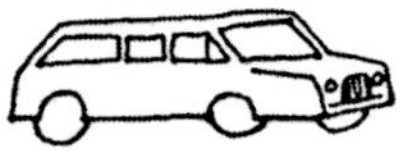

RECREATION VEHICLE
good shape
mint condition
3 years old
make offer
399-4339

Here are some ads.

Practice *Work with a partner. Talk about the ads above. See the example below.*

Student 1: What kind of equipment does the ...... have?
Student 2: It has ....

Practice *Work with a partner. Talk about the ads above. Use short answers. See the example below.*

Student 1: Does the .... ?
Student 2: Yes, it does. / No, it doesn't.

Does the pickup need work?

Practice *Work with a partner. Talk about the ads above. Use short answers. See the example below.*

Student 1: Is the .... ?
Student 2: Yes, it is. / No, it isn't.

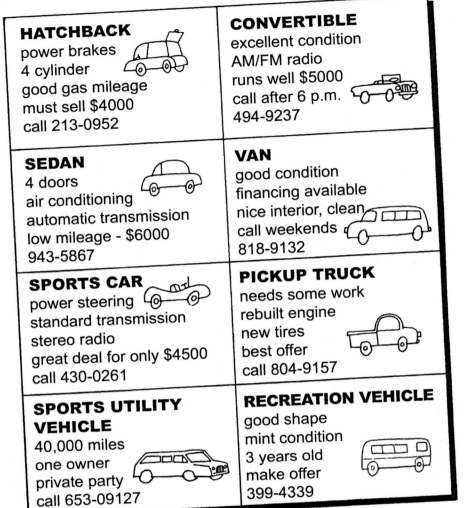

Is the recreational vehicle in good condition?
Yes, it is.

Read & Listen

Rita is calling about the sports car.

Rita: Hello, do you have a car for sale?
Seller: Yes, I do.
Rita: What kind of car is it?
Seller: It's a five-year-old domestic car.
Rita: What color is the car?
Seller: Beige.
Rita: What's the condition of the car?
Seller: It's in excellent condition.
Rita: How much are you asking for it?
Seller: $5500.
Rita: When can I see it?
Seller: Anytime. I'll be home all day. My address is 211 Olympic Drive.
Rita: Good. I'll be there soon.

Understand *Circle* ***True, False,*** *or* ***We don't know.***

1. ***"What are you asking?"*** means ***"How much does it cost?"***	True	False	We don't know.
2. The car costs $5500.	True	False	We don't know.
3. Rita knows the man's address.	True	False	We don't know.

Practice *Work with a partner. Use the signs in the car windows below. See the example below.*

Student 1: What's the price and condition of the car?
Student 2: It's .... and in ....

1.

2.

3.

4.

5.

6.

7.

8.

Read *Parts of a car.*

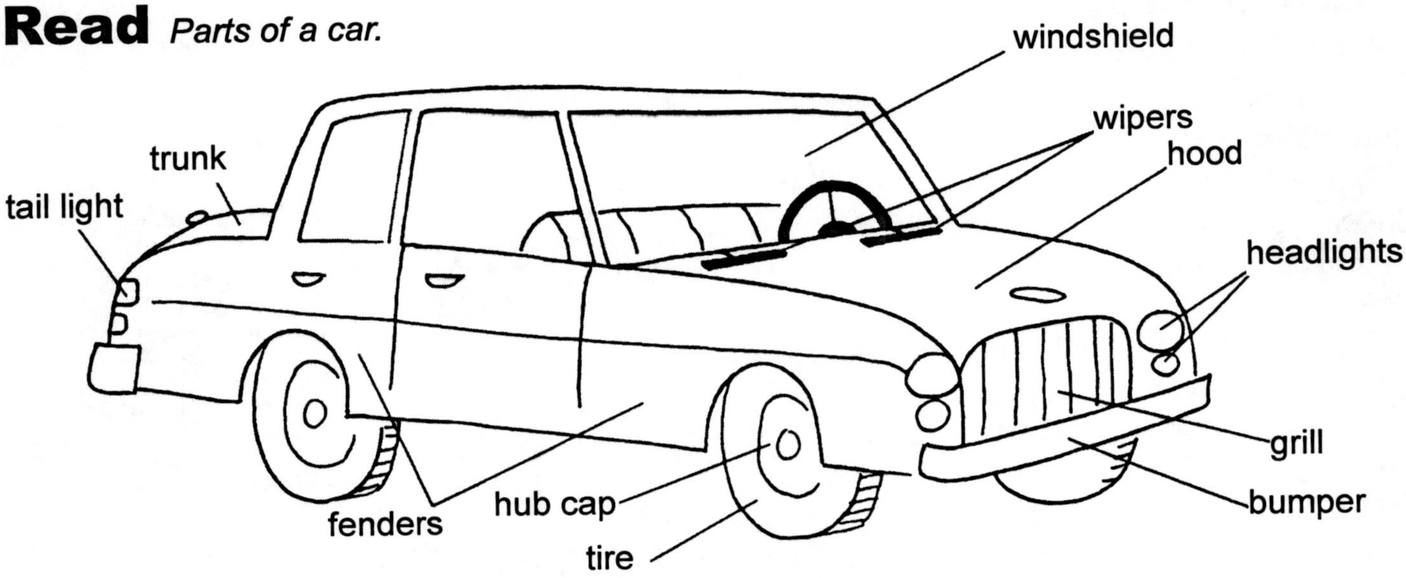

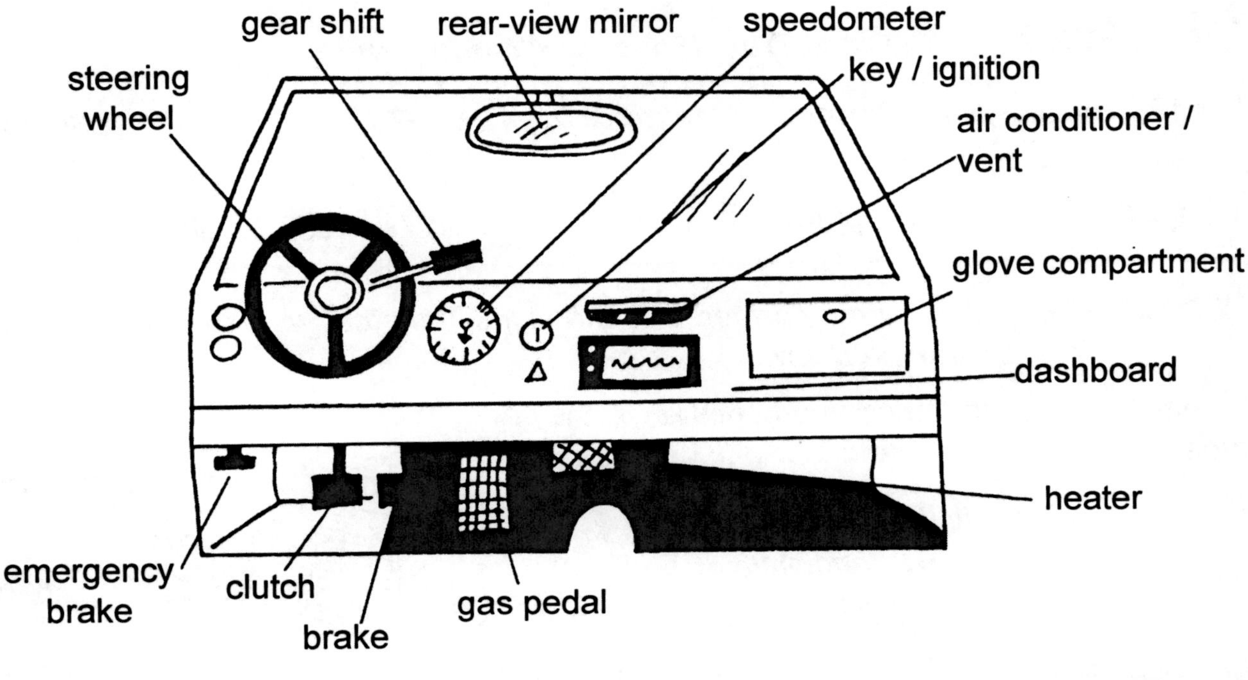

Practice *Work with a partner. Talk about the parts of a car. Use the prepositions in the box below to describe where the parts are. See the example below.*

on the outside of	in front of	on the side of
on the inside of	in the back of	at the corners of

Student 1: Where is / are ....?
Student 2: It's / They're ....

Where are the tires?
They're on the outside of the car.

Write

Help Rita ask questions about the car. The answers will help you write the questions.

Rita is looking at the sports car.

Rita: (1) *Do you have a car for sale?*
Seller: Yes, I have a car for sale.
Rita: (2) ______________________________
Seller: The tires are in very good condition.
Rita: (3) ______________________________
Seller: Yes, it has power brakes and power steering, too.
Rita: (4) ______________________________
Seller: 30,000 miles.
Rita: (5) ______________________________
Seller: I'm asking $5500 for this car.
Rita: (6) ______________________________
Seller: OK. You can have the car for $5000.

Dictation

Listen to the teacher or your partner read the dictation at the bottom of the next page. Write the sentences below. Then, check your writing.

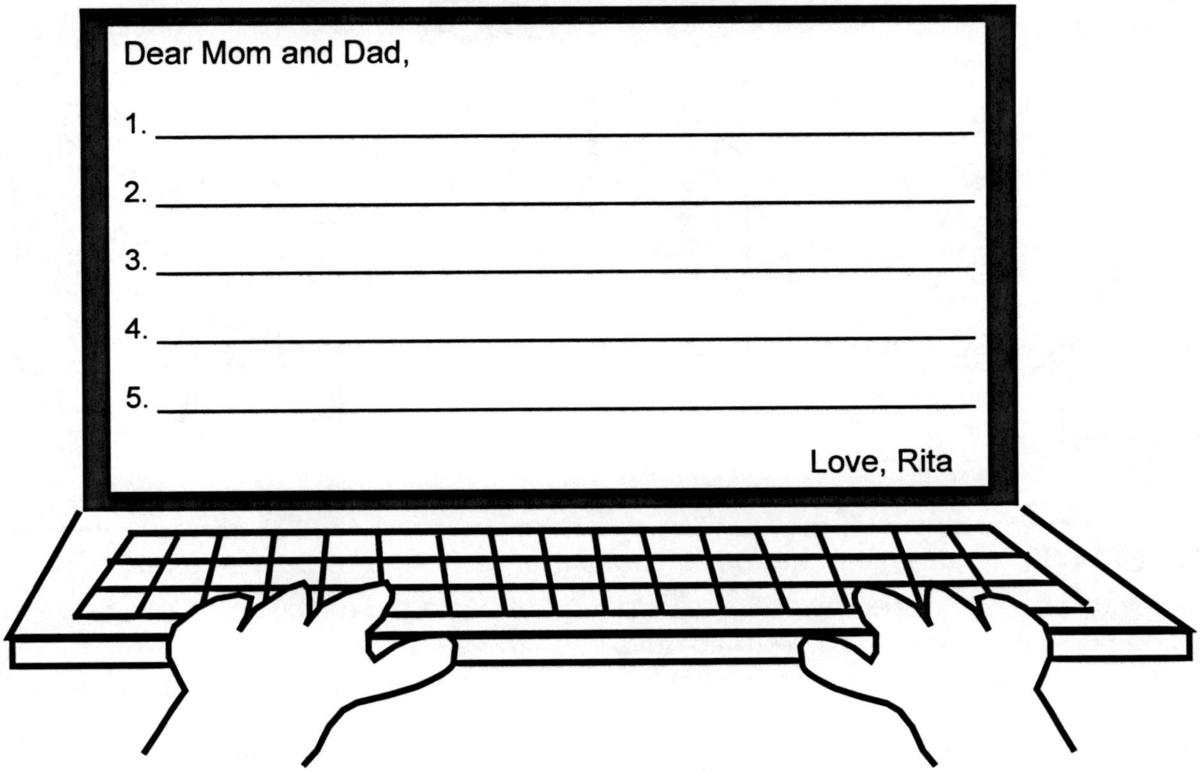
Dear Mom and Dad,
1. ______________________________
2. ______________________________
3. ______________________________
4. ______________________________
5. ______________________________
Love, Rita

Practice *Fold this page along the dotted lines. Practice with a partner.*

Student 1

Don't show your picture to your partner. Tell him / her where the signs are in your picture and what is on the sign. Your partner will write your information on the signs in his or her pictures.

Now you fill your signs with the information from your partner.

FOLD HERE

Student 2

Don't look at your partner's picture. Listen to your partner's information, then write the information on the signs in your picture.

Now you tell your partner where the signs are in your picture and what is on the signs.

FOLD HERE

Dictation *Read this dictation to your partner. (from the previous page.)*

1. I took my driving test yesterday and passed.
2. It took me only a few months to learn to drive.
3. I bought a used sports car, but it's in very good condition.
4. It has a radio, power brakes, and standard transmission.
5. I'll write you more about my new car later.

Word Building **The Suffix *-ward***

- The suffix ***-ward*** means ***in the direction***.
- It is pronounced the same as ***"word" /wərd/***.

Examples:

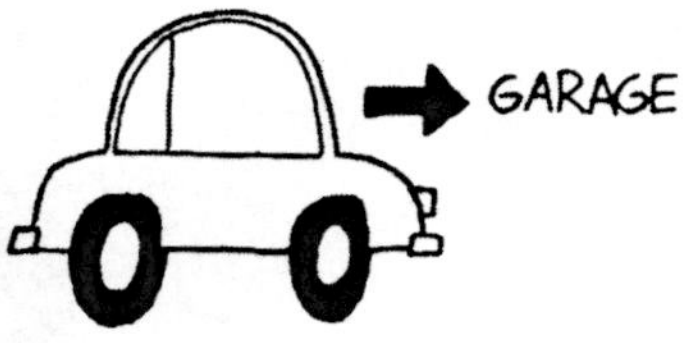

1. The car drove for<u>ward</u> to<u>ward</u> the garage.

2. The boy walked home<u>ward</u>.

3. The bus went north<u>ward</u>.

Write *Fill in the crossword puzzle with the <u>opposites</u> of the words on the left. See example.*

DOWN ↓

1. westward
3. inward
4. downward
6. eastward
7. outward

ACROSS →

2. backward
5. northward
8. upward
9. inward

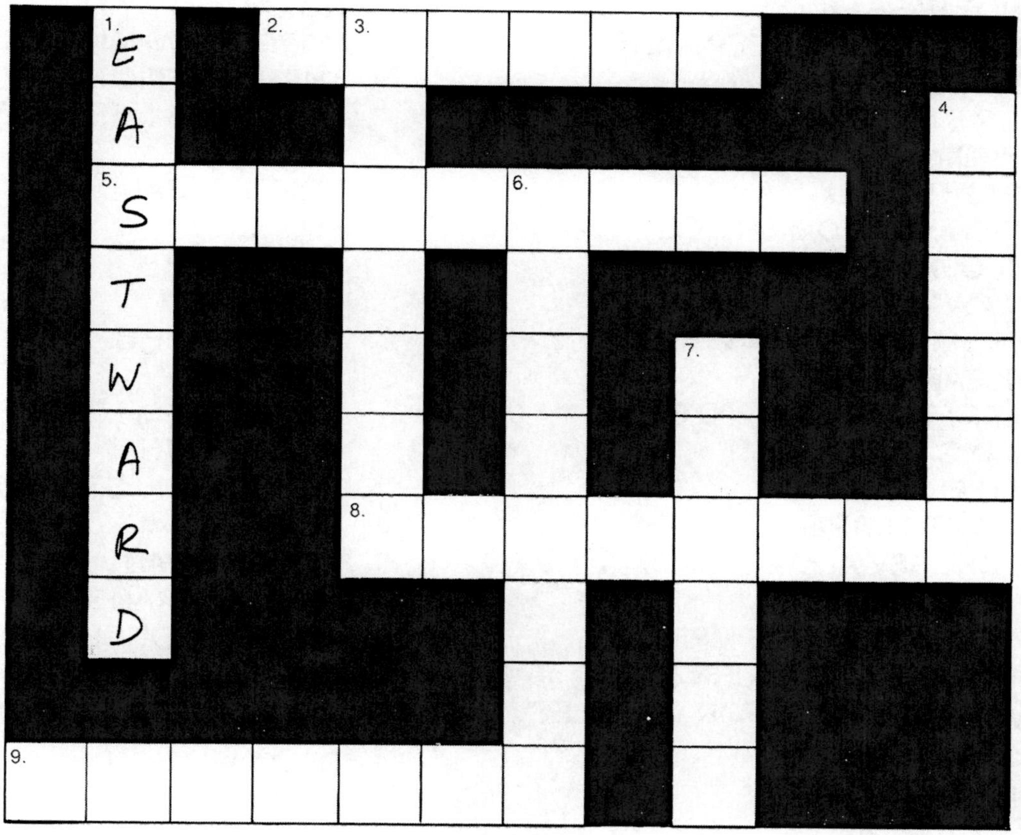

OTHER WORDS AND PHRASE USED IN ROAD SIGNS

Regulatory Signs

END 25 MILE ZONE
NO STOPPING ANY TIME
TRUCK ROUTE
NO PED CROSSING
LEFT TURN ON LEFT ARROW ONLY
TURNOUT 1/4 MILE
COMMERCIAL VEHICLES PROHIBITED
MAXIMUM SPEED LIMIT 55 MILES
LOAD LIMIT 10 TONS
NO PARKING ANY TIME
SPEED CHECKED BY RADAR
$500 FINE FOR LITTERING
SLOWER TRAFFIC USE TURNOUTS
NO BICYCLES
TWO-LANE TRAFFIC AHEAD
DO NOT PASS
SLOWER TRAFFIC KEEP RIGHT
U TURN OK
AFTER STOP RIGHT TURN PERMITTED ON RED
NO RIGHT TURN
NO FISHING FROM BRIDGE
PARK OFF PAVEMENT
TOW AWAY ZONE
EMERGENCY PARKING ONLY
PARK PARALLEL
NO LEFT TURN 4 P.M. TO 6 P.M.
PASSING LANE AHEAD
BEGIN FREEWAY
PASS WITH CARE
USE CROSSWALK
3-WAY SIGNAL
SIGNALS SET FOR 23 MPH
RIGHT LANE MUST TURN RIGHT
15 MPH ON BRIDGE FOR VEHICLES OVER 10 TONS
RIGHT TURN ONLY
LEFT TURN ONLY
NO TURNS
LEFT TURN LANE
PEDESTRIANS, BICYCLES, MOTOR DRIVEN CYCLES PROHIBITED
BUSES AND CAR POOLS ONLY

Guide Signs

HISTORICAL LANDMARK
ELEVATION 3000 FT
GAS FOOD LODGING
NEXT SERVICES 22 MILES
REST AREA

Warning Signs

ROAD NARROWS
SOFT SHOULDER
PAVEMENT ENDS
NARROW BRIDGE
RANGE CATTLE
DIVIDED ROAD
PED XING
CROSS TRAFFIC AHEAD
NO OUTLET
SLIPPERY WHEN WET
THRU TRAFFIC MERGE LEFT
LANE ENDS MERGE LEFT
DIP
DRIFTING SAND
FLOODED
EXIT 30 M.P.H.
SLIDE AREA
RAMP 30 M.P.H.
BIKE XING
ICY NEXT 4 MILES
BRIDLE PATH
SCHOOL BUS STOP 400 FT
BUMP
ROUGH ROAD
LOW CLEARANCE 12 FT 6 IN
NOT A THROUGH STREET
ONE-LANE BRIDGE

Construction Signs

DETOUR AHEAD
LOOSE GRAVEL
OPEN TRENCH
FLAGMAN AHEAD
ROAD WORK AHEAD
ROAD CLOSED TO THRU TRAFFIC
BRIDGE OUT
ROAD CLOSED
PREPARE TO STOP

CHAPTER 15

Do You Work Hard or Hardly Work?

SKILLS • Describing How People Work

GRAMMAR • Adjectives and Adverbs

• Regular and Irregular Forms of Adverbs

VOCABULARY • Common Adjectives and Adverbs

• Important Safety Signs

• ***hardly***

WORD BUILDING • The Suffix ***-tion*** and ***-sion***

SPELLING • Rules for adding ***-ly*** to Words

Read & Listen

David Morris and Paul Wilson are talking in the school hall.

Paul: Hi, David. How's it going?
David: Not bad. How about you?
Paul: OK. It's almost the end of the semester, and I have to give a final test. There are a lot of nervous students in my ESL class. How are your students?
David: Busy. Their final is a solar panel workshop project. They're doing it right now. Come on. I'll show you.
Paul: How are they working?
David: They're working steadily.
Paul: I can see that.
David: There's Vince Cartelli. He's a quick and accurate worker.
Paul: Oh, yes. David. He was in my class last year.
David: And there's Martin Ngon. He works a little slowly, but he's a very careful worker. He always does everything correctly. There's Joanne Vordale. She's an attentive and safe student. And next to her, there's Alberto Duran. He left his project temporarily because he's helping a slow student. Alberto explains directions very clearly. There's only one problem.
Paul: What's that?
David: The machines run too noisily.

Understand *Circle* ***True, False,*** *or* ***We don't know.***

1. ***"How's it going?"*** means ***"How are you?"***	True	False	We don't know.
2. Mr. Morris has a lot of nervous students.	True	False	We don't know.
3 All the students are working nicely.	True	False	We don't know.
4. Alfonse finished his project.	True	False	We don't know.
5. The machines don't run very quietly.	True	False	We don't know.

Grammar Adjectives and Regular Adverbs

- Adjectives modify nouns and precede them.
- Adjectives generally appear in answers to questions with ***What kind of ...?***
- Adverbs modify verbs and usually follow them.
- Many common adverbs are formed by adding the suffix ***-ly***.
- Adverbs generally appear in answers to questions with ***How ...?***

Examples:	***Adjectives***	***Nouns***	
There are a lot of	***nervous***	***students***	in my class
Vince's an	***accurate***	***worker.***	
Vince's a	***quick***	***worker.***	
Martin Ngon's a	***careful***	***worker.***	
Joanne Vordale is an	***attentive***	***student.***	
Joanne's a	***safe***	***student.***	

	Verbs		***Adverbs***
They	***'re working***		***steadily.***
Martin	***does***	everything	***correctly.***
Alberto	***left***	his project	***temporarily.***
He	***explains***	directions	***clearly.***
The machines	***run***		***noisily.***
The students	***are working***		***nicely.***

Read *Make logical complete sentences with the words in the box.*

Vince Martin Joanne Alberto It	is isn't	a an	quick accurate noisy careful attentive	person. machine. worker. man. woman

Vince Martin Joanne Alberto The students I	work on works on explain explains do does	directions his / her project his / her work everything nothing	carefully. clearly. nicely correctly. steadily. slowly.

Practice *Work with a partner. Talk about the people in the pictures below. Use your own verbs. Change the adjective to an adverb using* ***-ly.*** *See the example.*

Student 1: How does ....?
Student 2: He / She / It ....ly.

1. Vince is a quick worker.

2. Joanne's an attentive student.

3. Martin's a careful student.

4. Alberto's a clear speaker.

5. She is a steady worker.

6. It's a noisy machine.

Practice *Work with a partner. Talk about the people in the pictures below. Change the adverbs to adjectives. See the example below.*

Student 1: What kind of .... is ....?
Student 2: He / She / It is a ....

What kind of machine is this?

It's a noisy machine.

1. The machine works noisily.

2. Amir studies nervously.

3. This student is working steadily.

4. Paul's listening calmly.

5. Alberto speaks clearly.

6. Martin's working correctly.

7. Joanne works safely.

8. Vince works accurately.

Spelling Rules for Adding *-ly* to Words

• Most adverbs are formed by simply addlng ***-ly***.

Examples: quick → quickly attentive → attentively
slow → slowly correct → correctly

• The letter ***y*** changes to ***i*** before adding ***-ly***.

Examples: busy → busily temporary → temporarily
noisy → noisily steady → steadily

• When a word ends in ***le***, drop the ***e***, and simply add ***y***. The letter ***e*** is no longer pronounced.

Examples: comfortable → comfortably
terrible → terrlbly

• Do not drop a final ***l*** when adding ***-ly***.

Examples: careful → carefully
normal → normally

Write

Fill in the spaces with the opposite of the adverb in the question. Make sure that you spell the adverb correctly.

1. Do you have any careless students?
2. Do you have any slow students?
3. Are there any inaccurate students?
4. Are there any inattentive students?
5. Do any students work incorrectly?
6. Do they work noisily?
7. Do they work nervously?
.8 Do the machines run quietly?

All my students work ____________________.
No, they all work ____________________.
No, they all work ____________________.
No, they listen ____________________.
No, they work ____________________.
No, they work ____________________.
No, everybody works ____________________.
No, they run too ____________________.

Read

Paul Wilson and David Morris are talking about Alberto Duran.

Is Alberto a good, hard worker?
He sure is! He works hard, fast and well. He hardly ever stops.

Grammar Irregular Adverbs

• Unlike most adverbs, ***well***, ***fast***, and ***hard*** do not end in ***-ly***.

Example: ***How*** does Alberto work? He works ***hard***.

• Don't confuse ***hard*** with ***hardly.***

1. ***Hardly*** is an adverb of manner
2. ***Hardly*** is often used with ***ever***.
3. ***Hardly*** answers the question ***How often ...?*** It means ***almost never***.

Examples:

How often	does he stop?	He	***hardly***	stops.
How often	do you eat out?	We	***hardly ever***	eat out.

Read *Make logical complete sentences with the words in the box.*

Alberto I We The students She	works work study studies learn learns	well. hard. fast.

Do you	study play work listen	hard,	or	do you	hardly	study? play? work? listen?

Challenge *Answer the questions you made with the words in the box above.*

Practice

Work with a partner. Talk about the pictures below. Use ***well***, ***hard***, *or* ***fast*** *in the answers. See the example below.*

Student 1: How should a .... work?
Student 2: He / She / It should work ...

1. construction worker

2. word processor

3. surgeon

4. machine

5. miner

6. assembly line worker

7. pilot

8. athlete

9. nurse

10. dentist

11. mail carrier

12. student

Practice

Work with a partner. Talk about the activities in the phrases below. Use original answers with ***often*** *or* ***hardly ever*** *in the answers. See the example below.*

Student 1: How often do you ......?
Student 2: I .... often / hardly ever ....

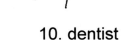

1. go to a restaurant
2. go to the movies
3. spend a lot of money on clothes
4. buy expensive presents
5. get gifts
6. take long trips
7. go shopping at night
8. watch TV in the morning
9. get a raise
10. *(Use your own words.)*

Challenge *Tell what the signs in the picture mean.*

Challenge *How many dangerous situations can you identify in the picture above? List them below.*

1. ______________________________
2. ______________________________
3. ______________________________
4. ______________________________
5. ______________________________
6. ______________________________
7. ______________________________
8. ______________________________
9. ______________________________
10. ______________________________
11. ______________________________
12. ______________________________

Word Building **The Suffixes *-tion* and *-sion***

- The suffex ***-tion*** is the most common and are all nouns.
- We usually pronounce the suffixes ***-tion*** as ***/sh-n/*** or ***/ch-n/***.
- We always use ***-tion*** after the words ending in ***-a*** or ***-ate***.
- We use ***-tion*** after any consonant except ***-l, -n,*** or ***-r.***

accommodation	competition	mention	position	revolution
action	completion	moderation	promotion	solution
addition	condition	nation	protection	station
attention	invitation	occupation	rejection	suggestion
communication	location	population	relation	vocation

- Not that many nouns have ***-sion*** endings.
- We pronounce ***-sion*** as ***/sh-n/***, ***/zh-n/***, and ***/ch-n/*** (as in ***question***).
- They are often formed from verbs which end with ***-d, -de, -se, -t***.

collision	decision	infusion	pension	suspension
comprehension	explosion	occasion	persuasion	television

- When words end in ***-ss*** or ***-mit*** just add ***–ion***.
- When words end in ***-cede / -ceed*** change to ***-ssion***

admission	confession	expression	mission	possession
commission	discussion	impression	permission	transmission

Pronunciation *Practice reading the following sentences aloud.*

1. When we studied mathematics, we learned addition, subtraction, multiplication and division.
2. How is my pronunciation and intonation when I ask questions?
3. Joanne got some direction at the information section of the train station.
4. There are a lot of exceptions and variations in English spelling.
5. I am on a mission to get an invitation to the political convention in the mansion.
6. My boss made a decision to give me a promotion because I have good communication skills.

Write *Fill in the word with the correct word. The pictures hold clues.*

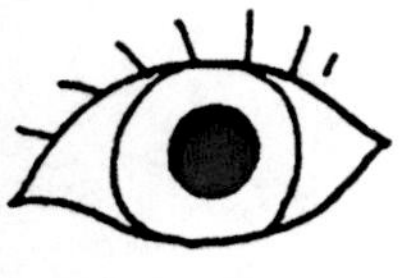

1. Optometrists check people's vision.

2. Do you have a ______________ for me?

3. The United States is big ______________.

4. Please give me ______________s to your house.

5. This new house is under ______________.

6. Fllying airplanes is his ______________.

7. The subway ______________ is underground.

8. The surgeon is performing an ______________.

9. Please fill out this job ______________.

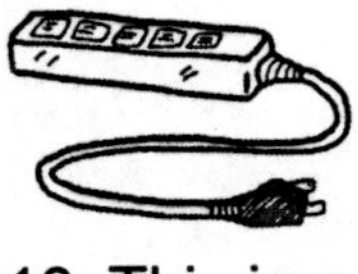

10. This is an ______________ cord.

CHAPTER 16

English for a Better Job

• Review Chapter

• Final Test

Read & Listen

It's break time at school. A few students are talking.

Joanne: Did you hear?
Rita: No, what?
Joanne: Vince Cartelli lost his job.
Rita: No kidding! What happened?
Joanne: His company laid him off.
Rita: Why?
Joanne: The economy!

Understand *Circle **True, False,** or **We don't know.***

1. ***"A few"*** means ***"over 100."***	True	False	We don't know.
2. Vince Cartelli has a job.	True	False	We don't know.
3. ***"No kidding!"*** means ***"Really?!"***	True	False	We don't know.
4. Vince lost his job because he doesn't work hard.	True	False	We don't know.

Write *Rewrite the verbs under the lines in the past tense.*

Here comes Vince.

Joanne: Hi, Vince. How's it going?
Vince: Not too well. I (1) lost my job.
lose
Joanne: What (2) ____________?
happen
Vince: I (3) ________ this morning, and I (4) ________ everything as usual. When
get up **do**
I (5) ____________ at work, I (6) ________ a pink piece of paper on my time
arrive **find**
card. It (7) ________ to see the personnel manager, so I (8) ________ to
say **go**
the office and I (9) ________ to her. She (10) ________ me that business
speak **tell**
(11) ________ bad and that they (12) ________ lay off fifty percent of the
is **have to**
work force. Now I have to find a new job.

Read

Write

Fill in an application for a job.

APPLICATION

(Please print.)

Name: Mr. / Mrs. / Ms. / Miss (circle one)

____

Last *First* *Middle*

Address: ____

Street Number *Street* *Apartment Number*

City: ______________________ State: __________ Zip Code: ______

Telephone Number: __________ __________ E-mail: ______________

Home *Cell*

Place of Birth: __________ __________ Sex: *(Check one)* Male ☐ Female ☐

City *Country*

Date of Birth: ______/______/______ Age: __________

Month *Date* *Year*

Marital Status: *(Underline one)* Married / Single / Divorced / Separated / Widowed

Are you a citizen of this country? *(Circle one.)* YES NO

What is your present occupation? ______________________________

References: Name: ______________________ Phone Number __________

Name: ______________________ Phone Number __________

Today's Date: __________________ Signature: __________________

Write *Fold this page down the middle along the dotted line. Do this exercise with a partner. Each of you will select a side. Tell your partner what messages there are on your bulletin board, and your partner will write them on his or her bulletin board. Then reverse roles. Compare your messages only after you both finish.*

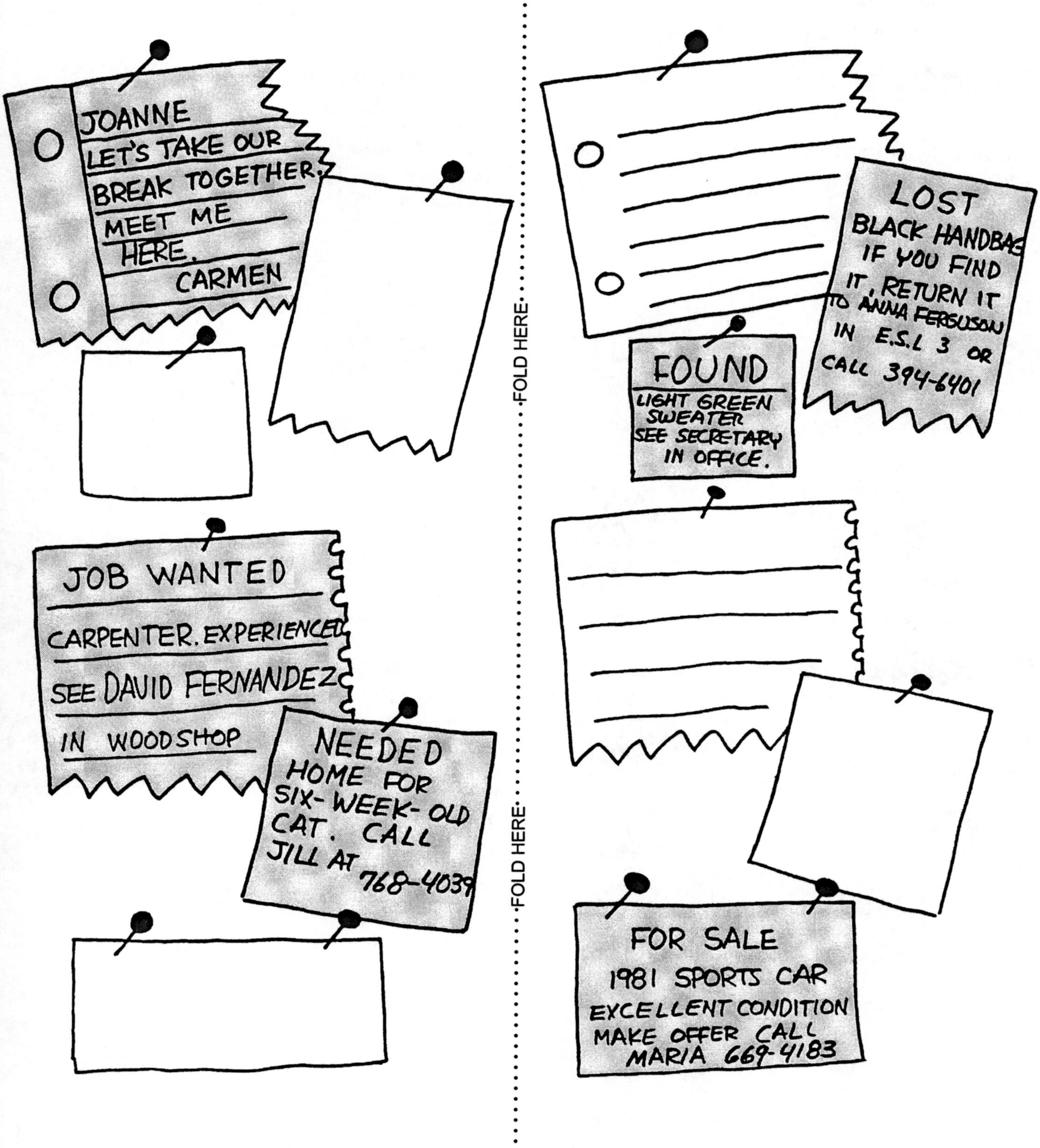

Read

The students are back in class after the break.

Joanne: It's almost the weekend. We have two days off.
Rita: Maybe, but I have to do my housework. What are you going to do?
Joanne: I'm going to go to a party.

Practice

Work with a partner. Talk about the activities in the phrases below. Use the expressions with the word ***do*** *in the answers. See the example below.*

Student 1: What do you have to do tomorrow?
Student 2: I have to ....

What do you have to do tomorrow?
I have to do some housework.

1. some housework

2. the cooking

3. the dishes

4. the shopping

5. the laundry

6. the ironing

7. the vacuuming

8. the dusting

Practice

Work with a partner. Talk about the activities in the phrases below. Use the expressions with the word ***get*** *in the answers. See the example below.*

Student 1: What are you going to do?
Student 2: I'm going to get ....

What are you going to do?
I'm going to get a haircut.

CLIP
CLIP

1. a haircut

12

2. up late

MAIL

3. the mail

$

4. a check

5. new clothes

6. ready for the party

TAXI

7. a taxi

8. there on time.

Read

Did you see Rita's new car?

No, I didn't. Where is it?

It's in the parking lot next to Mike's station wagon and Martin's sedan.

Owner: Mike & Mary Breyer

Kind: Station Wagon

Model: Panther

Color: Black

Age: 2 years old

Owner: Rita Lachance

Kind: Sports Car

Model: XZ-1000

Color: White

Age: 5 years old

Owner: Martin Ngon

Kind: Sedan

Model: Executive

Color: Gray

Age: 6 months old

Practice *Work with a partner. Talk about the cars above. See the example below.*

Student 1: What model is ..*(name)*..'s car?

or

How old is ..*(name)*.'s car?

Student 2: It's

What model is Mike's car?

It's a Panther.

Practice *Work with a partner. Talk about the cars above. Use short answers. See the example below.*

Student 1: Whose car is?

Student 2: ..*(name)*.'s car is.

Whose car is gray?

Martin's car is.

Read

Rita: How are you getting home?
Vince: I'm walking.
Rita: I have a car. Do you want a ride?
Vince: Oh, "si." I mean, yes.
How do you say "yes" in French?
Rita: "Oui." We pronounce it /wē/.

Understand *Circle **True, False,** or **We don't know.***

1. David has a car.	True	False	We don't know.
2. Rita speaks French.	True	False	We don't know.
3. Vince will walk home tonight.	True	False	We don't know.

Practice *Work with a partner. Talk about the phrases below. See the example below.*

Student 1: How do you say "..............." in your language?
Student 2: We say "............"

1. yes
2. no
3. hello
4. good-bye
5. please
6. thank you
7. how are you?
8. man
9. woman
10. *(Use your own words.)*..............................

Practice *Work with a partner. Review the names of the letters of the alphabet before doing this exercise. See the example below.*

Student 1: How do you spell ".........."?
Student 2: "................."

1. your first name
2. your last name
3 your middle name
4. the name of your street
5. the name of your city or town
6. the name of your state
7. the name of your country
8. the name of your profession
9.the month of your birth
10. the *(Use your own words.)*..............................

Read & Listen

Vince Cartelli and Mr. Wilson are talking in the hall in front of the ESL classroom. The students are taking their final exam.

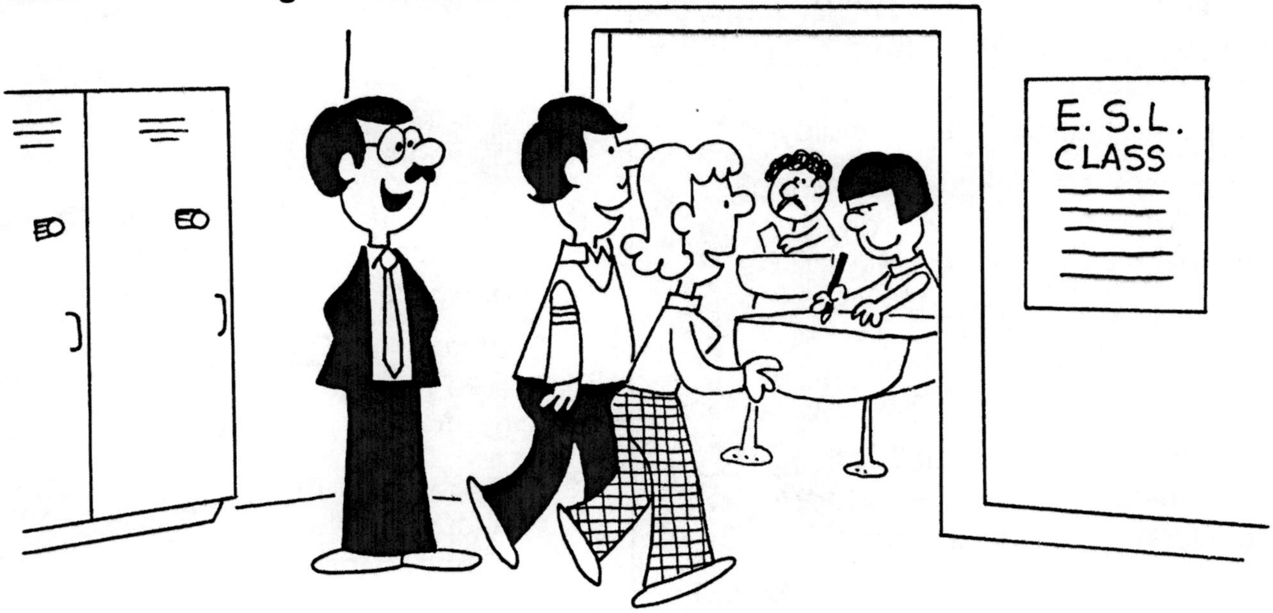

Vince: How are you, Mr. Wilson?
Paul: Pretty good. How are you doing?
Vince: Not so good. I lost my job today.
Paul: I'm sorry to hear that.
Vince: How are your students doing?
Paul: They're very nervous about their final test.
Vince: I remember that you gave our class a hard final last year. I really learned a lot when I was in your class.
Paul: Thanks for the compliment.
Vince: Now I can speak English good. I'll need it to find a job.
Paul: If you speak English "good," you don't speak English "well."
Vince: Oh, sorry! But my English is improving. Don't you think so?
Paul: Yes, I do.
Vince: I remember you said, "Learn better English for a better job."
Paul: So true! So true!

Understand *Circle* ***True, False,*** *or* ***We don't know.***

1. Vince was in Mr. Wilson's class last year.	True	False	We don't know.
2. Vince's English isn't improving.	True	False	We don't know.
3. Vince doesn't need English to find a job.	True	False	We don't know.
4. Your English is better every day.	True	False	We don't know.

Final Test *Circle the correct answers.*

1. How __________ do you come to school?
   a. sometimes c. never
   b. often d. seldom

2. Vince doesn't have a job; he's __________.
   a. temporary c. employed
   b. permanent d. unemployed

3. When people are sick, they don't feel ___.
   a. hard c. hardly
   b. weak d. well

4. Vince ________ get a job.
   a. has c. have
   b. has to d. have to

5. How's the weather outside? Is it ________?
   a. raining c. expensive
   b. working d. cheap

6. Joanne doesn't _______ work on Sunday.
   a. has c. have
   b. has to d. have to

7. What kind of car does Joanne ________?
   a. has c. have
   b. has to d. have to

8. He'll call the boss _____ask about a job.
   a. for c. in
   b. too d. to

9. ________ David find a good job?
   a. Going c. Want
   b. Will d. Need

10. The company ________ close.
    a. no c. no will
    b. not d. won't

11. Will that be all? _______________
    a. Please, yes. c. Yes, I will.
    b. Yes, that's all. d. Thank you.

12. When ___________ on our next picnic?
    a. we going c. are we going
    b. are going d. we are going

13. We're _____ to have the picnic as usual.
    a. go c. go to
    b. going to d. going

14. Will you take a walk with me? No, not now. Maybe later. I _______ to rest now.
    a. want c. won't
    b. will d. going to

15. Many students __________ at the picnic.
    a. was c. were
    b. where d. wear

16. How _________ the weather yesterday?
    a. was c. were
    b. where d. wear

17 What kind _____________ was there?
    a. of food c. foods
    b. off food d. food

18. This test isn't very __________; it's easy.
    a. complicated c. really
    b. understand d. directions

19. Please don't __________ that box.
    a. spill c. tall
    b. drop d. fell

20. Rita ___________ to buy a new car.
    a. decide c. will
    b. decided d. want

21. _____________ car did Sami paint?
    a. How much c. Whose
    b. Who d. How

22. When ________ you arrive here?
    a. are c. was
    b. did d. were

23. Betty's sister _________ her two theater tickets for a show in New York.
    a. buy c. buyed
    b. will buys d. bought

24. Can I ask you a few questions? Yes, __________.
    a. I can c. can
    b. you can d. can't

25. Do you have any relatives here? Yes, __________.
    a. I did c. I does
    b. I was d. I do

26. Please _______ the the machine before you try to fix it.
    a. place c. unplug
    b. turn d. plug

27. Turn______ the light; I can't see.
    a. of c. in
    b. on d. away

28. All the members of the family _______ the shopping.
    a. do c. make
    b. does d. makes

29. Please don't __________ any mistakes.
    a. do c. make
    b. does d. makes

30. James ________some new shoes at the store a few months ago.
    a. got c. buy
    b. get d. getted

31. Carmen ________ the bus after a long ride home.
    a. go off c. get off
    b. got off d. get on

32. She looked _______ to see the airplane.
    a. on c. at
    b. up d. to

33. Please throw the garbage ________ .
    a. out c. off
    b. way d. why

34. Please take ______ your coat.
    a. on c. of
    b. up d. off

35. Please get me a ________ milk.
    a. bottle c. bottles
    b. of bottle d. bottle of'

36. You can find the milk in ________10.
    a. Information c. Directory
    b. Section d. Piece

37. There are 16 ounces in a _______.
    a. pint c. quart
    b. pound d. kilo

38. I _________ to make an appointment.
    a. would c. 'd like
    b. will d. likes

39. Where ________ it hurt?
    a. do c. is
    b. does d. was

40. I have ________ in my left hand.
    a. some weak c. some pain
    b. some hurt d. weak

41. People can get immediate help in an ________ room.
    a. operating c. waiting
    b. emergency d. lab

42. I ________ that Vince lost his job.
    a. was hear c. heard
    b. heared d. hear

43. What did the doctor _______ to Alice?
    a. said c. told
    b. tell d. say

44. He _____ her that she had a little arthritis.
    a. said c. told
    b. tell d. say

45. Please turn left at that "one way" ______.
    a. sign c. picture
    b. signs d. directions

46. What kind of _____ does Rita's car have?
    a. standard c. equipment
    b. cylinders d. conditions

47. Her car is in excellent ________.
    a. standard c. brakes
    b. condition d. power

48. The workshop students work very ______.
    a. careful c. careless
    b. carefully d. quick

49. The students are ________ workers.
    a. careful c. carelessly
    b. carefully d. quickly

50. If you speak English "good," you don't speak English ______.
    a. will c. good
    b. very d. well

After you correct the test, calculate your grade below.

1. Write the number of correct answers in the box below.

CORRECT ANSWERS ➔ ➔ ➔ ➔ ➔ ☐

2. Multiply the number of correct answers by 2.

CORRECT ANSWER ☐ x 2 = ☐

3. Find your letter grade below.

90% to 100%	= A	(excellent)
75% to 89%	= B	(above average)
60% to 74%	= C	(average)
45% to 59%	= D	(below average)
0% to 44%	= F	(failure)

4. Write your final grade in the box below.

MY FINAL GRADE: ☐

Detailed Teaching Notes and Answer Keys, Workbook 2

Although most activities are self-explanatory, the instructor's notes give suggestions for class presentations and additional activities.

It is strongly recommended that the instructor consider the teaching suggestions in the Introduction at the beginning of this book. They contain tips and techniques that can help the students progress smoothly through each lesson. Being familiar with Workbook 1 will also help.

CHAPTER 1

PAGE 2

• Use the methodology for teaching a dialog described in the Teaching Notes. (page viii).

Answers for Understand:

1. True, 2. True, 3. We don't know. 4. True, 5. True, 6. True

PAGE 4

• Use the schedule of classes as a silent reading activity. Explain that the students must read the schedule of classes by themselves and underline all the words that they do not know.

• After the students have read the schedule of classes at least twice, discuss any new vocabulary.

• Instead of the teacher asking questions about the schedule of classes, reverse the roles and ask the students to try to stump the teacher by asking original questions.

• With the help of a student, demonstrate how to do the Practice exercise using the schedule of classes in the Read exercise, Then have the students continue by working in pairs.

• Play a game. Divide the class into two teams. Teams take turns asking original questions about the schedule of classes. If one team asks a question that the second team cannot answer, then it gets a point. If the answer is correct, then no points are given. The team with the most points wins.

PAGE 5

• Use the methodology for teaching a dialog described in the Teaching Notes. (page viii).

• With the students' books closed, practice the mini-dialogs in the Practice exercises orally with the whole class.

• Have the students open their books and continue the exercise by working in pairs or small groups.

PAGE 6

• Use the methodology for teaching a dialog described in the Teaching Notes. (page viii).

• Use the text in the balloon in the Write exercise as a silent reading comprehension exercise.

• Ask general comprehension questions about the information in the balloon.

• As a follow-up activity, instead of the teacher asking all the comprehension questions about the dialog, reverse the roles and ask the students to try to stump the teacher by asking difficult questions.

• Review the meanings of the abbreviations in the box.

• Have the students fill out the application in the write exercise by using the information in the balloon,

Answers for Understand:

1. False, 2. We don't know., 3. False, 4. True.

PAGE 7

• Read the texts in the balloons. Review the use of the final ***s*** in the third person singular of the present habitual/simple tense. (You may want to refer to Workbook 1, Chapter 5, page 82 and Chapter 6, page 95 for more detailed grammar rules.)

• Model the pronunciation of the verbs with final ***s***:

a. Add ***-es*** to verbs that end in ***s, sh, ch, z,*** and ***x***.

b. When words end in ***g*** preceded by a consonant, change the ***y*** to ***i*** and add ***-es.*** This is the same rule for forming plural nouns.

c. Add ***-s*** to most other verbs.

Examples:
She start<u>s</u> work early.
She punch<u>es</u> in at 8 a.m.
She finish<u>es</u> at 5 p.m.
She go<u>es</u> home and gets ready for school.
She stud<u>ies</u> in the evening.

• For additional exercises, refer to Workbook 1, Chapter 6, page 99.

• Explain how to fill in the words in the Write exercises at the bottom of the page. Read the directions, and do a few examples with the whole class.

Answer Key: First Write exercise:

1. lives, doesn't live; 2. rents, doesn't rent; 3. works, doesn't work

Answer Key: Second Write exercise:

1. Does, does
2. Does, doesn't
3. Does, does
4. Does, doesn't
5. Does, does

• As a follow-up activity, dictate the Write exercises as a short quiz.

PAGE 8

• Use the dialog as a silent reading activity. Explain that the students must read the text in the balloon in the Read exercise by themselves and underline all the words that they do not know.

• After the students have read the text at least twice, discuss any new vocabulary.

• Ask general comprehension questions.

• Explain how to fill in the sentences in both Write exercises as described on page 6.

Answer Key: First write exercise:

1. come, don't come	*3. live, don't live*
2. have, don't have	*4. drive, don't drive*

Answer Key: Second write exercise:

1. Does ... come, does	*4. Do ... live, don't*
2. Do ... come, don't	*5. Do ... live, do*
3. Does ... have, does	*6. Does ... drive, does*

PAGE 9

• Review the use of the present continuous tense as described on page 166 of Workbook 1.

a. Use the present continuous to describe an action that is happening now.

b. We form the present continuous with the verb to be *(am, is, are)* and the present participle *(-ing form)* of the main verb.

c. Do not use these verbs describing mental or physical conditions in the continuous: *want, like, need, know, believe, see, hear.*

• Explain how to fill in the words in the Write exercise. Read the directions and do a few examples with the whole class. Correct the exercise and have volunteers act out the dialog in front of the class.

Answer Key:

1. are...doing, 2. 'm doing, 3. are ... doing, 4. is resting, 5. is having, 6. is eating, 7. is running, 8. is helping, 9. are trying, 10. is standing, 11. is talking, 12. is telling, 13. are leaving

• As a follow-up activity, dictate a part of the Write exercise as a short quiz.

• Continue the Group Discussion activity by having the students role-play the following situations silently (without words as in a pantomime game):

a. calling a waitress or waiter
b. leaving a tip
c. how to eat correctly in a restaurant
d. asking for the bill

PAGE 10

• Review the use of object pronouns, possessive pronouns, and possessive adjectives. (Refer to pages 102 in Chapter 6 and page 179 in Chapter 13 of Workbook 1.)

• Explain how to fill in the words in the Write exercise. Read the directions and do a few examples with the whole class. Correct the exercise.

Answer Key:

1. He, 2. His, 3. him, 4. She, 5. Her, 6. her, 7. He, 8. He, 9. His, 10. him, 11. We, 12. our, 13, us

• As a follow-up activity, dictate the Write exercise as a short quiz.

PAGE 11

• Contrast the use of the past continuous and present habitual tenses.

• Explain how to fill in the words in the dialogs in the Write exercise. Read the directions and do a few examples with the whole class. Correct the exercise and have volunteers act out the dialog in front of the class.

Answer Key:

1. is working, 2. is she working, 3. works, 4. Does she like, 5. does, 6. are you reading, 7. am reading, 8. Do you like, 9. do, 10. like, 11. is he doing, 12. is looking for, 13. does he need, 14. wants, 15. are waiting, 16. are waiting, 17. Do you come, 18. do, 19. want

• As a follow-up activity, dictate the Write exercise as a short quiz.

PAGE 12

• Introduce the new vocabulary and expressions: *electronics assembler, catch a bus, take a bus, bus schedule*

• Use the methodology for teaching a dialog described in the Teaching Notes (page viii).

• Read the bus schedule at the bottom of the page.

• Teach the mini-dialog in the Practice exercise and read the bus schedule at the bottom of the page. Demonstrate how to do this activity with the help of a student, Then have the students continue the exercise by working in pairs.

• As a follow-up activity, repeat the activity above with a real bus schedule.

PAGE 13

Use the dialog as a silent reading activity. Explain that the students must read the dialog by themselves and underline all the words that they do not know. When they have finished, tell them to do the Understand exercise.

• After the students have read the dialog at least twice, discuss any new vocabulary.

• Correct and discuss the Understand exercise.

Answer Key: *1. True, 2. False*

• Have the students practice the dialog in pairs.

• Have volunteers read or act out the dialog in front of the class.

• Teach the mini-dialogs in both Practice exercises and review the names of the places in the directory. Demonstrate how to do this activity with the help of a student. Then have the students continue the exercise by working in pairs.

• Have the students alphabetize the directory in their notebooks or on another piece of paper.

• As an additional activity, have the students make a directory of a local shopping center.

PAGE 14

• Use the methodology for teaching a dialog described in the Teaching Notes. (page viii).

• Read through the application and discuss any new vocabulary.

• Instead of the teacher asking comprehension questions about the dialog, reverse the roles and ask the students to try to stump the teacher by asking difficult, original comprehension questions.

• Read through the blank application form and have the students fill it out in class. Pair up the students and have them talk about the application by practicing asking questions about their occupation.

• Before having the students fill out the application form, point out the following items that may cause confusion:

1. the meaning of Mr., Mrs., Miss, and Ms.
2. the last name preceding the first name on many forms and applications
3. the street number preceding the street name
4. apartment numbers written as #6, Apt. 6, or Apt. #6 and placed after the street name
5. telephone area codes and prefixes
6. the month as the first element of the date which is expressed either by word or number. Caution students not to use Roman numerals.
7. illegal questions: In the United States, it is against the law to ask certain questions on employment appplications (i.e., race, religion, sex, and age),

• Have the students fill in the application, then have them pair up again to practice asking questions about the information on their application.

PAGE 15

Explain how to fill in the words in the Write exercise. Read the words in the box below the picture, read the directions, and do a few examples with the whole class. Correct the exercise and have volunteers act out the dialog in front of the class.

Answer Key:
1 am, 2 Is, 3 Do, 4 do, 5 ’m, 6 do, 7 Are, 8 ’m, 9 don’t, 10 ’m, 11 can, 12 Can, 13 can, 14 ’s, 15 is.

• As a follow-up activity, dictate part of the dialog in the Write exercise as a short quiz.

• As another follow-up activity, explain the importance of the following:
a. punctuality for appointments*
b. eye contact
c. good grooming and hygiene
d. appropriate language usage
e. courtesy and polite language (both written and oral)
f. a firm handshake

**** Cultural Note: Time***

Being on time is very important to most people living in the United States. People wear watches or have a cell phone so they are not late, Most school and work schedules, business appointments, and social engagements are exact times. However, it is usually permitted to be ten or even twenty minutes late for some social invitations such as a dinner party. Professionals who meet a lot of people during the day are often not on schedule, but people arriving for a business appointment usually try to arrive a few minutes early.

PAGE 16

• Have the students pair up and put all writing material away. Stress that this is a speaking and not a writing exercise. Explain the following directions.

• Demonstrate how the students must fold the page in half where indicated.

• Tell them that they must look at only one side of the page.

• One student asks the questions and the other answers by finding the answers in the schedule.

• The students reverse roles for the second exercise. The second student must write the information that the first student will give on the identification card.

• When the students have finished, discuss the answers with the whole class and pose more questions about the schedule and identification card.

PAGE 17

• Use the Group Activity as a "mixer" exercise in which students have to talk to other students to get the necessary information. Tell the students to stand up, walk around the room, and find other students who fit the qualities described in the exercise.

• As a homework exercise, have the students find as many words as they can.

• Point out the examples with the class.

CHAPTER 2

PAGE 19

• Introduce the new vocabulary and expressions: *badge, personnel manager, once, wear, midmorning twice, legal, mid-afternoon, introduce, punch in, get a paycheck, punch out, get a raise.*

• Use the methodology for teaching a dialog described in the Teaching Notes. (page viii).

Answers for Understand:
1. True, 2. True, 3. We don't know., 4. True, 5. True, 6. True.

• As a follow-up activity, discuss official, local, state, and national holidays when people traditionally do not work. Make a list on the board as a whole class exercise.

PAGE 20

• Use the methodology for teaching grammar described in the Teaching Notes (page ix).

• Other common adverbs of frequency include *rarely, not ever, frequently,* and *occasionally.*

Direct the students to make as many correct sentences as possible using the words in the boxes in the Read exercise at the top of the page. Expand this activity by having the students compose original sentences.

• With the students' books closed, do the Practice exercise as an oral drill.

• Use the methodology for conducting oral drills in the Teaching Notes (page ix).

• Then, tell the students to open their books and repeat the drill with a partner.

Have them extend the exercise by using original phrases.

PAGE 21

• Use the methodology for teaching grammar described in the Teaching Notes (page ix).

• Other common adverbial expressions of time:

now and then	*once in a while*	*bimonthly*
every two weeks	*all the time*	*most of the time*
at no time	*several times*	*daily*
weekly	*monthly*	*yearly*
annually	*from time to time*	

• Direct the students to make as many correct sentences as possible using the words in the boxes in the Read exercise at the top of the page. Expand this activity by having the students compose original sentences.

• With the students' books closed, do the Practice exercises as an oral drills.

• Use the methodology for conducting oral drills in the Teaching Notes (page ix).

• Then, tell the students to open their books and repeat the drill with a partner.

Have them extend the exercise by using original phrases.

PAGE 22

• Read through Carmen's calendar at the top of the page. Then, with the help of a student, demonstrate how to do the Practice exercises using the calendar in the Read exercise at the top of the page. Have the students continue by working in pairs.

PAGE 23

Introduce the new vocabulary and expressions:

wet	*weather*	*cool*	*clear*
terrible	*rain*	*wind*	*winter*
storm	*hard*	*warm*	*sunny*
nice	*snow*	*smoggy*	*degree*
season	*summer*	*daytime*	*cloudy*
favorite	*Fahrenheit*	*foggy*	*centigrade*

• Use the methodology for teaching a dialog described in the Teaching Notes. (page viii).

Answers for Understand: *1. False, 2. True, 3. True, 4. True*

• Have the students do the Challenge as a homework exercise using the formula provided at the bottom of the page. The answer is about l7 degrees C.

• As a follow-up exercise, bring a real thermometer to school and check it every day at the beginning of the class for at least a week.

PAGE 24

• Examine the picture of the thermometer at the top of the page. Centigrade is shown to the right and Fahrenheit to the left.

• Quiz the students by asking questions about the thermometer. Practice finding the equivalent degrees by looking across the thermometer.

• Read through the questions in the questionnaire. Then tell the students to fill it out as homework.

• On the following day, discuss the answers to the questionnaire.

Answer Key:

1. answers will vary	*8. hot*
2. about 72 degrees F.	*9. warm*
3. answers will vary	*10. cool*
4. answers will vary	*11. cold*
5. answers will vary	*12. freezing*
6. 96.6 degrees F.	*13. about 61 degrees F.*
7. yes	

• With the help of a student, demonstrate how to do the Practice exercise using the thermometer in the Read exercise. Then have the students continue by working in pairs.

PAGE 25

• Read the weather report at the top of the page with the whole class. Practice the pronunciation of the names of the cities. Find the cities on the map below the weather report. (Use a large wall map if available.)

• With the help of a student, demonstrate how to do the Practice exercises using the weather forecast in the Read exercise. Then have the students continue by working in pairs.

• As an extension of the Challenge exercise, repeat the Practice exercises by using an actual weather report from your local newspaper.

• As a follow-up map activity, have the students name the states in which the cities in the weather report are found.

• Inexpensive commercially available map puzzles of the United States are an excellent supplement to this lesson.

PAGE 26

• Introduce the new vocabulary and expressions:

able	*percent*	*necessary*
important	*department*	*dangerous*
circuit board	*train (verb)*	*pass inspection*
try	*throw away*	*fix*
parts	*send*	*interesting*
possible	*electronics*	*challenging*
easy	*shipping*	

• Use the dialog as a silent reading activity. Explain that the students must read the dialog by themselves and underline all the words that they do not know. When they have finished, tell them to do the Understand exercise at the bottom of the page.

• After the students have read the dialog at least twice, discuss and read it aloud. Discuss any additional vocabulary.

• Correct and discuss the Understand exercise.

Answer Key: *1. True, 2. True, 3. False, 4. False, 5. False*

• Instead of the teacher asking comprehension questions about the dialog, play a game, Divide the class into two teams. Teams take turns asking difficult questions about the dialog. If one team asks a question that the second team cannot answer, then it gets a point. If the answer is correct, then no points are given. The team with the most points wins.

PAGE 27

• Use the methodology for teaching grammar described in the Teaching Notes (page ix).

• Direct the students to make as many correct sentences as possible using the words in the boxes in the Read exercise in the middle of the page. Expand this activity by having the students compose original sentences.

• Explain how to make negative prefixes in the Word Building exercise.

• Direct the students to make as many correct sentences as possible using the words in the boxes in the Read exercise at the bottom of the page. Expand this activity by having the students compose original sentences.

PAGE 28

• Read and discuss the short dialog in the Read exercise at the top of the page.

• Talk about the students' or the students', friends' and relatives' experiences in finding a job in this country.

• With the students' books closed, do the Practice exercise as an oral drill.

• Use the methodology for conducting oral drills in the Teaching Notes (page ix).

• Then, tell the students to open their books and repeat the drill with a partner.

• Have them extend the exercise by using original phrases.

• Have students break up into small groups and do the exercise in the Group Discussion. Then bring the whole class back together to discuss various answers.

• As a follow-up activity, ask for volunteers to go to the front of the class to be interviewed by the whole class.

• Tell the students to use the structures in the Practice and Discussion exercises as models.

PAGE 29

• Read the dialog in the Read exercise at the top of the page. Point out the uses of *enough* and *too*.

• Use the methodology for teaching grammar described in the Teaching Notes (page ix).

• Direct the students to make as many correct sentences as possible using the words in the boxes in the Read exercise at the bottom of the page. Expand this activity by having the students compose original sentences.

PAGE 30

• Read the words below the pictures and practice the mini-dialog in the Practice exercise. Next, show how to do this exercise with the help of a student. Practice the activity until the students understand what to do. Then tell the students to continue the exercise by working in pairs.

• Explain how to fill in the words in the Write exercise. Read the words in the box at the beginning of the exercise, read the directions, and do a few examples with the whole class. Correct the exercise and have volunteers act out the dialog in front of the class.

Answer Key:

1. always	*5. usually*
2. never	*6. too expensive*
3. hours a day	*7. twice a month*
4. twice a day	*8. once a year*

• As a follow-up activity, dictate the Write exercise as a short quiz.

PAGE 31

• Explain how to put the sentences in the Write exercise in the correct order. Read the directions and do a few examples with the whole class. Correct the exercise and have volunteers act out the dialog in front of the class.

Answer Key: *8, 5, 2, 9, 3, 7, 4, 1, 6*

• Use the methodology for doing a dictation described in the Teaching Notes (page xi).

PAGE 32

Have the students pair up and put all writing material away. Stress that this is a speaking and not a writing exercise. Explain the following directions.

• Demonstrate how the students must fold the page in half where indicated.

• Tell them that they must look at only one side of the page.

• One student asks the questions and the other answers by finding the answers in the picture.

• The students reverse roles for the second exercise.

• When the students have finished, discuss the answers with the whole class and pose more questions about the temperature chart and the thermometer.

• As a follow-up or homework activity, have the students complete the exercise in writing.

PAGE 33

• Read the rules in the Word Building box at the top of the page. Then slowly read the examples. Point out the additional rules in the footnote at the bottom of the box.

• Explain the directions of the first Write exercise. Do a few examples with the whole class.

Answer Key:

1. snowy	*4. foggy*	*7. stormy*
2. icy	*5. smoggy*	*8. cloudy*
3. hazy	*6. windy*	*9. rainy*

• Explain the directions for the last Write exercise at the bottom of the page.

• Have the students write complete sentences. Do a few examples with the whole class.

Answer Key:

1. It's a rainy day.	*5. It's a snowy day.*
2. It's a cloudy day.	*6. It's a smoggy day.*
3. It's a sunny day.	*7. It's a windy day.*
4. It's a foggy day,	*8. It's an icy day.*

• As a follow-up activity, have the students use the words above in original sentences describing the weather in your area at different times of the year.

CHAPTER 3

PAGE 35

• Introduce the new vocabulary and expressions:

take out	*garbage*	*have to*
go out with	*skills*	*really hard*
part-time	*if*	*Don't you want ...?*
interview	*I guess so.*	

• Use the methodology for teaching a dialog described in the Teaching Notes. (page viii).

Answers for Understand:
1. False, 2. False, 3. We don't know., 4. False, 5. True

• Have students underline ***have to*** and ***has to*** whenever they appear in the dialog.

PAGE 36

• Use the methodology for teaching grammar described in the Teaching Notes (page ix).

• Direct the students to make as many correct sentences as possible using the words in the boxes in the Read exercise at the top of the page. Expand this activity by having the students compose original sentences.

• Have the students write questions and answers at the bottom of the page.

• As a group discussion, ask for volunteers to write their question the board. Discuss them and have other volunteers write the answers.

PAGE 37

• With the students' books closed, do the Practice exercises as an oral drills.

• Use the methodology for conducting oral drills in the Teaching Notes (page ix).

• Then, tell the students to open their books and repeat the drills with a partner.

• Have them extend the exercise by using original phrases.

PAGE 38

• Introduce the new vocabulary and expressions: *decide, soon, plans, counselor, medicine, engineer.*

• Use the methodology for teaching a dialog described in the Teaching Notes. (page viii).

• Read and model the pronunciation of the careers and subjects below the dialog. Then, help the students learn the careers and the corresponding subjects by drilling with flash cards. Expand this exercise by helping the students list on the blackboard additional subjects for each career.

Answers for Understand: *1. False, 2. True, 3. We don't know.*

• With the help of a student, demonstrate how to do the Practice exercise using the list of careers and subjects in the Read exercise. Then have the students continue by working in pairs.

PAGE 39

• Use the methodology for teaching a dialog described in the Teaching Notes. (page viii).

• With the help of a student, demonstrate how to do the Practice exercise. Then have the students continue by working in pairs.

• Use the page from the appointment book as a silent reading activity. Explain that the students must read the information by themselves and underline all the words that they do not know.

• Discuss any new vocabulary.

• Instead of the teacher asking comprehension questions about the page from the appointment book, play a game. Divide the class into two teams. Teams take turns asking difficult questions with have to about the information on the page. If one team asks a question that the second team cannot answer, then it gets a point. If the answer is correct, then no points are given. The team with the most points wins.

• With the help of a student, demonstrate how to do the Practice exercise using the appointment book in the Read exercise. Then have the students continue by working in pairs.

PAGE 39

• Introduce the new vocabulary and expressions:

in order to	*attend*	*UCLA*
average	*special*	*grades*
take a test	*pass a test*	

• Use the methodology for teaching a dialog described in the Teaching Notes. (page viii).

Answers for Understand:
1. We don't know. 2. True, 3. False, 4. False, 5. False

PAGE 41

• Use the methodology for teaching grammar described in the Teaching Notes (page ix).

• You may want to expand this Grammar section by contrasting the uses of *because, to (in order to),* and *for.*

• Note that a sentence follows *because*, a noun or gerund follows *for*, and a verb follows *to*.

Example:
Why did you go to a restaurant?
<u>Because</u> I wanted to eat dinner.
<u>For</u> dinner.
<u>To</u> eat dinner.

• Have the students ask one another personalized questions. Some examples:

Why do you go to the library, hairdresser, drugstore?
Why do you sleep, eat, exercise, study, read?
Why do people work, save money?
Why do you wear shoes, a watch, glasses, a coat?
Why do we have police, fire-fighters, doctors, friends?
Why do we need laws, the media, phones, books?

• You may want to practice the structure *What ... for?* which is commonly used in conversation.

Example: <u>What</u> did you go to the restaurant <u>for</u>?

• *How come?* is often used in conversation. Students should at least have a passive recognition of this form.

• Note that *how come* does not take the normal question pattern. Compare: *How come you went home?* and *Why did you go home?*

• Direct the students to make as many correct sentences as possible using the words in the boxes in the Read exercise. Expand this activity by having the students compose original sentences.

• With the students' books closed, do the Practice exercise as an oral drill.

• Use the methodology for conducting oral drills in the Teaching Notes (page ix).

• Then, tell the students to open their books and repeat the drill with a partner.

• Have them extend the exercise by using original phrases.

PAGE 42

• Read the dialog in the Read section and point out the use of *to (in order to).*

• With the students' books closed, practice the mini-dialog in the Practice orally with the whole class.

• Repeat the dialog by substituting the objects found in the pictures.

• Have the students open their books. Review the vocabulary in the box at the beginning of the Practice exercise and identify the items in the pictures. Tell the students to repeat the exercise by working in pairs. Encourage the students to expand the exercise by using original phrases.

PAGE 43

• Introduce the new vocabulary and expressions:

tired	*enroll*	*find*	*fast*
widower	*stay with*	*relatives*	*sure*

• Use the methodology for teaching a dialog described in the Teaching Notes. (page viii).

Answers for Understand:
1. False, 2. True, 3. True, 4. We don't know., 5. True

• Have the students underline the word ***so*** wherever it appears in the dialog.

PAGE 44

• Use the methodology for teaching grammar described in the Teaching Notes (page ix).

• Show the students how to make as many correct sentences as possible using the words in the box in the Read exercise. Expand this activity by having the students compose original sentences.

• With the students' books closed, do the Practice exercise as an oral drill.

• Use the methodology for conducting oral drills in the Teaching Notes (page ix).

• Then, tell the students to open their books and repeat the drill with a partner.

• Have them extend the exercise by using original phrases.

PAGE 45

• Explain how to fill in the appointment book in the Write exercise with sentences containing ***have to*** and ***don't have to***. Read the directions and do a few examples with the whole class.

• Compare the answers and have volunteers write some of the best ones on the board.

• With the help of a student, demonstrate how to do the Practice exercises using the Appointment Book in the Write exercises or the students' list on the board. Then have the students continue by working in pairs.

PAGE 46

• Explain how to put the sentences in the Write exercise in the correct order. Read the directions and do a few examples with the whole class. Correct the exercise and have volunteers act out the dialog in front of the class.

Answer Key: *6, 2, 9, 1, 4, 10, 5, 7, 3, 8*

• Use the methodology for doing a dictation described in the Teaching Notes (page xi).

PAGE 47

• Have the students pair up and explain the following directions.

• Demonstrate how the students must fold the page in half where indicated.

• Tell them that they must look at only one side of the page.

• One student asks the questions and the other answers by finding the answers on the school report card.

• The students reverse roles for the second exercise.

• Now the second student must write what he/she has to do at the time the first student tells him/her.

• When the students have finished, discuss the answers with the whole class and pose more questions about the report card and list of things to do.

• As a follow-up or homework activity, have the students complete the first exercise in writing.

PAGE 48

• Read the rules and examples in the word Building at the top of the page.

Ask the students to identify other words that follow the rule, and write them on the board, Some words:

manager	*builder*	*programmer*
swimmer	*reporter*	*painter*
teacher	*reader*	*waiter*
writer	*driver*	*speaker*
worker	*learner*	*runner*

Explain how to fill in the words in the Write exercise. Read the directions and do a few examples with the whole class.

As a follow-up activity, dictate the Write exercise as a short quiz.

Read through the other suffixes in the second Word Building exercise, then have the students write as many occupations that they can find using the suffixes in the first Challenge exercise.

Use the second Challenge exercise as a group activity. Tell the students to stand up, walk around the room, and ask other students in the class for their occupation.

After the students have gathered their information, discuss the different occupations, have volunteers write them on the board, and drill the correct pronunciation of each.

CHAPTER 4

PAGE 51

• Introduce the new vocabulary and expressions:

going to	*birthday*	*golf*	*toy*
party	*afterwards*	*picnic*	

• Use the methodology for teaching a dialog described in the Teaching Notes. (page viii).

Answers for Understand:

1. We don't know, 2. We don't know., 3. True, 4. True, 5. False

• Have the students underline all the verbs in the present continuous tense in the dialog.

PAGE 52

• Use the methodology for teaching grammar described in the Teaching Notes (page ix).

• You might want to use some of the following expressions of time in some of the exercises in this chapter:

tomorrow	in a while
tomorrow morning	the week after next
tomorrow afternoon	the after tomorrow
tomorrow night	a week from today
next week	a week from tomorrow
next month	after school/class
next year	after work
next Saturday	soon
next summer	later
in fifteen minutes	after breakfast
in a few minutes	after lunch
in an hour	after dinner
in a day or two	after supper

• Direct the students to make as many correct sentences as possible using the words in the box in the Read exercise. Expand this activity by having the students compose original sentences.

With the students' books closed, do the Practice exercise as an oral drill.

• Use the methodology for conducting oral drills in the Teaching Notes (page ix).

• Then, tell the students to open their books and repeat the drill with a partner.

Have them extend the exercise by using original phrases.

PAGE 53

• Introduce the new vocabulary and expressions:

everything	*will*	*won't*	*million*
housework	*get ready for*	*make a cake*	*busy*
clean up	*make dinner*		

• Use the methodology for teaching a dialog described in the Teaching Notes. (page viii).

Answers for Understand:

1. True, 2, False, 3. We don't know., 4. We don't know., 5. False 6. True

• Have the students underline ***will, won't,*** and ***'ll*** in the dialog.

PAGE 54

• Use the methodology for teaching grammar described in the Teaching Notes (page ix).

• You may also want to show that won't is also used to express the idea of refusal such as *"I won't eat liver!"* Also point out that *will* is followed by the verb and not the infinitive. Contrast *"He will drive a car."* with *"He wants to drive a car."*

• In some English speaking countries *shall* is used instead of will with the pronouns *I* and *we*. In the United States, the use of shall is limited to questions such as *"Shall we go?" or "Shall we dance?"* in which the speaker seeks agreement or concurrence .

• Direct the students to make as many correct sentences as possible using the words in the boxes in the Read exercise. Expand this activity by having the students compose original sentences.

PAGE 55

• Practice the short dialog in the Read exercise with the students. Stress the use of *maybe*.

• Read the names of the items in the pictures and practice the mini-dialog in the Practice, Next, show how to do this exercise with the help of a student. Practice the activity until the students understand what to do.

• Then tell the students to continue the exercise by working in pairs.

• Practice the short dialog in the second Read exercise, Stress the use of *"I'll take it."* and *"That'll be $...."*

• Use the same methodology described for doing the Practice exercise at the top of the page.

PAGE 56

• Practice the short dialog in the Read exercise at the top of the page. Stress the use of *"He'll be...."*

• Teach the mini-dialog in the first Practice exercise. Then demonstrate how to do this activity with the help of a student. Have the students continue the exercise by working in pairs.

• Practice the short dialog in the second Read exercise. Identify the items in the pictures and practice the mini-dialog in the Practice exercise at the bottom of the page. Next, show how to do this exercise with the help of a student. Practice the activity until the students understand what to do. Then tell the students to continue the exercise by working in pairs.

• Discuss the questions in the Group Discussion. You may want to contrast what is culturally acceptable in the United States with other cultures.

PAGE 57

• As a homework assignment, have the students fill in the diary in the Write exercise at the top of the page.

• On the following day, correct the Write exercise by having individuals write their answers on the board.

• Use the methodology for teaching a dialog described in the Teaching Notes. (page viii).

• Teach the birthday song.

Answers for Understand: *1. We don't know., 2. False, 3. True*

PAGE 58

• Use the Read exercise as a silent reading activity. Explain that the students must read the itinerary by themselves and underline all the words that they do not know.

• After the students have read the itinerary at least twice, discuss any new vocabulary.

• As a follow-up activity, instead of the teacher asking comprehension questions about the itinerary, reverse the roles and ask the students to try to stump the teacher by asking difficult questions.

• Expand the activity by having the students label the locations of the cities that Betty will visit on the map below the itinerary. Use a wall map.

• With the help of a student, demonstrate how to do the Practice exercise using the itinerary in the Read exercise. Then have the students continue by working in pairs.

• Have the students repeat the Practice exercise by having them substitute *you* and *I* with *she*.

PAGE 59

• Use the methodology for teaching grammar described in the Teaching Notes (page ix).

• Practice the mini-dialogs in the Practice exercises and read the words below the pictures. Next, show how to do this exercise with the help of a student. Practice the activity until the students understand what to do. Then tell the students to continue the exercise by working in pairs.

• You may want to expand this section by teaching a lesson on basic word order. English word order usually follows the pattern below.

SUBJECT	VERB	OBJECT	LOCATION	MEANS	TIME
Betty	bought	it	downtown		yesterday.
Nancy	will travel		to Boston	by bus	next month.
She	sent	it	to Miami	by plane	on Tuesday.

• Expressions of time and expressions of location are sometimes placed at the beginning of the sentence for emphasis or style.

• When two expressions of time or location appear in the same sentence, the word order progresses from specific to general (e.g., at 8 o'clock in the morning; in San Juan, Puerto Rico).

• Drill correct word order. In order to insure that essential word-order combinations are elicited, ask the following types of questions:

How can you go to [place]?
When did you go to [place]?
How and when will you go to [place]?

• Continue drilling by asking personalized questions beginning with *"Where and when did / do / will you....?"*

• The following vocabulary may be useful in formulating such questions:

eat (lunch)	*study meet (Tony)*
play (football)	*speak to (Kim)*
speak (English)	*break your (arm)*
get married	*find (the money)*
do your shopping	*do your homework*
buy your (coat)	*see (Mary)*
mail (the letter)	

• Additional expressions of time, means of transportation, and location may be used to expand the lesson. Note the use of the prepositions and articles in the examples below.

downstairs/upstairs	at lunch
outside/inside	on [day/date/holiday]
here/there	in [month,season/year]
to school/class	on one's birthday
t0 bed	by taxi/cab
to church	by subway
to jail/prison	by jet
to the market/bank	by helicopter
in the afternoon/evening	by boat
at night	by train
at noon/midnight	By motorcycle
at break	on foot

• For further practice, scramble the word order of a sentence. Then have the students write the sentences in the correct order.

PAGE 60

• Introduce the new vocabulary and expressions:

going to	*lake*	*bring*	*meat*
drinks	*salads*	*desserts*	*plates*
paper goods	*cups*	*tablecloth*	*napkins*
plastic utensils			

• Use the methodology for teaching a dialog described in the Teaching Notes. (page viii).

Answers for Understand:
1. False, 2. True, 3. True, 4. False, 5. We don't know., 6. True

PAGE 61

• Use the methodology for teaching grammar described in the Teaching Notes (page ix).

• You may want to review the lesson on going to in Workbook 1, pages 173 and 174.

• Direct the students to make as many correct sentences as possible using the words in the box in the Read exercise. Expand this activity by having the students compose original sentences.

• With the help of a student, demonstrate how to do the Practice exercises. Then have the students continue by working in pairs.

PAGE 62

• Read the names of the people, and identify the food items on the picnic list in the Read & Listen exercise at the top of the page.

• With the help of a student, demonstrate how to do the Practice exercises using the picnic list in the Read exercise. Then have the students continue by working in pairs.

PAGE 63

Explain how to fill in the sentences in the Write exercise. Read the directions and do a few examples with the whole class. Correct the exercise and have volunteers act out the dialog in front of the class.

Answer Key:
1. They are going to eat.
2. She's going to fill it.
3. She's going to go swimming.
4. He's going to drink.
5. He's going to stop eating.
6 & 7. Answers will vary.

PAGE 64

• Explain how to fill in the words in the Write exercise. Read the directions and do a few examples with the whole class. Correct the exercise and have volunteers act out the dialog in front of the class.

Answer Key:
4. want, 5. want, will, 6. will, 7. want, 8. want, 9. won't, 10. Will, 11. want, 12. want, 13. Will, 14. will, 15. won't, 16. want, 17. will

• As a follow-up activity, dictate the Write exercise as a short quiz.

PAGE 65

• As a homework assignment, have the students write what they are going to do next week, Read the directions and write a few examples with the whole class.

• On the following day, correct the Write exercise by having individuals write some of their sentences on the board.

• Have the volunteers write their names next to their sentences.

• Instead of the teacher asking comprehension questions about the information on the board, play a game, Divide the class into two teams, Teams take turns asking difficult questions about the sentences on the board. If one team asks a question that the second team cannot answer, then it gets a point. If the answer is correct, then no points are given. The team with the most points wins.

• With the help of a student, demonstrate how to do the Practice exercise using the list of activities in the Write exercise at the top of the page. Then have the students continue by working in pairs.

• On a subsequent day, dictate some of the sentences that the students wrote the board as a surprise quiz.

PAGE 66

• Explain how to put the sentences in the Write exercise in the correct order. Read the directions and do a few examples with the whole class. Correct the exercise and have volunteers act out the dialog in front of the class.

Answer Key: *6, 3, l, 7, 2*

• Use the methodology for doing a dictation described in the Teaching Notes (page xi).

PAGE 67

• You might want to have a wall map of the U.S. for this activity.

• Read through the name of the states and have the students repeat the names after you. Stress the pronunciation as many are difficult to say.

• Tell the students to write the number of the state in front of the corresponding name of the state.

• Expand the activity by having a general discussion about the geography, history, and different cultures and accents found in the U.S.A.

Answer Key:

19 Alabama	27 Louisiana	18 Ohio
50 Alaska	1 Maine	33 Oklahoma
42 Arizona	9 Maryland	47 Oregon
28 Arkansas	4 Massachusetts	11 Pennsylvania
46 California	23 Michigan	5 Rhode Island
39 Colorado	31 Minnesota	11 South Carolina
6 Connecticut	24 Mississippi	36 South Dakota
8 Delaware	29 Missouri	20 Tennessee
19 Florida	41 Montana	32Texas
15 Georgia	35 Nebraska	43 Utah
49 Hawaii	45 Nevada	2 Vermont
44 Idaho	3 New Hampshire	12 Virginia
25 Illinois	7 New Jersey	48 Washington
22 Indiana	38 New Mexico	17 West Virginia
30 Iowa	10 New York	26 Wisconsin
34 Kansas	13 North Carolina	40 Wyoming
21 Kentucky	37 North Dakota	

• Read the names of the major cities found on the second map. Have the students repeat the names after you. Again, stress correct pronunciation.

• With the help of a student, show how to do the Practice exercise. Then, let the students work in pairs.

• Challenge exercise: Tell the students to plan a trip using the map in the Practice exercise. Read the directions and let the students work in small groups.

• Ask for volunteers to answer questions about their trip routes.

PAGE 68

• Have the students address the envelope and answer Betty's questions from the Dictation on the previous page. Explain the following:

1. In English-speaking countries, domestic addresses are traditionally written in the following order:

Line 1: person or name of company
Line 2: street number, street name, apartment number
Line 3: city, state or province, zip or postal code

2. Make students aware of the current domestic and international postal rates.

• On the board, list the abbreviations below. Drill for pronunciation. Allow the students sufficient time to study the list. Then erase the non-abbreviated forms. Divide the class into two teams. Alternately have one member of a team come to the board. Select a word from the list of abbreviations and tell the student to write the word beside the corresponding abbreviation. For each correct answer, give one point to the appropriate team. Insist on complete accuracy including spelling and capitalization.

#	*number*	*Jr.*	*junior*
Apt.	*apartment*	*Ln.*	*lane*
Ave.	*avenue*	*N.*	*north St.*
Blvd.	*boulevard*	*P.O.*	*Post Office*
CA	*California*	*Pl.*	*place*
Cir.	*circle*	*Rd.*	*road*
Co.	*company, county*	*Rm.*	*room*
Ct.	*court*	*S.*	*South*
DC	*District of Columbia*	*St.*	*street*
Dr.	*doctor*	*Ste.*	*suite*
Dr.	*drive*	*TX*	*Texas*
E.	*east*	*W.*	*west*
Hwy.	*highway*		

• Two-letter postal codes for states are not technically abbreviations. Therefore, CA for California and TX for Texas are not followed by periods.

• On a subsequent day, have the students bring a post card or envelope to school. Have them prepare a message, and then address and mail the card or letter.

• Cultural Note: Make students aware of the street address patterns used in your city. In many English-speaking countries, cities are usually organized in blocks. Each block generally contains one hundred addresses. Odd numbers are used on one side of the street and even numbers on the other side. Some cities such as Washington, D.C., utilize a grid system dividing the city into N.E., N.W., S.E., and S.W.

PAGE 69

• Have the students pair up and explain the following directions.

• Demonstrate how the students must fold the page in half where indicated.

• Tell them that they must look at only one side of the page.

• One student asks the questions and the other answers by finding the in the picture.

• The students reverse roles for the second exercise.

• For the second part of the exercise, one student writes what he/she is going to do at the time the other student indicates.

• When the students have finished, discuss the answers with the whole class and pose more questions about the itinerary and list of activities.

• As a follow-up or homework activity, have the students complete the first part of the exercise in writing.

PAGE 70

• Read the rules in the box at the top of the page. Then slowly read the words below the pictures. Tell the students to pay attention to the double consonant combinations in each word. Read the words a second time.

• Model the words again and have the students repeat each word several times.

• Encourage students to think of other words that contain the double consonant combination, Make a list on the board.

• Explain the directions for the Write exercise at the bottom of the page. Then have the students fill in the missing letters. Do a few examples with the whole class.

Answer Key:
1. I will call the boss and tell him to fill all the tall wine glasses.
2, Dolls and balls sell well in the fall.
3. Please clean off the mess on the wall across from the bell in the hall.

• Have students try to make "crazy" sentences using as many of the words in the lesson above as possible. Ask for volunteers to write their sentences on the board.

• As a follow-up activity, have the students use the words above in original sentences.
• As a dictionary activity have the students find the missing words in the Challenge exercise.

Answer Key: *1. off, 2. staff, 3. off, 4. cliff*

CHAPTER 5

PAGE 72

Introduce the new vocabulary and expressions: *were, was, fantastic, how long, wonderful, That's too bad.*

• Use the methodology for teaching a dialog described in the Teaching Notes. (page viii).

Answers for Understand:
1. False, 2. True, 3. True, 4. True, 5. False, 6. We don't know.

Have the students underline ***was, were, wasn't,*** and ***weren't*** in the dialog.

PAGE 73

• Use the methodology for teaching grammar described in the Teaching Notes (page ix).

• Teach a short lesson on describing emotions. Have the students explain how they feel when the following things happen. Have the students use the structure ***"I feel [emotion] when...."*** Some emotions are as follows: *happy, nervous, afraid, sad, excited, embarrassed, bored, lonely.*

hear about an accident	*see a mouse*
give a speech	*meet new people*
make a mistake	*go to a wedding*
get a letter from home	*see a horror film*
go on vacation alone	*see a comedy*
see an old friend	*say goodbye to an old friend*
win money	*find money*
dance	*see a movie 10 times*
hear a bad singer	*forget someone's name*
cry	*attend the first day of school*

• Direct the students to make as many correct sentences as possible using the words in the boxes in the Read exercise. Expand this activity by having the students compose original sentences.

PAGE 74

• Practice the mini-dialogs in the Practice exercise and read the vocabulary below the pictures, Next, show how to do this exercise with the help of a student. Practice the activity until the students understand what to do. Then tell the students to continue the exercises by working in pairs.

PAGE 75

Read the dialog in the Read exercise at the top of the page. Then have the students identify and label the items in the picture. (Tell the students that they may refer to the correct spelling in the list of words in the Practice exercise below the picture.)

• With the help of a student, demonstrate how to do the Practice exercise using the items in the picture in the Read exercise. Then have the students continue by working in pairs.

• Explain how to fill in the questions in the Write exercise. Read the directions and do a few examples with the whole class. Correct the exercise and have volunteers act out the dialog in front of the class.

Answer Key: *(Answers will vary slightly.)*
1. Were you at the picnic?
2. How was the weather?
3. Were all the students there?
4. Was David there?
5. Was Carmen there, too?
6. Why weren't you there?

• As a follow-up activity, dictate the Write exercise as a short quiz.

PAGE 76

• Introduce the new vocabulary and expressions: *overtime, complicated, again, confusing, surprise, quiz*

• Use the methodology for teaching a dialog described in the Teaching Notes. (page viii).

Answers for Understand: *1. True, 2, False, 3. True, 4. True.*

• Practice the mini-dialog in the Practice exercise and read the vocabulary below the pictures. Next, show how to do this exercise with the help of a student. Practice the activity until the students understand what to do. Then tell the students to continue the exercise by working in pairs.

PAGE 77

• Explain how to match the sentences in the write exercise. Read the directions and do a few examples with the whole class. Correct the exercise on the board.

Answer Key: 1-e, 2-d, 3-a, 4-c, 5-b

• Review the vocabulary in the box in the Write exercise, and read through the questions in the questionnaire. Tell students to fill out the questionnaire as a homework assignment.

• On the following day, discuss the answers to the questionnaire by having volunteers write their answers on the board.

PAGE 78

• Introduce the new vocabulary and expressions: *principal, equipment, robbery, officer, police, department, security guard, to report, on duty*

• Use the methodology for teaching a dialog described in the Teaching Notes. (page viii).

Answers for Understand:
1. We don't know., 2. We don't know., 3. False, 4. True

• Explain how to fill in the words in the Write exercise. Read the directions and do a few examples with the whole class. Correct the exercise and have volunteers act out the dialog in front of the class.

Answer Key:
1. was, 2. was, 3. wasn't, 4. was, 5. was, 6. was, 7. Was, 8. weren't.

• As a follow-up activity, dictate the Write exercise as a short quiz.

PAGE 79

• Read the short dialog and the vocabulary in the picture at the top of the page.

• Have students identify which objects are missing in the second picture. Make a list of all the missing items on the board.

• At this point, you may want to review the use of common prepositions. Try the following activity.

• Draw a simple picture consisting of a room containing a table, door, and a window on the board. Then have the class tell you or a student volunteer (who might have better drawing skills) what items to add to the picture and where to place them. Tell the students to use the vocabulary in the lesson and some of the following prepositions:

in front of	*between*	*outside*
to the right of	*inside*	*next to*
above	*behind*	*under*
beside	*over*	*on*
in back of	*on top of*	*across from*
to the left of	*in*	*below*

• Model a few examples such as:

Please draw a computer on the table.
Please draw a printer next to the computer.

• After a sufficient number of prepositions and vocabulary items have been used, reverse the exercise by having the students tell you (Or another student) what to erase. Model the examples:

Please erase the printer (that's) next to the computer.
Please erase the computer (that's) on the table.

• This is an effective way to subtly introduce and drill the relative pronoun ***that***.

• With the help of a student, demonstrate how to do the Practice exercise using the pictures in the Read exercise. Then have the students continue by working in pairs.

PAGE 80

• With the help of a student, demonstrate how to do the Practice exercise using the pictures in the Read exercise on the previous page. Then have the students continue by working in pairs.

• Explain how to unscramble the sentences in the write exercise. Read the directions and do a few examples with the whole class. Correct the exercise and have volunteers act out the dialog in front of the class.

Answer Key:
2. What kind of information do you have?
3. There was a strange man behind the school last night.
4. What time was he there?
5. He was there at about eleven p.m.
6. How do you know this?
7. I can see the school from my bedroom window.
9. Sure, I'll know him.
10. Thanks for your help.

• As a follow-up activity, dictate the Write exercise as a short quiz.

PAGE 81

• Read the short dialog at the top of the page.

• Explain how to fill in the words in the Write exercise. Read the directions and do a few examples with the whole class. Correct the exercise and have volunteers act out the dialog in front of the class.

Answer Key:
1. were, 2. was, 3. Were, 4. were, 5. Were, 6. weren't, 7. were, 8. were, 9. wasn't, 10. was, 11. was

• As a follow-up activity, dictate the Write exercise as a short quiz.

• Read the short dialog at the bottom of the page.

• As a follow-up activity, try the following role play.

• Tell the students that you are a detective conducting an investigation. Tell them that they have to answer your questions. Question individuals as to where they were at a specific time. For example, ask:

When were you at the bank?
When was the last time you were at the bank?
Where were you at midnight?
Where were you on Friday night?

PAGE 82

• Have the students pair up and put all writing material away. Stress that this is a speaking and not a writing exercise. Explain the following directions.

• Demonstrate how the students must fold the page in half where indicated.

• Tell them that they must look at only one side of the page.

One student asks the questions and the other answers by finding the in the picture.

• The students reverse roles for the second exercise.

• When the students have finished, discuss the answers with the whole class and pose more questions about the picture of the office and information in the appointment book.

• As a follow-up or homework activity, have the students complete the exercise in writing.

PAGE 83

• Explain that we make the ***w*** sound with the lips rounded and the tongue high and back at the beginning of the sound. It's voiced. We make the ***v*** sound by the upper teeth touching the lower lip.

• Slowly read the words below the pictures. Tell the students to pay attention to the ***w*** and ***v*** sounds that are underlined in each word. Read the words a second time.

• Model the words again and have the students repeat each word several times.

• Encourage students to think of other words that contain ***w*** and ***v*** sounds. Make a list on the board. Then, have the students use these words in original sentences.

• Practiced the pronunciation of the lists of words in the Practice exercise. If they are unfamiliar with any of the words, have the students use a dictionary, a computer, or their smart phone to look up the meanings.

• Ask the students to make complete sentences with the words in the Practice exercise.

• Explain the directions for the write exercise at the bottom of the page. Then have the students fill in the missing letters. Do a few examples with the whole class.

Answer Key:
1. Why were you with that woman for five weeks on your vacation?
2. How will the weather be on November eleventh and twelfth?
3. He works very well without visits from lawyers.
4. Those seven women will visit his wife every Wednesday.
5. We want you to open the west window in the evening.

• Practice the pronunciation of these sentences.

• Challenge the students to make "crazy" sentences using words containing ***v*** or ***w***. Use the sentences in the Write exercise as models. Have volunteers write their sentences on the board to practice pronunciation.

CHAPTER 6

PAGE 85

• Introduce the new vocabulary and expressions: *attend, try, pick up, laugh, improved, stay, happen, drop, joke, great, earn, use, spill, wait, extra, kind, wipe off, until, decide, mix, terrible, dry, skill, enough, guys, repaint*

• Use the methodology for teaching a dialog described in the Teaching Notes. (page viii).

Answers for Understand:
1. True, 2, True, 3. True, 4, We don't know., 5. False

PAGE 86

• Use the methodology for teaching grammar described in the Teaching Notes (page ix).

• Direct the students to make as many correct sentences as possible using the words in the boxes in the Read exercise, Expand this activity by having the students compose original sentences.

PAGE 87

• Read the rules in the box at the top of the page. Then slowly read the words below the pictures. Tell the students to pay attention to the endings of each word. Read the words a second time.

• Model the words again and have the students repeat each word several times.

• Model the words in the Read exercise and have the students repeat each word.

• Have volunteers read rows and ask the class to check which words if any were mispronounced. Let students try to correct the mistakes.

• Repeat the exercise by having students make complete sentences with the words in the lists. (Challenge exercise at the bottom of the page.)

• Encourage students to think of other regular past tense verbs. Make a list of them on the board and repeat items in the steps above.

• For future practice, write the words in the Read exercise and any new words on flash cards. For results, drill them frequently.

PAGE 88

• Read the sentences in the Read & Listen exercise.

• Stress the pronunciation of the ***-ed*** ending. Have the class as a whole, then individuals, repeat the sentences.

• With the help of a student, demonstrate how to do the Practice exercises using the sequence of events in the Read exercise. Then have the students continue by working in pairs.

PAGE 89

• With the help of a student, demonstrate how to do the first Practice exercise. Then have the students continue by working in pairs.

• With the students' books closed, do the Practice exercise as an oral drill.

• Use the methodology for conducting oral drills in the Teaching Notes (page ix).

• Then, tell the students to open their books and repeat the drill with a partner.

• Have them extend the exercise by using original phrases.

• Practice the mini-dialog in the Practice exercise at the bottom of the page and read the vocabulary in the box above the pictures. Next, show how to do this exercise with the help of a student. Practice the activity until the students understand what to do. Then tell the students to continue the exercise by working in pairs.

• As an additional activity, have the students label each picture in writing.

PAGE 90

• Explain how to match the questions and answer in the write exercise at the top of the page, Read the directions and do a few example with the whole class. Correct the exercise and have volunteers act out the dialog in front of the class,

Answer Key: *1-d, 2-b, 3-a, 4-g, 5-h, 6-c, 7-e, 8-f*

• Read and discuss the vocabulary on the time card.

• Instead of the teacher asking comprehension questions about the dialog, reverse the roles and ask the students to try to stump the teacher by asking difficult questions.

• With the help or a student, demonstrate how to do the Practice exercises using the time card in the Read exercise. Then have the students continue by working in pairs.

PAGE 91

• Introduce the new vocabulary and expressions: *semester, UCLA, return, visit, enjoy, miss, translator, dormitory, arrive, campus, both, travel*

• Use the methodology for teaching a dialog described in the Teaching Notes. (page viii).

Answers for Understand:

1. Yes, she did.	*3. No, she didn't.*	*5. No, she didn't.*
2. Yes, she did.	*4. Yes, she did.*	*6. Yes, she did.*

• As a review of the past, present, and future, have the students underline all verbs in the past, circle all verbs in the present habitual, and put a box around all verbs in the future.

PAGE 92

• Explain how to fill in the sentences in the write exercise. Reed the directions and do as few examples with the whole class. Correct the exercise by having the students write the answers non the board. Then have volunteers act out the dialog in front of the class.

Answer Key: (Answers may vary slightly.)

1. *When did Yoshi arrive?*
2. *Why did she come?*
3. *What did you study?*
4. *Where did you study.*
5. *What time/when did your class start?*
6. *What time/when did it end?*
7. *Where did you travel/go?*
8. *When did Yoshi return to Japan?*
9. *Why did you stay?*

• As a follow-up activity, dictate part of the Write exercise as a short quiz.

PAGE 93

Introduce the new vocabulary and expressions: *answer, really busy, senior citizens, nursing home, move*

• Use the methodology for teaching a dialog described in the Teaching Notes. (page viii).

Answers for Understand:

1. True, 2. False, 3. We don't know., 4. True, 5. True

• Explain how to fill in the answers to Amir's questions in the Write exercise with short answers. Read the direction: and do a few examples with the whole class. Correct the exercise by having individuals write their answers on the board, Then have volunteers act out the dialog in front of the class.

• Repeat the exercise above by having the students change the words ***you*** and ***I*** to ***Yuri*** and ***she***.

PAGE 94

• Read the entries on Yuri's calendar. Then reread the entries having the students make complete sentences using the past tense. Stress tho correct pronunciation of the ***-ed*** endings.

• With the help of a student, demonstrate how to do the Practice exercises using the calendar. Then have the students continue by working in pairs.

PAGE 95

• With the students' books closed, do the Practice exercise as an oral drill.

• Use the methodology for conducting oral drills in the Teaching Notes (page ix).

• Then, tell the students to open their books and repeat the drills with a partner.

• Read through the words in the box in the last Practice exercise.

• Have them extend the exercise by using original phrases in the last Practice exercise. Discuss the words in the box and ask for examples of sentences in which they are used. Have the students continue the exercise in pairs.

PAGE 96

Explain how to fill in the words in the Write exercise. Read the directions and do a few example with the whole class. Correct the exercise and have volunteers act out the dialog in front of the class.

Answer key:

1. did	*9. ed*	*17. Did*	*25. Did*
2. nothing	*10. Did*	*18. nothing*	*26. nothing*
3. d	*11. nothing*	*19. ed*	*27. did*
4. did	*12. did*	*20. didn't*	*28. Did*
5. nothing	*13. Did*	*21. nothing*	*29. nothing*
6.d	*14. nothing*	*22. Did*	*30. ed*
7. Did	*15. didn't*	*23. nothing*	*31. ed*
8. didn't	*16. ed*	*24. did*	

• As a follow-up activity, dictate the Write exercise as a short quiz.

PAGE 97

• Read the rules and examples in the Spelling section.

• Ask the students to think of other verbs that would use the rules described. Make a list of them on the board.

• Some Verbs: *live, arrive, like, try, decide, practice, move, study, apply*

• Explain how to fill in tho words in the Write exercise. Read the directions and do a few examples with the whole class. Correct the exercise by having individuals write the words on the board. Then have volunteers read the text orally. Stress the pronunciation of the ***-ed*** ending.

Answer key:

1. lived	*2. worked*	*3. liked*	*4. decided*
5. moved	*6. stayed*	*7. arrived*	*8. applied*
9. started	*10. registered*	*11. want*	*12. tried*
13. needed	*14. practiced*	*15. studied*	*16. asked*

• As a follow-up activity, dictate the Write exercise as a short quiz.

PAGE 98

• Read the questions in the questionnaire in the Write exercise. As a homework assignment, have the Students fill out the questionnaire.

• On the following day, correct tho questionnaire by having volunteers write their answers on the board. Discuss other possible answers.

CHAPTER 7

PAGE 100

• Introduce the new vocabulary and expressions: *vent, ate, show, saw, drove, had, drank, lucky, sat, left, especially, delicious, champagne, Broadway, afterward, took, gave, got, forgot, did, famous, bought, began, row, didn't*

• Use the methodology for teaching a dialog described in the Teaching Notes. (page viii).

Answers for understand:

1. True, 2. False, 3. False, 4. We don't know. 5. True 6. False

PAGE 101

• Use the methodology for teaching grammar described in the Teaching Notes (page ix).

• You may want to list these irregular verbs on flash cards for drilling. Write the present habitual form on one side of the card and the irregular form on the other side. Have the students make complete original sentences with the verbs, transform sentences from affirmative to negative or questions, or use them for spelling bees.

• Direct the students to make as many correct sentences as possible using the words in the boxes in the Read exercise. Expand this activity by having the students compose original sentences.

• Have the students underline all the irregular verbs in the dialog on page 100.

PAGE 102

Read the sequence of events in the Read exercise at the top or the page. Point out the irregular verbs. Model the sentences and have the students repeat than after you.

With the help of a student, demonstrate how to do the Practice exercises using the calendar in the Read exercise. Then have the students continue by working in pairs.

PAGE 103

• With the students' books closed, do the Practice exercise as an oral drill.

• Use the methodology for conducting oral drills in the Teaching Notes (page ix).

• Then, tell the students to open their books and repeat the drill with a partner.

• Have them extend the exercise by using original phrases.

• Explain how to fill in the words in the Write exercise. Read the directions and do a few samples with the whole class. Correct the exercise by having the students write the sentence: on the board. Have volunteers act out the dialog in front or the class.

Answer Key:

1. Did, ate	*5. Did, didn't see*
2. Did, took	*6. Did, didn't drive*
3. Did, lent	*7. Did, left*
4. Did, gave	*8. Did, bought*

• As a follow-up activity, dictate the Write exercise as a short quiz.

PAGE 104

Explain how on fill in the words in the Write exercise. Read the words in the box at the top of the page, read the directions, and do a few examples with the whole class. Correct the exercise by having the students write the mini-dialogs on the board, have volunteers act Out the dialog in front of the class.

Answer key:

First Dialog	**Second Dialog**	**Third Dialog**
1. did you go	*8. did yo eat*	*14. drank*
2. went	*9. ate*	*15. Did you drink*
3. did you go	*10. ate*	*16. didn't drink*
4. went	*11. Did you eat*	*17. drank*
5. did you go	*12. didn't eat*	*18. drink*
6. went	*13. ate*	*19. drank*
7. didn't go		

• As a follow-up activity, dictate the dialogs as a short quiz.

PAGE 105

Do the exercises on this page the same way as those on page 104.

Answer key:

First Dialog	**Second Dialog**	**Third Dialog**
1. Did ... give	*8. did you see*	*15. Did you have*
2. gave	*9. saw*	*16. had*
3. did you give	*10. Did you see*	*17. Did you have*
4. gave	*11. didn't see*	*18. didn't have*
5. Did you give	*12. saw*	
6. didn't give	*13. did you see*	
7. gave	*14. saw*	

PAGE 106

• Introduce the new vocabulary and expressions: *restful, sat, deserts, slept, sightseeing, passengers, relaxed, scenery, spoke, read, cities, met, wrote, mountains, made*

• Use the methodology for teaching a dialog described in the Teaching Notes. (page viii).

Answers to Understand

1. True, 2. We don't know., 3. True 4. False 5. True

PAGE 107

• Use the methodology for teaching grammar described in the Teaching Notes (page ix).

• Have the students underline all the irregular verbs in the dialog on page 106.

• Direct the students to make as many correct sentences as possible using the words in the boxes in the Read exercise. Expand this activity by having the students compose original sentences.

• Review the use of ***was*** and ***were*** on page 73.

• Explain how to fill in the words in the Write exercise. Read the directions and do a few examples with the whole class. Correct the exercise and have volunteers act out the dialog in front of the class.

Answer Key:

1. Were	*4. were*	*7. Were*
2. was	*5. Were*	*8. were*
3. Was	*6. were*	*9. were*

• As a follow-up activity, dictate the Write exercise as a short quiz.

PAGE 108

• Read the pages from Betty's diary at the top of the page. Have the students make complete sentences using the information given (e.g., "Betty left New York on Saturday."). Stress the use of irregular verbs.

• As a follow-up activity, instead of the teacher asking comprehension questions about the dialog, reverse the roles and ask the students to try to stump the teacher by asking difficult questions.

• With the help of a student, demonstrate how to do the Practice exercises using the diary in the Read exercise. Then have the students continue by working in pairs.

PAGE 109

• Read the names of the cities and states on the map at the top of the page.

• Identify the states through which the train tracks cross. You may want to review the names of the states on page 67.

• Have the students practice using prepositions such as north of, south of, east of, west of, far from, near and close to, by asking questions about the position of one city relative to another. Model the sample questions and responses such as, *"Where's Boston? It's north of New York City."*

• Repeat the exercise above using a large wall map. Tell students to speak about additional place names. Expand the exercise to include *northeast of, northwest of, southwest of,* and *southeast of.*

• Show that the adjectives corresponding to north, south, east, and west are formed by adding the suffix ***-ern.*** using the map, have the students tell you the location of each city. For example, ask *"In what part of the United States is San Francisco?"* The students should respond, *"It's in the western part."*

• Explain that place names are always capitalized.

• With the help of a student, demonstrate how to do the Practice exercises using the map exercise. Then have the students continue by working in pairs.

• As a Challenge exercise, have the students fill in the missing names of the states on the map.

PAGE 110

• Explain how to fill in the words in the Write exercise. Read the words in the box at the top of the page, read the directions, and do a few examples with the whole class. Correct the exercise by having the students write the mini-dialogs on tho board. Have volunteer act out the dialog in front of the class.

Answer Key:

First Dialog	Second Dialog	Third Dialog
1. Did you sleep	*7. Did you write*	*12. did you meet*
2. didn't sleep	*8. wrote*	*13. met*
3. slept	*9. Did you write*	*14. met*
4. Did you sleep	*10. didn't write*	*15. did you meet*
5. did	*11. wrote*	*16. met*
6. slept		

• As a follow-up exercise, dictate the dialogs as a short quiz.

PAGE 111

• Explain how to unscramble words below the lines in the Write exercise. Read the directions and do several examples with the whole class. Correct the exercise and have volunteers read parts of the letter for the class.

• Instead of the teacher asking comprehension questions about the letter, play a game. Divide the class into two teams. Teams take turns asking difficult questions about the email. If one team asks a question that the second team cannot answer, then it gets a point. If the answer is correct, then no points are given. The team with the most points wins.

Answer key:

1. had	*6. wrote*	*11. met*	*16. went*
2. took	*7. met*	*12. were*	*17. was*
3. gave	*8. saw*	*13. spoke*	
4. slept	*9. had*	*14. gave*	
5. read	*10. forgot*	*15. bought*	

PAGE 112

• Have the students pair up and put all writing material sway. Stress that this is a speaking and not a writing exercise. Explain the following directions.

• Demonstrate how the students must fold the page in half where indicated.

• Tell them that they must look at only one side or the page.

• One student asks the questions and the other answers by using the irregular verbs in the box.

The students reverse roles for the second exercise.

• When the student: have finished, discuss the answers with the whole class and pose more questions modeled on the structures given.

•As a follow-up or homework activity, have the students complete the exercise in writing.

PAGE 113

• Read the rules in the box at the top of the page.

Then slowly read the words below the pictures. Tell the students to pay attention to the prefix ***re-***. Read the words a second time.

• Model the words again and have the students repeat each word several tines.

• Encourage students to think or other words that contain the prefix ***re-***. Make a list on the board.

• Have the students make as many original sentences as possible using the new words.

• Explain the directions for the Write exercises. Then have the students fill in the missing sentences or words. Do a few examples with the whole class.

Answer Key:

First exercise:
1. *Amir repainted his car.*
2. *Betty reread the book.*
3. *Amir retold the story.*
4. *The students retook the tests.*
5. *Betty rewrote the letter.*
6. *Yuri revisited the senior center.*
7. *Betty's sister reinvited her.*

Second exercise:
1. *rewashed*
2. *remade*
3. *remixed*
4. *relearned*
5. *redid*

CHAPTER 8

PAGE 115

• Read the short dialog in the Read & Listen section at the top of the page.

• Review the use of short answers in the present continuous, present habitual, past, and future.

• Explain how to fill in the words in the Write exercises. Read the directions and do a few examples with the whole class. Correct the exercises and have volunteers act out the dialog in front of the class.

Answer Key:

First exercise	Second exercise
1. *you can.*	1. *Are*
2. *I am.*	2. *Do*
3. *I didn't.*	3. *Is*
4. *it is.*	4. *Do*
5. *I do.*	5. *Did*
6. *I don't.*	6. *Are*
7. *it is.*	7. *Is*
8. *it is.*	8. *Will*

• As a follow-up activity, dictate the write exercise as a short quiz.

PAGE 116

• Explain how to fill in the questions in the first Write exercise and the answers in the second. Read the directions, and do a few examples with the whole class. Correct the exercise by having the students write the answers on the board. Then have volunteers act out the dialog in front of the class.

Answer Key:

First exercise: (Answers will very slightly.)
1. *Why are you asking me these questions?*
2. *What do you want to know?*
3. *Where do you work?*
4. *When will the article be in the newspaper?*
5. *How many people do you have to interview?*

Second exercise: (Answers will vary.)

• As a follow-up activity, dictate the write exercise as a short quiz.

• As the basis of a group activity, tell the students to interview another person in the class using the questions in the write exercises as a model.

PAGE 117

• Review the use of the preposition: ***in, on,*** and ***at***.

• Explain how to fill in the words in the write exercise. Read the directions and do a few examples with the whole class. Correct the exercise.

• Instead of the teacher asking comprehension questions about the story, play a game. Divide the class into two teams. Teams take turns asking difficult questions about the story. If one team asks a question that the second team cannot answer, then it gets a point. If the answer is correct, then no points are given. The team with the most points wins.

• Explain how to match the questions and answers in the last Write exercise. Read the directions and do a few examples with the whole class. Correct the exercise.

• ***Answer Key:*** *1-c, 2-a, 3-f, 4-b, 5-d, 5-e*

As a follow-up activity, dictate part of the first Write exercise as a short quiz.

PAGE 118

• Read the short dialog and the information in the calendar in the Read exercise at the top of the page. Then have the students make complete sentences with the information. Point out that all the verbs are in the past and some are irregular.

Examples:
a. *Stephen arrived in the U.S.A. in April.*
b. *He moved to an apartment in May.*
c. *He got a job in June.*

• Instead of the teacher asking comprehension questions about the information in the calendar, reverse the roles and ask the students to try to stump the teacher by posing original questions.

• With the help of a student, demonstrate how to do the Practice exercise using the calendar in the Read exercise. Then have the students continue by working in pairs.

PAGE 119

• Read the dialog in the Read exercise at the top of the page. Ask general comprehension questions about what Manuel said.

• Review the use of ***have to, has,*** and ***had*** to by having the students sake sentences with had to using the information in Manuel's speech balloon.

• With the help of a student, demonstrate how to do the Practice exercise using the information in Manuel's speech balloon in the Read exercise. Then have the students continue by working in pairs.

• Explain how to fill in the short questionnaire about "Things I Had to Do" in the Write exercise at the bottom of the page. Correct the exercise by having individuals write their sentences on the board.

• Repeat the two Practice exercises using the information that the students supplied.

• As a follow-up activity, dictate some of the sentences that the students wrote on the board as a short quiz.

PAGE 120

• Use the methodology for teaching a dialog described in the Teaching Notes. (page viii).

• Explain how to complete the sentences in the write exercise. Read the directions and do a few examples with the whole class. Correct the exercise by having volunteers write their sentences on the board. Discuss other possible answers.

• As a follow-up activity, dictate some of the students' answers an a surprise quiz.

PAGE 121

Read the speech balloons in the Read exercise at the top of the page, review how to express the future in Chapter 4, and discuss your students' future plans.

• With the help or a student, demonstrate how to do the Practice exercise using the information in the Read exercise. Then have the students continue by working in pairs.

• As a homework assignment, have the student: write what they will and will not do in the future in the space provided.

• On the following day, correct the exercise by having some volunteers write their sentences on the board.

PAGE 122 123

• Read through the questions in the questionnaire with the whole class. Explain any unfamiliar vocabulary.

• Tell the students that they are to pretend that they are reporters and must interview someone.

• Have the students pair up for the interview. Encourage students to pair up with someone they do not know well.

• Tell the students to write the information they gather on the questionnaire.

• Encourage the students to ask additional questions. When the students finish the interview, discuss the questions and the answers with the whole class.

PAGE 123

• Tell the students to write an article about the person they interviewed based on the questionnaire. On the board, help the students begin their articles by writing two or three lines.

• Ask for volunteers to read their articles in front or the class.

• Challenge the students to repeat the interviewing and articled-writing process by interviewing an English-speaking friend or neighbor.

PAGE 124

Answer Rey:

ACROSS	DOWN	
3. off	*1. hot*	*10. fat*
4. beautiful	*2. much*	*11. happy*
7. go	*4. big*	*15 up*
12. after	*5. used*	*16. from*
13. empty	*6. understand*	*17. far*
14. down	*8. over*	*19. slow*
17. for	*9. many*	
18. quietly		
20. remember		

PAGES 125-126

Answer Key to Test

1. b	8. a	15. d	22. c	29. c	36. a
2. d	9. c	16. c	23.b	30. c	37. c
3. d	10. c	17. b	24. b	31. b	38. a
4. b	11. b	18. d	25. a	32. b	39. a
5. a	12. c	19. c	26. a	33. a	40. a
6. b	13. d	20. d	27. b	34. b	
7. c	14. b	21. b	28. b	35. a	

CHAPTER 9

PAGE 128

• Introduce the new vocabulary and expressions: *bookcases, screwdriver, remove, nails, bottom, position, attach, insert, assembled, hammer, make sure, wood, side, natch, tighten, adjust, unassembled, follow, include, top, shelves, ends, lift, instructions, steps, screws, board, place (v.), holes, upright*

• Use the methodology for teaching a dialog described in the Teaching Notes. (page viii).

• Use the instructions to assemble the bookcase as a silent reading activity. Explain that the students must read the instruction: by themselves and underline all the words that they do not know. When they have finished, tell them to do the Understand exercise at the bottom of the page.

• After the students have reed the instructions at least twice, discuss any new vocabulary.

• Correct and discuss the Understand exercise.

Answer Key:
1. True, 2. True, 3. True, 4. False, 5. True

PAGE 129

• Use the methodology for teaching grammar described in the Teaching Notes (page ix).

• Review the pronunciation of the ***-ed*** ending on page 86.

• Read the sequence of events in the Read exercise. Have the students describe the sequence in the past tense.

• Practice yes/no type questions about the sequence.

• With the help of a student, demonstrate how to do the Practice exercise using the sequence of events in the Read exercise. Then have the students continue by working in pairs.

PAGE 130

• Explain how to fill in the words in the Write exercise. Read the words in the box, read the directions, and do a few examples with the whole class. Correct the exercise by having volunteers write the words on the board. Then have volunteers read the dialog aloud in class.

Answer Key:

1. followed	*4. included*	*7. attached*	*10. lifted*
2. removed	*5. placed*	*6. tightened*	*11. inserted*
3. checked	*6. positioned*	*9. nailed*	*12. adjusted*

• Explain how to label the different parts of the bookcase. Read the directions and the words in the box, and do a few examples with the whole class.
Correct the exercise by having individuals write the words on the board.

Answer Key:

1, aide	*3. back*	*5. top shelf*	*7. screws*
2, shelf	*4. bottom shelf*	*6. nails*	*8. box*

• Have the students use the new vocabulary in original sentences.

PAGE 131

• Introduce the new vocabulary and expressions: *electrical, unplug, burned out, turn on, equipment, light bulb, lamp shade, plug, throw away, turn off, unscrew, outlet.*

• Use the methodology for teaching a dialog described in the Teaching Notes. (page viii).

Answers for Understand:
1. False, 2. False, 3. True, 4. False, 5. We don't know.

PAGE 132

• Read the sequence of events in the Read exercise. Then tell the students to describe the events in the past tense. Ask general comprehension questions about the pictures. Have the students use the new vocabulary items in original sentences.

• You my want to point out the impersonal use of the word ***you***.

• With the help of a student, demonstrate how to do the Practice exercises using the events in the Read exercise. Then have the students continue by working in pairs.

PAGE 133

• Explain how to fill in the words in the Write exercise. Read the directions and the words in the box at the top of the page. Do a few examples with the whole class. Correct the exercise by having individuals write the answers on the board.

Answer key:

1. turn off	*4. unscrew*	*7. screw*	*10. turn on*
2. unplug	*5. check*	*8. place*	
3. remove	*6. get*	*9. plug*	

• Explain how to label the items in the Write exercise. Read the directions and the words in the box. Then do a few examples with the whole class. Correct the exercise by having the students write the words on the board. Ask volunteers to act out the dialog in front of the class.

Answer key:

1. a cord	*3. plug*	*5. switch*
2. light bulb	*4. outlet*	*6. socket*

PAGE 134

Identify what Rita is doinq in the pictures in the Write exercise at the top of the page. Then tell the students to write sentences tor each picture.

Answer Key: (Answers will vary slightly.)
1. She's turning on the lamp.
2. She's plugging in the cord (plug).
3. She's screwing in the light bulb.
4. She's unplugging the cord (plug)
5. She's placing (putting) the lamp on the table.
6. She's removing the lamp shade.

• Have the students put the pictures in the correct order.

Answer Key: 4, 5, 6, 3, 2, 1

• As a follow-up activity, dictate the write exercise as a short quiz.

• For further practice, bring a lamp to school and have the students show and describe how to replace a light bulb.

• Explain how to fill in the words in the write exercise. Read the words in the box, read the directions, and do a few examples with the whole class.

• Correct the exercise by having individuals write the words on the board. Then have volunteers read the sequence aloud in front of the class.

Answer Key:

1. turn off 3. remove 5. close 7. throw away
2. open 4. replace 6. turn on

• As a follow-up activity, dictate the Write exercise as a short quiz.

• Challenge the students to name as many electrical machines and appliances as they can. Write them on the board. Discuss how the machines work, where they are found, what they are used for, and the names of their various parts.

PAGE 135

Use the dialog and the instructions for using the photocopy machine as a silent reading activity. Explain that the students must read the dialog and instructions by themselves and underline all the words that they do not know. When they have finished, tell them to do the Understand exercise at the bottom of the page,

Some new vocabulary:

deposit, button, lit, original, select, copy, size, coin return, press, legal

•After the students have read the dialog and instructions at least twice, discuss any new vocabulary.

• Correct and discuss the Understand exercise.

Answer Key:

1. False, 2. True, 3. We don't know., 4. False, 5. False

PAGE 136

• Read the sequence of events in the Read exercise. Then tell the students to describe the events in the present continuous tense.

• Ask general comprehension questions about the pictures.

• Have the students use the new verbs in original sentences.

• With the help of a student, demonstrate how to do the Practice exercises using the events in the Read exercise. Then have the students continue by working in pairs.

• Practice changing the sentences in the Read exercise to the past tense. Tell the students to pay special attention to the use of articles. Then have the students rewrite the sequence of events on the lines provided.

Answer Key:

1. First, she deposited the money.
2. Then, she opened the lid.
3. She placed the paper on the glass surface.
4. She closed the lid.
5. She selected the size.
6. She pressed the button to start.
7. She waited for the light.
8. She opened the lid.
9. She removed the original and the copy.

PAGE 137

• Read through the sentences in the four exercises. Then explain how to put the sentences in the Write exercise in the correct order. Read the directions and do a few examples with the whole class. Correct the exercise by having individuals read the right order aloud.

Answer Key:

Coffee Machine 4, 3, 1, 5, 2
Microwave Oven: 6, 7, I, 5, 2, 1, 3
Washing Machine: 7, 4, 6, 1, 8, 2, 3, 5

• Discuss what the machines are used for, how they are used, and where they are found, and the names or their various parts.

PAGE 138

• As a whole class activity, read and discuss the questions in the questionnaire in the Write exercise at the top of the page,

• Have the student: continue the activity by answering the questions in writing as a homework assignment. On the following day, ask volunteers to write their answers on the board. Correct the sentences and discuss other possible answers.

• As a follow-up activity, stage mock job interviews between an employer and a prospective employee. Use the questionnaire as the basis of some of the questions.

• Challenge your students to explain how to replace a battery in a smoke detector. (Use an actual smoke detector player if available.) Read the vocabulary in the box. Have the students make original sentences using the words. As a written exercise, tell the students to write the sequence on the lines provided. Correct the sentences by having students write the sequence on the board. Discuss other possible answers.

PAGE 139

• Have the students pair up and put all writing material away. Stress that this is a speaking and not a writing exercise. Explain the following directions.

• Demonstrate how the students must fold the page in half where indicated.
Tell them that they must look at only one side of the page.

• One student asks the questions and the other answers by finding the answers in the picture.

• The students reverse roles for the second exercise.

• When the students have finished, discuss the answers with the whole class and pose more questions about the bookcase and the lamp.
As a follow-up or homework activity, have the students complete the exercise in writing.

PAGE 140

• Read the rule in the box at the top or the page. Then read the two sentences below the pictures. Tell the students to pay attention to the two adjectives with the suffix ***-al.*** Read the sentences a second time.

• Encourage the students to think of other words that contain the suffix ***-al.*** Make a list on the board and have the students use them in original sentences.

• Explain the directions for the first two Write exercises. Then have the students rewrite the words with the suffix ***-al.*** Do a few examples with the whole class.

Answer Key:

First Write exercise:

1. national	*3. original*	*5. magical*
2, practical	*4. instrumental*	*6. classical*

Second Write exercise

1. technical	3. personal	5. electrical
2. political	4. musical	

• Read and explain the words in the last Write exercise at the bottom of the page. Have the students make original sentences with the words. Then have them write their sentences on the lines provided. Ask individuals to write their sentences on the board. Have other students correct any mistakes.

CHAPTER 10

PAGE 142

• Introduce the new vocabulary and expressions: *vacuum, ironing, meal, housework, gardening, both, noise, cleaning, mess, share, dusting, pretty good, laundry, even*

• Use the methodology for teaching a dialog described in the Teaching Notes. (page viii).

Answers for Understand:
1. We don't know., 2. False, 3. True, 4. We don't know., 5. True, 6. True

Ask the students to help write a list of the Wilson family's duties on the board.

Paul	***Nancy***	***Theresa***	***Steve***	***Everybody***
cook	cook	dust	make bed	shop
garden	laundry	dishes	help others	clean
vacuum	bathrooms	make bed		

• Instead of the teacher asking comprehension questions about the family's duties in the dialog, play a game. Divide the class into two teams. Teams take turns asking difficult questions about the dialog. If one team asks a question that the second team cannot answer, then it gets a point. If the answer is correct then no points are given. The team with the most points wins.

PAGE 143

• Use the methodology for teaching grammar described in the Teaching Notes (page ix).

• Direct the students to make as many correct sentences as possible using the words in the boxes in the Read exercise. Expand this activity by having the students compose original sentences.

PAGE 144

Explain how to match the sentences in the dialogs. Read the directions and do a few examples with the whole class.

Answer Key:
Exercise 1: 1-c, 2-g, 3-h, 4-f, 5-e, 6-b, 7-d, 8-a
Exercise 2: 1-f, 2-a, 3-b, 4-d, 5-g, 6-e, 7-c

• Have pairs of students read the dialogs aloud in front of the class.

PAGE 145

• Read the vocabulary in the note on the bulletin board. Then have the students make sentences with ***do*** and ***make*** using the information. Point out the use of the past, present habitual, and future tenses.
For example: Betty made dinner last Saturday.
Betty will make dinner this Saturday.
Betty always makes dinner on Saturday.

• With the help of a student, demonstrate how to do the Practice exercise using the note. Then have the students continue by working in pairs.

PAGE 146

• With the students' books closed, do the Practice exercise as an oral drill.

• Use the methodology for conducting oral drills in the Teaching Notes (page ix).

• Then, tell the students to open their books and repeat the drill with a partner.

• Have them extend the exercise by using original phrases.

• Explain that the students must list their personal or family household responsibilities at the bottom of the page. Do a few examples with the whole class. Correct the exercise by having individuals write their responsibilities on the board. Discuss other possible responsibilities or duties.

• As an follow-up activity, dictate some of the sentences that the students used in the Write exercise as a short quiz.

• For further practice, repeat the Practice exercises on page 145 using the students' list of responsibilities.

PAGE 147

• Explain how to fill in the phrases in the Write exercise. Read the phrases in the box at the top of the page, read the directions, and do a few examples with the whole class. Correct the exercise and have volunteers act out the dialog in front of the class.

Answer key:

1. did the housework	*7. did the ironing*
2. did the work	*8. did the cleaning*
3, did a good job	*9. did the bathroom*
4. did the cooking	*10. did the dishes*
5. did the shopping	*11. did the gardening*
6. did the laundry	*12. made a mess*

• As a group exercise, discuss the questions in the Discussion activity at bottom of the page.

PAGE 148

• Introduce the new vocabulary and expressions: *get the door, get thirsty, get a haircut, ATM (automatic money machine), get the mail, get ready for, get home*

• Use the methodology for teaching a dialog described in the Teaching Notes. (page viii).

Answers for Understand:
1. We don't know. 2. True 3. We don't know. 4. False 5. True

PAGE 149

• Use the methodology for teaching grammar described in the Teaching Notes (page ix).

• Direct the students to make as many correct sentences as possible using the words in the box in the Read exercise. Expand this activity by having the students compose original sentences.

• Explain how to match the sentences in the Write exercise. Read the directions and do a few examples with the whole class. Correct the exercise and have volunteers act out the dialog in front of the class.

Answer Key: *1-c, 2-f, 3-a, 4-e, 5-b, 6-d*

• As a follow-up activity, dictate the Write exercise as a short quiz.

PAGE 150

• Discuss the sequence of events in the Read exercise. Tell the students to describe the events using ***get***.

• Instead of the teacher asking comprehension questions about the sequence, reverse the roles and ask the students to try to stump the teacher by asking difficult questions.

• Have students label each picture with a phrase using ***get***.

• With the help of a student, demonstrate how to do the first Practice exercise using the events in the Read exercise. Then have the students continue by working in pairs.

• With the students' books closed, do the Practice exercise as an oral drill.

• Use the methodology for conducting oral drills in the Teaching Notes (page ix).

• Then, tell the students to open their books and repeat the drill with a partner.

• Have them extend the exercise by using original phrases.

PAGE 151

• With the help of a student, demonstrate how to do the Practice exercises at the top of the page. Then have the students continue by working in pairs.

• Explain how to unscramble the questions in the questionnaire. Read the directions and do a few examples with the whole class. Correct the exercise by having volunteers write their questions on the board. Discuss the questions as a whole class activity.

Answer Key:
1. What do you get your guests when they visit you?
2. Do you get enough money to pay your bills?
3. How often do you get sick?
4. What time do you get to work or school?
5. What do you usually get at the supermarket every week?

• Have the students write their answers to the questions. Correct the answers by using the some methodology described above.

PAGE 152

• Explain how to fill in the words in the Write exercise. Read the directions and do a few examples with the whole class. Correct the exercise and have volunteers say the dialog aloud.

Answer key:

1. got up	*6. got tired*	*11. got home*
2. got ready	*7. didn't get*	*12. got ready*
3. got	*8. got*	*13. got*
4. got	*9. got a haircut*	*14. got*
5. got	*10. got the mail*	

PAGE 153

• Review the vocabulary in the box and have the students make original sentences with the phrases orally.

• As a homework assignment, tell the students to write a short story in the past tense about their weekend using as many of the phrases as possible.

• On the following day, have volunteers read their stories to the class. Have the other students listen for any errors. Correct and discuss the mistakes.

• As an additional activity, ask the students to write about an English-speaking friend or his/her past weekend.

PAGE 154

• Read the rules in the box at the top of the page. Then slowly read the sentences below the pictures. Tell the students to pay attention to the fact that gerunds appear in both subject and object positions. Read the sentences a second time.

• Model the sentences again and have the students repeat each several times.

• Encourage students to think of other words that contain the suffix ***-ing***. Make a list on them board.

• Have the students make as many original sentences as possible using the new words.

• Review the rule for adding ***-ing*** to a verb.

• Explain the direction for the Write exercise. Then have the students fill in the missing words. Do a few examples with the whole class.

Answer Key: *(Answers will vary. The words in parentheses are examples.)*

1. I like dancing.
2, I don't like (dancing).
3. I hate eating (liver).
4. I love (resting/doing nothing).
5. (Watching a movie) is fun.
6. (Doing homework) is difficult.
7. (Buying / fixing a car) is expensive.
8, (Smiling) is easy.
9. (Learning English) is important.

CHAPTER 11

PAGE 156

• Use the dialog as a silent reading activity. Explain that the students must read the dialog by themselves and underline all the words that they do not know. When they have finished, tell them to do the Understand exercise st the button of the page.
• After the students have read the dialog at least twice, discuss any new vocabulary.

Some new vocabulary: *wake up, throw away, broken, day off, put on (clothes), take off (clothes), punch in/out, drop, run back, turn on/off, clean up, get on/off (bus), set up (equipment)*

• Correct and discuss the Understand exercise.

Answer key:
1. False, 2. We don't know., 3. False, 4. False, 5. True

PAGE 157

• Instead of the teacher asking comprehension questions about the dialog, play a game. Divide the class into two teams. Teams take turns asking difficult questions about the dialog. If one team asks a question that the second team cannot answer, then it gets a point. It the answer is correct, then no points are given. The team with the most points wins.

• Use the methodology for teaching grammar described in the Teaching Notes (page ix).

• Direct the students to make as many correct sentences as possible using the words in the boxes in the Read exercise. Expand this activity by having the students compose original sentences.

PAGE 158

• Discuss the sequence of events in the Read exercise. Tell the students to describe the events using the past tense.

• Instead of the teacher asking comprehension questions about the sequence, reverse the roles and ask the students to try to stump the teacher by asking difficult questions.

• With the help of a student, demonstrate how to do the Practice exercises using the events in the Read exercise. Then have the students continue by working in pairs.

PAGE 159

• Use the methodology for teaching grammar described in the Teaching Notes (page ix).

• Direct the students to make as many correct

sentences as possible using the words in the box in the Rend exercise. Expand this activity by having the students compose original sentences.

• Discuss the sequence of events in the Read exercise. Tell the students to describe the events using the past tense.

• Ask general comprehension questions about the events.

• With the help of a student, demonstrate how to do the Practice exercise using the events in the Read exercise. Then have the students continue by working in pairs.

PAGE 160

• Use the methodology for teaching grammar described in the Teaching Notes (page ix).

• Direct the students to make as many correct sentences as possible using the words in the boxes in the Read exercise. Expand this activity by having the students compose original sentences.

PAGE 161

With the students' books closed, do the Practice exercises as oral drills.

• Use the methodology for conducting oral drills in the Teaching Notes (page ix).

• Then, tell the students to open their books and repeat the drills with a partner.

• Have them extend the exercise by using original phrases.

PAGE 162

• With the students' books closed, do the Practice exercise as an oral drill.

• Use the methodology for conducting oral drills in the Teaching Notes (page ix).

• Then, tell the students to open their books and repeat the drill with a partner.

• Have them extend the exercise by using original phrases.

• Explain how to fill in the questions with the words from the box and then match the questions and answers in the Write exercise. Read the directions and do a few examples with the whole class.

• Correct the exercise and have volunteers read the dialog aloud.

Answer key:

1. up	*1-c*	*4. away*	*4-h*	*7. on*	*7-e*
2. on	*2-g*	*5. for*	*5-b*	*8. up*	*8-i*
3. up	*3-a*	*6. on*	*6-d*	*9. up*	*9-f*

PAGE 163

• Explain how to fill in the words in the Write exercise. Read the words in the box at the top of the page, read the directions, and do a few examples with the whole class. Correct the exercise and have volunteers act out the commands in front of the class.

Answer Key:

Command #1:
Line 1: off, down, up
Line 2: back, up
Line 3: away, on, back

Command #2:
Line 1: up, in, out
Line 2: off, on,
Line 3: back, down

Command #3:
Line 1: out, for
Line 2: up, back
Line 3: back, around, back

Command #4
Line 1: up, around, for, up
Line 2: on, off, back, back
Line 3: down

• As a follow-up activity, dictate one or two of the commands as a short quiz.

• Challenge the students to write their own commands. Correct them by having the students write them on the board. Have the students act them out.

PAGE 164

• Explain how to fill in the words in the Write exercise. Read the directions and do a few examples with the whole class. Correct the exercise and have volunteers read the dialog aloud in front of the class.

Answer key:

1. woke up	7. wasn't	13. got out	19. gave
2. didn't ring	8. got in	14. began	20. arrived
3. got up	9. turned on	15. helped	21. was
4. too	10. didn't work	16. realized	22. had to
5. put on	11. stopped	17. didn't have	23. guessed
6. went	12. didn't have	18. was	24. got

PAGE 165

• Have the students pair up and put all writing material away. Stress that speaking and not a writing exercise. Explain the following directions.

• Demonstrate how the students must fold the page in half where indicated. Tell them that they must look at only one side of the page.

• One student asks the questions and the other answers by finding the answers in the picture.

• The students reverse roles for the second exercise.

• When the students have finished, discuss the answers with the whole class and pose more questions about the pictures.

• As a follow-up or homework activity, have the students complete the exercise in writing.

PAGE 166

• Read the rules in the box at the top of the page. Then slowly read the words below the pictures. Tell the students to pay attention to the ***/ər/*** sound in each word. Point out the underlined letters in each word. Read the words a second time .

• Model the words again and have the student repeat each word several times.

• Encourage the students to think of other words that contain the ***/ər/*** sound on the board.

• Have the students make original sentences with the list.

• Explain the directions of the Listen exercise. Tell the students that the teacher will say three words.

• The students must circle the word that contains the ***/ər/*** sound. Do a few examples with the whole class.

Answer key:

1. skirt	*4. doctor*	*7. November*	*10. learn*
2. first	*5. third*	*8. were*	
3. teacher	*6. Thursday*	*9. dollar*	

• Explain the directions tor the Write exercise at the bottom of the page. Then have the students fill in the missing letters. Do a few examples with the whole class.

Answer Key:
1. I saw a picture of her mother and father at church on November third.
2. The store clerk showed the two girls some new summer skirts.
3. The nurse worked late for the doctor on Thursdays and Saturdays for only a few dollars.
4. The thirsty farmer changed his dirty shirt before dinner.

• Challenge the students to make more 'crazy' sentences using words with the ***/ər/*** sound. Write them on the board and practice their pronunciation.

CHAPTER 12

PAGE 168

• Introduce the new vocabulary and expressions: *shopping list, check-out counter, shopping cart, ad, section, push, coupon, minus, bag, total, clerk, receipt*

• Use the methodology for teaching a dialog described in the Teaching Notes. (page viii).

Answers for Understand:
1. We don't know., 2. True, 3. We don't know., 4. False, 5. True, 6. False

PAGE 169

• Read and identify the items in the directory and in the picture.

• Have the student: practice making sentences using the information in the directory. Point out the use of ***is*** and ***are*** for singular and plural.

For example: Candy is in section 6.
Toys are in section 35.

• Have the students practice making sentences about the location of the people and items in the picture of the market. Stress the use of common prepositions such as ***next to, beside, in front of, behind, over, under, on, in,*** and ***between.***

For example: The cash register is on the check stand.
The cashier is behind the check stand.

• With the help of a student, demonstrate how to do the Practice exercises using the directory in the Read exercise. Then have the students continue by working in pairs.

• As a Challenge exercise, have the students alphabetize the directory using their notebooks or another piece of paper.

PAGE 170

• Explain how to match the questions or sentences with the pictures in the Write exercises. Read the directions and do a few examples with the whole class.

Answer Key:
Exercise 1: 1-d, 2-b, 3-h, 4-a, 5-e, 6-f, 7-g, 8-c
Exercise 2: 1-b, 2-e, 3-f, 4-g, 5-a, 6-c, 7-d, 8-h

PAGE 171

• Read and identify all the items on the counter. Point out the use of the preposition ***of***.

• Have the students practice making sentences about the location of the people and items in the picture of the market. Stress the use of common prepositions such as ***next to, beside, in front of, behind, over, under, on, in,*** and ***between***.

• With the help of a student, demonstrate how to do the Practice exercises using the items in the Read exercise. Then have the students continue by working in pairs.

PAGE 172

• Use the methodology for teaching grammar described in the Teaching Notes (page ix).

• Direct the students to make as many correct sentences as possible using the words in the box in the Read exercise. Expand this activity by having the students compose original sentences.

• Practice the mini-dialog in the Practice exercise and identify the objects in the pictures. Next, show how to do this exercise with the help of a student. Practice the activity until the students understand what to do. Then ell the students to continue the exercise by working n pairs.

Challenge your students to name store items that come in the containers listed.

Correct the Challenge exercise by having volunteers write the items in lists on the board. Practice the pronunciation of the items.

Repeat the last two Practice exercises on page 171 using the items on the board.

AGE 173

Read and identify all the items on the counter. Point out the use of the preposition ***of***.

Have the students practice making sentences about the location of the people and items in the picture of the market. Stress the use of common prepositions such as ***next to, beside, in front of, behind, over, under, on, in,*** and ***between.***

• With the help of a student, demonstrate how to do the Pair exercises using the items in the Read exercise. Then have the students continue by working in pairs.

Challenge the students to identify items that come in the measurements shown.

• Correct the Challenge exercise by having volunteers list the items on the board. Practice the pronunciation of the items.

• Repeat the last Practice using the list on the board.

PAGE 174

• Read and explain the liquid measurements in the Read exercise at the top of the page. Have the students practice making sentences with there are using the units of measurement. Point out the abbreviations.

For example: *There are 3 teaspoons in 1 tablespoon.*
There are 16 tablespoons in one cup.

• On the board, list the abbreviations below. Drill for pronunciation.

• Allow the students sufficient time to study the list. Then erase the non-abbreviated forms. Divide the class into two teams. Alternately have one member of a team come to the board, Select a word from the list of abbreviations and tell the students to write the word beside the corresponding abbreviation. For each correct answer, give one point to the appropriate team. Insist on complete accuracy including spelling and capitalization.

teaspoon tsp.	*gallon gal.*	*bottle btl.*
tablespoon Tb.	*ounce oz.*	*package pkg.*
pint pt.	*pound lb.*	*carton ctn.*
quart qt.	*kilogram kg.*	*vegetable veg.*

• With the help of a student, demonstrate how to do the Practice exercise using the information in the Read exercise. Then have the students continue by working in pairs.

• Challenge the students to list what liquid measurement or weight the items in the list come in. Answers will vary.

• As an additional exercise, have the students calculate their weight in pounds.

To determine pounds from kilograms, multiply the numbers of kilograms by 2.2 since one kilogram equals 2.2 pounds.

Example: *70 (kilograms) X 2.2 = 154 pounds.*

• To expand the lesson, select additional units of measure from the list below.

plate	*pot*	*liter*	*bouquet*	*container*
glass	*pan*	*pinch*	*sheet*	*stick*
dish	*book*	*spoonful*	*gram*	

PAGE 175

• Use the recipe as a silent reading activity. Explain that the students must read the recipe by themselves and underline all the words that they do not know.

• After the students have read the recipe at least twice, discuss any new vocabulary.

New vocabulary: *yogurt, mix, unsweetened, vanilla, strawberries, immediately, blender, servings*

• Ask general comprehension questions about the recipe.

•With the help of a student, demonstrate how to do the Practice exercises using the recipe in the Read exercise. Then have the students continue by working in pairs.

• As a homework assignment, have students write down their favorite recipe in English.

• On the following day, discuss the recipe and have a student write one recipe on the board. Read and discuss it, Then repeat the Practice exercises using the new recipe.

PAGE 176

• Introduce the new vocabulary and expressions: *salami, by, quarter, half, delicatessen*

• Use the methodology for teaching a dialog described in the Teaching Notes. (page viii).

Answers for Understand:
1. We don't know., 2. True, 3. False, 4. True

• Practice the mini-dialog in the first Practice exercise, read the words in the box, and identify the items in the pictures. Next, show how to do this exercise with the help of a student. Practice the activity until the students understand what to do. Then tell the students to continue the exercise by working in pairs.

•With the students' books closed, do the Practice exercise as an oral drill.

• Use the methodology for conducting oral drills in the Teaching Notes (page ix).

• Then, tell the students to open their books and repeat the drill with a partner.

• Have them extend the exercise by using original phrases.

PAGE 177

• Read and identify the items in both the shopping list and the directory.

• Ask volunteers to read the items in the shopping list. Have them substitute the number ***1*** with the article ***a***.

• Also practice pronouncing the vocabulary in the directory. Have students practice describing where the items are located in the store.

Example: *The dairy products are in section 10.*
Coffee and tea are in section 6.

• For further practice, have the students decide which are food and nonfood items.

• With the help of a student, demonstrate how to do the Practice exercise using the shopping list and directory in the Read exercise. Then have the students continue by working in pairs.

• As a Challenge exercise, have the students alphabetize the directory using their notebooks or a separate sheet of paper.

• Ask the students to write a shopping list for their next visit to their favorite store. Then have a group discussion by comparing the students' lists.

PAGE 178

• Read and explain the items in the ads and coupons, their sizes, and the abbreviations in the box to the right.

• Have students make sentences modeled on the structure below:

A/an [size] of [item] costs [price].

Examples:
An eight ounce bottle of shampoo costs one dollar and ninety-nine cents.
A forty-nine ounce box of detergent costs two dollars and twenty-five cents.

• Repeat exercise above using the abbreviated form for reading prices.

Examples:
An eight ounce bottle of shampoo costs one ninety-nine.
A forty-nine ounce box of detergent costs two twenty-five.

• With the help of a student, demonstrate how to do the Pair exercise using the ads in the Read exercise. Then have the students continue by working in pairs.

• As a group discussion, compare the prices of the items in the ad and their actual cost today,

To integrate math skills, have the students do simple math problems.

Addition: *How much is a ... of ...?*

Subtraction: *With a ... cent coupon, how much does a ... of ... cost?*

Multiplication: *How much do eight ... cost?*

Division: *A ... of ... costs ... cents. How much does one cost? / What is the unit price?*

Percent: *... costs ... cents and 6 percent tax. How much does it cost?*

Discount: *... is on sale for 20% off. How much does the ... cost?*

PAGE 179

• Explain how to fill in the sentences in the Write exercise. Read the directions and do a few examples with the whole class. Correct the exercise and have volunteers act out the dialog in front of the class.

Answer Key: *(Answers may vary.)*

2. It's in the dairy section.	5. Yes, that's fine.
3. No, I didn't.	6. Here you are.
4. A large size.	7. Thank you.

• As a follow-up activity, dictate the Write exercise as a short quiz.

• Challenge the students to write a dialog. Read the directions and help the students write the first few lines. Tell them to use the dialog in the Write exercise as a model. Then, have volunteers present their dialogs.

PAGE 180

• Use the methodology for doing a dictation described in the Teaching Notes (page xi).

• Have the students write a note to a person in their home. The students must tell him/her to go to the supermarket and buy some food. Help the students write a few lines, Tell them that they may use the Dictation as a model.

• Correct the Write exercise by having volunteers write their note on the board. Then have them read the notes aloud.

PAGE 181

• Have the students pair up and put all writing material away. Stress that this is a speaking and not a writing exercise. Explain the following directions. Demonstrate how the students must fold the page in half where indicated. Tell them that they must look at only one side of the page. One student asks the questions and the other answers by finding the answers in the picture. The students reverse roles for the second exercise. When the students have finished, discuss the answers with the whole class and pose more questions about the items in the pictures.

• As a follow-up or homework activity, have the students complete the exercise in writing.

• As another follow-up activity, take a field trip to the supermarket. Here's a suggestion: Do your weekly shopping with the students in your class. Write on individual slips of paper the items you need to buy. Pass the slips of paper out to your students and have them go around the supermarket and find the items. Tell the students to bring the items to your basket.

• As an additional activity, plan to have a luncheon with your students after your field trip. Decide on a menu, write out a shopping list, and assign each student one item to buy.

PAGE 182

• Read the rule in the box at the top of the page. Then slowly read the sentences below the pictures. Model the sentences again and have the students repeat each sentence several times.

• Direct the students to the word lists containing adjectives for nationalities, color, appearance and behavior. Again, model the words and explain any new words.

• Have the students make original sentences using the new words. Write a few on the board. Then, have volunteers read them aloud.

• Next, model the sentences in the second pronunciation exercise. Then, practice saying the sentences aloud.

• Explain the directions for the Write exercise. Then identify each item in the pictures. Have the students write sentences with adjectives using the suffix ***-ish.*** Do a few examples with the whole class. Answers will vary.

CHAPTER 13

PAGE 184

• Introduce the new vocabulary and expressions: *patient, cancellation, hold, hurt, would like, booked up, make an appointment, physical examination.*

• Use the methodology for teaching a dialog described in the Teaching Notes. (page viii).

Answers for Understand:

1. True, 2. True, 3. False, 4. True, 5. We don't know., 6. True

PAGE 185

• Use the methodology for teaching grammar described in the Teaching Notes (page ix).

• Direct the students to make as many correct sentences as possible using the words in the box in the Read exercise. Expand this activity by having the students compose original sentences,

• Practice the mini-dialog in the Practice exercise, read and explain the vocabulary below the pictures, and read the directions. Next, show how to do this exercise with the help of a student. Practice the activity until the students understand what to do. Then tell the students to continue the exercise by working in pairs.

PAGE 186

• Use the short dialog and the form as a silent reading activity. Explain that the students must read the dialog by themselves and underline all the words that they do not know, When they have finished, tell them to do the Understand exercise at the bottom of the page.

• Here are some new words: *print, drugs, insurance, pain, reason, policy*

• Correct and discuss the Understand exercise.

Answer Key:

1. True, 2. False, 3. True, 4. True, 5. False

• Instead of the teacher asking comprehension questions about the form, play a game. Divide the class into two teams. Teams take turns asking difficult questions about the form. If one team asks a question that the second team cannot answer, then it gets a point. If the answer is correct, then no points are given. The team with the most points wins.

PAGE 187

• Read the short dialog and the health examination record. Explain the information on the form and practice the pronunciation of the items on the form.

• With the help of a student, demonstrate how to do the Practice exercise using the health examination record. Then have the students continue by working in pairs.

PAGE 188

• Read the short dialog at the top of the page.

• Explain how to match the questions and answers in the Write exercise. Read the directions and do a few examples with the whole class. Correct the exercise and have volunteers act out the dialog in front of the class.

Answer Key: *1-f, 2-c, 3-b, 4-d, 5-g, 6-e, 7-h, 8-i, 9-a*

• Practice the mini-dialog in the Practice exercise, read the vocabulary below the pictures, and read the directions, Next, show how to do this exercise with the help of a student. Practice the activity until the students understand what to do. Then tell the students to continue the exercise by working in pairs.

PAGE 189

• Before having the students fill out the form on this page, demonstrate on the board the meaning of check, ***underline, print, circle,*** and ***cross out.***

• Have the students take a piece of paper. Dictate each instruction below. Then demonstrate each appropriate action on the board.

1. On line one, print your name.
2. Write 1-10 on the second line.
3. Underline your last name.
4. Circle your first name.
5. Check the first line.
6. Cross out number 6.
7. Underline number 9.
8. Circle number 1.
9. Cross out number 10.
10. Check the second line.

• Have the students fill out the form. Tell them that they may use the forms on pages 186 and 187 as models.

PAGE 190

Introduce the new vocabulary and expressions: *matter, laboratory, results, wrist, X-ray, notice, urine, prescription, blood*

• Use the methodology for teaching a dialog described in the Teaching Notes. (page viii).

Answers for Understand:
1. False, 2. False (True is possible), 3. We don't know., 4. True, 5. True, 6. We don't know.

PAGE 191

• Read and explain the different parts of the body. Practice the pronunciation of the vocabulary.

Have volunteers go to the board and draw parts of the body. As they draw a part, they have to name the part.

Play "Simon Says." Have all the students stand up. The leader says, "Simon says to touch your "..." The students have to obey. If the order is not preceded by the words "Simon says," then the students must not move. If they do, they are out of the game and have to sit down. The person who remains standing wins. Make the game more challenging by having the leader touch one part of the body and call another.

• With the help of a student, demonstrate how to do the Practice exercise using the chart of body parts in the Read exercise. Then have the students continue by working in pairs.

PAGE 192

• Read the short dialog and the directory in the Read exercise at the top of the page. Explain what is done in each area listed in the directory. Practice the pronunciation of the vocabulary in the directory.

• Drill the information in the directory by having the students practice the following questions:

Examples: ***Where is...? It's in / on....***

Where is surgery? It's in room 101.
Where are the wards? They're on the 3rd,4th, and 5th floors.
Where is the emergency room? It's in the basement.

Examples: ***What do they do in...?***

What do they do in surgery? They operate on patients.
What do they do in the X-ray lab? They take pictures of the inside of your body.

• Have the students alphabetize the directory using their notebooks or on a sheet of paper.

• Explain how to match the questions and answers in the Write exercise. Read the directions and do a few examples with the whole class.

Answer key: *1-e, 2-f, 3-b, 4-h, 5-d, 6-a, 7-g, 8-c*

PAGE 193

• Introduce the new vocabulary and expressions: *hear/heard, think/thought, understand/understood, write/wrote, remember, feel/felt, say/said, tell/told, prescription, ill, know/knew, concerns, give/gave, forget/forgot*

• Use the methodology for teaching a dialog described in the Teaching Notes. (page viii).

• Instead of the teacher asking comprehension questions about the dialog, reverse the roles and ask the students to try to stump the teacher by asking difficult questions.

Answers for Understand:
1. We don't know., 2. False, 3. True, 4. True

• Have the students underline the word ***that*** in the dialog. Also have them circle all irregular verbs.

PAGE 194

• Use the methodology for teaching grammar described in the Teaching Notes (page ix).

• Direct the students to make as many correct sentences as possible using the words in the box in the Read exercise. Expand this activity by having the students compose original sentences.

• With the students' books closed, do the Practice exercise as an oral drill.

• Use the methodology for conducting oral drills in the Teaching Notes (page ix).

• Then, tell the students to open their books and repeat the drill with a partner.

• Have them extend the exercise by using original phrases.

PAGE 195

• Explain how to fill in the words in the Write exercise. Read the words in the box at the top of the page, read the directions, and do a few examples with the whole class. Correct the exercise by having the students write the dialog on the board. Have volunteers act out the dialog in front of the class.

1. *know*	7. *Did ... forget*	14. *Did ... think*
2. *knew*	8. *did*	15. *didn't think*
3. *knew*	9. *forgot*	16. *thought*
4. *didn't know*	10. *did ... forget*	17. *Did ... think*
5. *Did ... know*	11. *forgot*	18. *did*
6. *didn't*	12. *Did ... forget*	19. *thought*
	13. *didn't forget*	

• As a follow-up exercise, dictate part of the dialog as a quiz.

PAGE 196

• Explain how to fill in the words in the Write exercise. Read the words in the box at the top of the page, read the directions, and do a few examples with the whole class. Correct the exercise by having the students write the dialog on the board. Have volunteers act out the dialog in front of the class.

Answer Key:

1. *Did ... understand*	9. *did ... hear*	17. *felt*
2. *did*	10. *heard*	18. *Did ... feel*
3. *understood*	11. *did ... hear*	19. *didn't.*
4. *Did ... understand*	12. *heard*	20. *felt*
5. *did*	13. *Did ... hear*	21. *Did ... hear*
6. *didn't understand*	14. *didn't hear*	22. *felt*
7. *did ... hear*	15. *heard*	
8. *heard*	16. *did ... feel*	

• As a follow-up exercise, dictate the dialogs as a short quiz.

PAGE 197

• Use the telephone message as a silent reading activity. Explain that the students must read the message by themselves and underline all the words that they do not know.
After the students have read the message at least twice, discuss any new vocabulary. Have individuals read the message aloud.

• Instead of the teacher asking comprehension questions about the message, play a game. Divide the class into two teams. Teams take turns asking difficult questions about the message using the following words: ***say, show, tell, hope, believe, think, know.***

• Answers must be given using the word ***that***. If one teams asks a question that the second team cannot answer, then it gets a point, If the answer is correct, then no points are given. The team with the most points wins.

• Explain how to complete the sentences in the Write exercise. Read the directions and do a few examples with the whole class. Correct the exercise by having volunteers write their answers on the board.

Answer key:

2. *... that Alice doesn't have any serious problems.*
3. *... that she was in good health.*
4. *... that her hand is better.*
5. *... that it's a mild case of arthritis.*
6. *... that it is serious.*
7. *... (The answers will vary.)*

• As a follow-up activity, dictate the Write exercise as a short quiz.

PAGE 198

• Use the methodology for teaching grammar described in the Teaching Notes (page ix).

• Direct the students to make as many correct sentences as possible using the words in the box in the Read exercise. Expand this activity by having the students compose original sentences.

• Practice the mini-dialog in the Practice exercise, read the speech balloons in the pictures, and read the directions. Next, show how to do this exercise with the help of a student. Practice the activity until the students understand what to do. Then tell the students to continue the exercise by working in pairs.

PAGE 199

• Explain how to fill in the words in the Write exercise. Read the directions and do a few examples with the whole class. Correct the exercise and have volunteers act out the dialog in front of the class.

Answer Key:

1. *say*	5. *told*	9. *said*	13. *told*
2. *said*	6. *tell*	10. *said*	
3. *tell*	7. *said*	11. *told*	
4. *told*	8. *told*	12. *told*	

• Have the students reread the dialog, but delete the word ***that*** from the clauses.

• As a follow-up exercise, dictate the dialogs as a short quiz.

PAGE 200

• Read the rule at the top of the page. Then slowly read the sentences below the pictures. Tell the students to pay attention to the words containing the silent ***gh***.

• Model the sentences again and have the students repeat each sentence several times.

• Next, model the pronunciation of the sentences in the pronunciation exercise. Then, have them practice saying the sentences aloud.

• Then, explain that there are only a few words in English in which gh is pronounced as /f/.

• Tell the students to find the words in the sentence in dictionary or on their smart phone and try to pronounce the words correctly in the sentences.

• As a follow-up, dictate the sentences as a dictation.

• For more advanced classes you might want to introduce additional words with a long /ō/ sound followed by a silent ***gh***:, *ought, sought, wrought, thought*.

Here is another group with a /aw/ sound followed by a silent ***gh***: *naughty, slaughter, taught, haughty*.

CHAPTER 14

PAGE 202

• Introduce the new vocabulary and expressions: *It takes..., motor, sign, vision, vehicles, traffic, manual, rules, road*

• Use the methodology for teaching a dialog described in the Teaching Notes. (page viii).

Answers for Understand:
1. True, 2. True, 3. We don't know., 4. True, 5. True

PAGE 203

• Use the methodology for teaching grammar described in the Teaching Notes (page ix).

• Direct the students to make as many correct sentences as possible using the words in the box in the Read exercise. Expand this activity by having the students compose original sentences.

• With the students' books closed, do the Practice exercise as an oral drill.

• Use the methodology for conducting oral drills in the Teaching Notes (page ix).

• Then, tell the students to open their books and repeat the drill with a partner.

• Have them extend the exercise by using original phrases.

PAGE 204

• Read and explain the road signs.

• On the board, draw the signs and write their meanings below them. (Overhead transparencies work well for this kind of exercise.)

• Drill for pronunciation. Then erase the meanings. Divide the class into two teams. Alternately have one member of a team come to the board. Have him/her select a sign and then write the meaning under it. For each correct answer, give one point to the appropriate team. Insist on complete accuracy including spelling and punctuation.

PAGE 205

Explain how to match the signs with their meanings. Read the directions and do a few examples with the whole class.

Answer Key: *1-a, 2-c, 3-b, 4-e, 5-d, 6-f, 7-h, 8-i, 9-j, 10-g*

PAGE 206

• Read and explain the meanings of the shapes and colors of road signs. You may want to use the same methodology described in item 2 on page 204 to drill the vocabulary.

• With the help of a student, demonstrate how to do the Practice exercise using the charts in the Read exercise. Then have the students continue by working in pairs.

PAGE 207

• Explain how to fill in the words in the Write exercise. Read the words in the box at the top of the page, read the directions, and do a few examples with the whole class. Correct the exercise by having volunteers read parts of the text aloud.

Answer Key:

1. 25	*6. stopped*
2. left	*7. railroad crossing*
3. right	*8. do not enter*
4. yield	*9. one way*
5. turned	*10. 2nd and A*

• As a follow-up activity, have the students bring in a map of the city. Ask them to find government buildings, fire department, hospital, schools, religious institutions, airports, bus stations, cultural and recreation facilities.

• Have them explain how to get to each place from the school and what kind of services each place provides.

PAGE 208

• Introduce the new vocabulary and expressions: *license, foreign, power brakes, air conditioner, mileage, equipment, stereo, cylinders, inexpensive, automatic, AM—FM radio, interior, domestic, transmission, steering, condition*

• Use the methodology for teaching a dialog described in the Teaching Notes. (page viii).

Answers for Understand:
1. True, 2, We don't know., 3. True, 4. False

• With the help of a student, demonstrate how to do the Practice exercise using Rita's list in the Read exercise. Then have the students continue by working in pairs.

PAGE 209

Read the car ads and explain the vocabulary in the Read exercise at the top of the page. Have the students try to make complete sentences using the information in the ads.

Examples:
The hatchback has power brakes.
The owners must sell the hatchback for $4000.
Call 231-0952 to buy the hatchback.

•With the help of a student, demonstrate how to do the Practice exercises using the ads in the Read exercise. Then have the students continue by working in pairs.

PAGE 210

• Introduce the new vocabulary and expressions: *for sale, anytime, soon*

• Use the methodology for teaching a dialog described in the Teaching Notes. (page viii).

Answers for Understand: *1. True, 2, True, 3. True*

• Practice the mini-dialog in the Practice exercise, read the information on the cars in the pictures, and read the directions. Next, show how to do this exercise with the help of a student. Practice the activity until the students understand what to do. Then tell the students to continue the exercise by working in pairs.

• Have the students bring in newspaper car ads from their local newspaper. Write a few of the ads on the board or project them with an overhead projector). Read and explain them. Then repeat the Practice exercise using the information on the board.

PAGE 211

• Read and explain the parts of the car shown in the pictures.

• Have the students practice the vocabulary by describing the location of the car parts. Use some of the following prepositions: ***on the outside of, on the inside of, in the front of, in the back of, on the side of,*** and ***at the corner of.***

• With the help of a student, demonstrate how to do the Practice exercise using the pictures in the Read exercise. Then have the students continue by working in pairs.

PAGE 212

• Explain how to fill in the sentences in the Write exercise. Read the directions and do a few examples with the whole class. Correct the exercise and have volunteers act out the dialog in front of the class.

Answer Key: *(Answers may vary.)*
1: Do you have a car for sale?
2: Are the tires in good condition?
3. Does it have power brakes?
4. How many miles does it have?/What's the mileage?
5. How much is it? / What are you asking?
6. I'll give you $5000. / I only have $5000.

• As a follow-up activity, dictate the Write exercise as a short quiz.

• Use the methodology for doing a dictation described in the Teaching Notes (page xi).

PAGE 213

• Read the directions carefully. Then demonstrate how to do the Practice exercise with the help of a student. Then have the students continue by working in pairs.

PAGE 214

• Read the rules in the box at the top of the page. Then slowly read the sentences below the pictures. Tell the students to pay attention to the words containing the suffix ***-ward***. Read the sentences a second time.

• Encourage students to think of other words that contain the suffix ***-ward.*** Make a list on the chalkboard. Have the students make as many original sentences as possible using the new words.

• Explain the directions for the crossword puzzle. Then have the students fill in the missing words. Do a few examples with the whole class.

Answer Key:

DOWN	ACROSS
1. eastward	2. toward
3. outrward	5. southward
4. upward	8. downward
6. westward	9. outward
7. inward	

PAGE 215

• Here are additional words and phrases used in road signs. Read through the names of the signs and have the students repeat after you.

• You may want to use this exercise as a word search activity using a dictionary or smart phone.

CHAPTER 15

PAGE 217

• Introduce the new vocabulary and expressions: final test, attentive, project, safe, steady, noisy, accurate

• Use the methodology for teaching a dialog described in the Teaching Notes. (page viii).

Answers for Understand:
1. True, 2. We don't know., 3. True, 4. False, 5. True

PAGE 218

• Use the methodology for teaching grammar described in the Teaching Notes (page ix).2.

• Direct the students to make as many correct sentences as possible using the words in the boxes in the Read exercise. Expand this activity by having the students compose original sentences.

PAGE 219

• Practice the mini-dialog in the Practice exercises,

read the sentences below the pictures, and read the directions. Next, show how to do this exercise with the help of a student. Practice the activity until the students understand what to do. Then tell the students to continue the exercises by working in pairs.

• Have the students ask personalized questions such as the following:

How do you work?
What kind of music do you prefer?
How do you do your homework?
What kind of musical instrument is a drum?
How do you speak?
What kind of person are you?
What kind of friends do you have?
How do you play games?
What kind of a person is a judge, a thief?
How should a person drive a car?

PAGE 220

• Read the rules in the box at the top of the page. Then slowly read the examples. Tell the students to pay attention to the suffix ***-ly***.

• Encourage students to think of other adjectives that can be made into adverbs. Make a list on the board.

• Have the students make as many original sentences as possible using the new words.

• Explain the directions for the Write exercises. Then have the students fill in the missing sentences or words. Do a few examples with the whole class.

Answer Key:

1. careful	*3. accurately*	*5. correctly*	*7. normally*
2. quickly	*4. attentively*	*6. quietly*	*8. noisily*

PAGE 221

• Read the dialog at the top of the page.

• Use the methodology for teaching grammar described in the Teaching Notes (page ix).

• Point out that ***hard*** is also used as an adjective meaning ***difficult*** as well as the opposite of ***soft***. Similarly, ***well*** can also be an adjective meaning ***healthy***.

• You may also want to show that ***well*** can be used with verbs to form compound adjectives such as:

well-mannered person
well-educated man
well-built house
well-done steak
well-cooked meal
well-prepared speech
well-written letter
well-made dress
well-dressed woman

• Have the students ask personalized questions such as the following using the irregular adverbs in the lesson.

How do you work?
How do you swim/run?
How do you study?
How do you like to dance?
What kind of cook are you?
What kind of car do you like?
What kind of music do you prefer?
What kind of worker/student are you?

• Direct the students to make as many correct sentences as possible using the words in the boxes in the Read exercise. Expand this activity by having the students compose original sentences.

PAGE 222

• Practice the mini-dialog in the first Practice exercise, read the vocabulary below the pictures, and read the directions. Next, show how to do this exercise with the help of a student. Practice the activity until the students understand what to do. Then tell the students to continue the exercise by working in pairs.

• With the students' books closed, do the Practice exercise as an oral drill.

• Use the methodology for conducting oral drills in the Teaching Notes (page ix).

• Then, tell the students to open their books and repeat the drill with a partner.

• Have them extend the exercise by using original phrases.

• You may want to expand this lesson by teaching descriptive adjectives.

• Place the names of the following common materials on the left side of the chalkboard: *plastic, gold, silver, metal, paper, leather, rubber, glass, cloth,* and *wood*.

• On the right side of the chalkboard write the following items: *ring, bag, ball, pen, hose, shoes, spoon, guitar, coat, plate, ashtray, purse, chair, coins,* and *cup*.

• Direct the students to the fifteen items on the board. Pose the question, *"What kind of rings are there?"* Model possible responses, *"There are gold rings," "There are silver rings,"* and *"There are metal rings."*

After drilling the examples several times, ask questions of individual students about a few more items. Continue the drill above by directing individual students to ask questions of other students using the remaining items.

• Note the existence of two parallel forms: ***gold/golden*** and ***wood/wooden***. Usage often leads to preference of one form over the other. Although the words ***gold*** and ***wood*** may be used as either nouns or adjectives, the words ***golde***n and ***wooden*** may only be used as adjectives.

You may want to expand the activity to include additional descriptive words and colors, The following words are examples of correct word order for such adjectives.

Descriptive Adjective	*Color*	*Material*	*Thing*
small	brown	wooden	spoon
long	green	plastic	comb

- Here's some additional adjectives: *big, small, long, short, heavy, light, hard, soft, new, old, strong, weak, broken, torn, used, clean, dirty*

- You may want to incorporate the following vocabulary:

diamond ring	*asphalt street*	*pearl necklace*
wool sweater	*dirty road*	*fur coat*
aluminum foil	*cotton blouse*	*brick wall*
steel pipe	*cardboard box*	*cement block*
iron chain	*silk stockings*	*chrome bumper*

PAGE 223

- Read and explain all the signs in the picture, Then ask the students to identify as many dangerous situations as they can.

- Have the students Practice asking questions about the pictures.

Example: Is the man working safely?
No, he's working dangerously,

- As a homework assignment, have the students list the situations in the space provided. Correct the situation by having volunteers write their sentences on the board.

- Here are some situations:

1. Boxes blocking the people's path.
2. The windows are broken.
3. The fire extinguisher is broken.
4. The fuse box on the wall in open and broken (the wires are hanging out).
5. Flammable liquid in the bottles on the shelf is tipped over and is dripping out.
6. The liquid is leaking onto the machine.
7. The ceiling is leaking.
8. The man is smoking near the flammable liquid.
9. The woman is eating near poisonous chemicals.
10. The woman is sitting on the barrel.
11. The people are ignoring the sign "Keep Out, No Admittance."
12. Poisonous chemicals are leaking out of the barrel.

PAGE 224

- Read the rules at the top of the page.

- Then slowly read the words below each explanation. Tell the students to pay attention to the suffixes ***-tion*** and ***-sion***. Read the words a second time.

- Explain the meaning of any unfamiliar words.

- Expand the exercise by discussing the root word or other related words for each noun with ***-tion*** and ***-sion*** in the lesson. Then, make a list on the board.

For example, the noun ***decision*** come from the verb ***decide***; ***transportation*** come from the verb ***transport***; etc. Encourage students to think of more words with ***-tion*** and ***-sion***. Make a list on the on the board.

- Direct the students to the Pronunciation exercise. Model the correct pronunciation of the sentences and have the students repeat. Do this several times.

- Tell the students to word in pairs or in small groups to practice saying the sentences.

- Challenge your students to volunteer saying some of the sentences without looking at the worksheet.

- Next, read the directions for the Write exercise. Then have the students fill in the missing words using the pictures as clues.

Answer key:

1. Optometrists check people's ***vision***.
2. Do you have a ***question*** for me?
3. The United States is big ***nation***.
4. Please give me ***directions*** to your house.
5. This new house is under ***construction***.
6. Flying airplanes is his ***profession***.
7. The subway ***station*** is underground.
8. The surgeon is performing an ***operation***.
9. Please fill out this job ***application***.
10. This is an ***extension*** cord.

- As a follow-up activity, give the sentences above as a dictation on a subsequent day.

CHAPTER 16

- This chapter is meant to review and test the students' knowledge of Chapters 1 through 15.

PAGE 226

- Review the vocabulary and expressions: *kidding, happen, laid off, economy.*

- Use the methodology for teaching a dialog described in the Teaching Notes. (page viii).

Answers for Understand:
1. False, 2. False, 3. True, 4. False

- Before doing the Write exercise you might want to review the use of regular and irregular verbs in the past tense in Chapters 6, 7, 9, and 13.

- Explain how to fill in the words in the Write exercise. Read the directions and do a few examples with the whole class. Correct the exercise and have volunteers act out the dialog in front of the class.

Answer Key:

1. lost	*5. arrived*	*9. spoke*
2. happened	*6. found*	*10. told*
3. got up	*7. said*	*11. was*
4. did	*8. went*	*12. had to*

PAGE 227

• Review the exercise described in item 1 for teaching page 189 of Chapter 13.

• Have the students fill out the application.

• Correct the application with a transparency and overhead projector (if available).

PAGE 228

• Explain how to dictate and write the notes in the Write exercise. Read the directions and do a few examples with the whole class.

• As a follow-up activity, dictate some of the notes as a quiz.

PAGE 229

• Read and discuss the short dialog at the top of the page.

• Before doing the Practice exercises, review the use of ***do*** and ***make*** on page 143 and ***get*** on page 149.

• Practice the mini-dialog in the Practice exercises, read the vocabulary below the pictures, and read the directions. Next, show how to do the exercises with the help of a student. Practice the activity until the students understand what to do. Then tell the students to continue the exercises by working in pairs.

PAGE 230

• Before doing the lesson on this page, you may want to review pages 209 and 210.

• Read the short dialog and the description of the cars in the picture.

• With the help of a student, demonstrate how to do the Practice exercise using the information about the cars in the picture. Have the students continue by working in pairs.

PAGE 231

• Use the methodology for teaching a dialog described in the Teaching Notes. (page viii).

Answers for Understand:

1. We don't know., 2. True, 3. False

• Before doing the Practice exercise, you may want to review pages 198 and 199.

• With the students' books closed, do the Practice exercise as an oral drill.

• Use the methodology for conducting oral drills in the Teaching Notes (page ix).

• Then, tell the students to open their books and repeat the drill with a partner.

• Have them extend the exercise by using original phrases.

PAGE 232

• Use the dialog as a silent reading activity. Explain that the students must read the dialog by themselves and underline all the words that they do not know. When they have finished, tell them to do the Understand exercise at the bottom of the page.

• After the students have read the dialog at least twice, discuss any new vocabulary.

• Correct and discuss the Understand exercise.

Answer Key:

1. True, 2. False, 3. False, 4. True, (We hope!)

• Instead of the teacher asking comprehension questions about the dialog, play a game. Divide the class into two teams. Teams take turns asking difficult questions about the dialog. If one team asks a question that the second team cannot answer, then it gets a point. If the answer is correct, then no points are given, The team with the most points wins.

• Have the students practice the dialog in pairs.

• Have volunteers read or act out the dialog in front of the class.

PAGES 233-234

Test Answers:

1 b	*11 b*	*21. c*	*31 b*	*41 b*
2 d	*12 c*	*22 b*	*32 b*	*42 c*
3 d	*13 d*	*23 d*	*33 a*	*43 b*
4 b	*14 a*	*24 b*	*34 d*	*44 c*
5 a	*15 c*	*25 d*	*35 d*	*45 a*
6 d	*16 a*	*26 c*	*36 b*	*46 c*
7 c	*17 a*	*27 b*	*37 b*	*47 b*
8 d	*18 a*	*28 a*	*38 c*	*48 b*
9. d	*19 b*	*29 c*	*39 b*	*49 a*
10 d	*20 b*	*30 a*	*40 c*	*50 d*

PAGE 235

• After the test has been corrected, help the students calculate their final grade.

• Read the directions and do an example on the board.

WORD LIST

CPSIA information can be obtained
at www.ICGtesting.com
Printed in the USA
LVOW09s1825151117
556397LV00009B/529/P

9 781537 605227